"I looked through your magazine and I was repelled by the title, *Semiotext(e)*. It's so dry, you just want to throw it in the trash, which I did. Listen: *Hatred of Capitalism* would be a much better title. It's stunning. The world is starving for thoughts. If you can think of something, the language will fall into place, but the thought is what's going to do it."
—Jack Smith

HATRED OF CAPITALISM

A READER

**edited by Chris Kraus
and Sylvère Lotringer**

SEMIOTEXT(E)

ACKNOWLEDGEMENTS

The editors would like to thank all the friends who helped us retype portions of this manuscript: Priyanka Basu, Shannon Durbin, Jim Fletcher, Giovanni Intra, D'Arcy Cook Jones, John Kelsey, Hedi El Kholti, Tessa Laird, Joan Laughlin, Allison Madigsohn, Keith Pirlot, Sara Reich, Steve Shimada, Tom Simpson, Mark Stritzel, Joel Tauber, John Tremblay, and Robert Hardwick Weston

Additional editing: Mark Von Schlegell

Assistant editors: Shannon Durbin and Tessa Laird

Designed at The Royal Academy of Nuts + Bolts, D.O.D.
www.TheRoyalAcademy.org

We gratefully acknowledge financial assistance in the publication of this book from the California Arts Council.

This work, published as part of a program of aid for publication, received support from the French Ministry of Foreign Affairs and the Cultural Services of the French Embassy in the United States.

Cover photo by Mark Borthwick
Text at top of back cover from *Algeria* by Kathy Acker

—

First *Semiotext(e)* edition published 2001
ISBN 1584350121

Semiotext(e) 2571 W. Street Los Angeles, California 90057
and 501 Philosophy Hall Columbia University New York, NY 10027

distributed by: The MIT Press, Cambridge, Massachusetts, and London, England

To the Memory of an Era
(1974–2002)

TABLE OF CONTENTS

GETTING & SPENDING

ECSTASY

BECOMING

LIFE IN THESE UNITED STATES

Introduction: The History of Semiotext(e)

Chris Kraus and Sylvère Lotringer

Introduction: The History of Semiotext(e)
Chris Kraus and Sylvère Lotringer

Part 1: Sylvère's First Dream

(June 12, '01 – Los Angeles California – 7:30 p.m.)

Chris Kraus: Could you tell me about the dream you had last night?

Sylvère Lotringer: What was the dream?

C: The dream about not having sex. Because, you see, I was disappointed ... I moved the bed around here in the room so that everything could be different.

S: But we *were* having sex. We were just, we didn't go beyond the crepuscular.

C: *Crepuscular Dawn*. That's the title I thought up for the book you're doing with Paul Virilio. It's very trans ... like a tequila sunrise, pineapple juice getting mixed up with grenadine. But I think the dream was about being middle aged.

S: Let me describe my dream. I never dream, but for the last two nights I remember my dreams. In both dreams, there is a communal situation – a big room like a loft or an office, with people coming and going. Nothing is private. And in the first dream I was trying to make out with someone. I just remember the white sheets pushed aside, the mattress on the floor. People were passing and I was kind of annoyed but somehow having sex didn't seem so important. Like in Kafka, *The Country Doctor*, I was looking between people passing by. The bodies themselves were not so important. And then last night, I was in another of these huge halls, but I was lying on my back with my sex erect –

C: You mean, your penis?

S: Awgggh, I hate the word "penis." As soon as you become physiological, it's not much fun.

C: Sylvère, that's all the fun.

S: I mean, I was like the Egyptian Needle.

C: You mean, you had a great big hard on.

S: Yeah. And you were hovering above me like the sky …And, how can you penetrate the sky?

C: That is a beautiful dream.

S: So then, it's not just you and me, it was people moving around doing their things and I was just trying to do mine and it didn't matter if it went anywhere or not. It was a feeling of energy and presence and there was a point. You don't always have to try to make a point –

C: So that is the history of *Semiotext(e)*.

S: Exactly. The Red Army Fraction wanted to make a point, and it was taken away from them. You can only take a disparate action… *Disparate Action / Desperate Action*… wasn't that the title of your first play?

C: Yeah – that was how I met you. Of the ten famous people I invited, you were the only one who came.

S: What was it about?

C: It was about coming to the East Village from Wellington, New Zealand and realizing there wasn't such a thing as politics any more. In New Zealand I was a teenage Maoist, working for trade unions ... there was a working class culture that was different from consumer culture, what you'd call "popular" in France... so we had that in common, even though we were different generations. I was wondering how to make sense, or maintain a sense of politics, in a situation that was inherently chaotic and apolitical. Regretting history. Of course that hardly is a topic anymore. But it was one of *Semiotext(e)*'s big topics. That's why I thought it was destiny that I should meet you.

S: I was never a Maoist. I only realized later on that in France I had been a Stalinist.

C: Yeah, well. How do you talk about the past without it seeming like an epitaph?

S: Hence my hatred of the penis. Hatred of capitalism.

C: Yeah, but I love dick, ya know? (laughs) What did you think, looking through the book today?

S: I felt that all of it was theory, even when theory wasn't there. It was so strong. Reading Assata's interview, *Prisoner in the United States*, made me think that while we're supposed to live such a privileged life in our glamorous vacuum it relies on the fact that 1.3 people in this country have just been put away. And that millions of people all over the world and in America are paying for this technological paradise. It's very upsetting. But the feeling I had was also strength – being connected to something very important, that hasn't disappeared. When I started *Semiotext(e)* in 1974 we were in the last gasp of Marxism, and I knew the terrorists were right, but I could not condone their actions. That is still the way I feel right now. What happened is that we forgot that capitalism even exists. It has become invisible because there's nothing else to see. When I told Baudrillard about this book, he said the title sounded too old-fashioned.

C: He didn't get the joke.

S: But capitalism hasn't disappeared. I was trying to disappear for years by doing interviews, but capitalism hasn't disappeared. Its repercussions are even more momentous than before, but no one can seem to grasp them.

(The phone rings. It's Mark Von Schlegell, who has edited sections of this book.)

C: Mark, what do you think about the book?

M: I think it's fine. I enjoyed the parts I read. I totally liked it.

C: Yeah, but do you think it's historical or speculative?

M: Probably a bit of both. I think it's hysterical. What do you want it to be?

C: I want it to be beautiful. (Mark hangs up.) Sylvère, should we move on to another topic? I wanted to say something about this direct, immediate tone of voice we publish in Native Agents. And how it relates to the entire project.

S: When I was doing a lot of interviews it was because I wanted theory to become ideas, that would have a direct impact. That would be grasped as naturally as you breathe.

C: Conversational theory.

S: Yeah. Interviews was one way of doing it. The other was to surround it with other stuff, til it became part of something more fluid and couldn't be isolated. Documents, images, quotes, ideas being part of some kind of movement that takes you from one thing to the next, and changes everything about the world.

C: Certain things need to be said over and over in order for anyone to hear them. I was reading an essay by Jill Johnston this afternoon, about meeting R.D. Laing. She'd noticed this enormous leap between *The Divided Self*, written in the late 1950s, and *The Politics of Experience*, which came out in 1965 or so, and she wanted to know how it happened. She wrote: "I concluded that Laing must've been protecting himself professionally by coming on as the high priest of madness without any direct personal information as to how he got there and I determined to ask him why." She was writing this in 1972, thinking that total disclosure on the part of everyone is the only way we can understand why things are the way they are. Thirty years later this is still so radical: "disclosure"'s gotten mixed up with "confession"…"confession" may be ridiculed but it is basically condoned because it implies personal guilt, the first step back towards the fold, some kind of cheap catharsis. "Disclosure," the mere statement of facts, bisects reality into cause and effect. This is much more disturbing. But the culture still considers "seriousness" immune from any sort of disclosure. Laing, or any other Great Man, would lose the power of myth if we understood how the myth was constructed.

S: The French avant-garde was looking for things extreme. Capitalism never goes to the extreme, and that's where you can get it. Can you put madness to some use? Hatred of capitalism is real madness.

C: Well Jill was crazy, and so are a lot of people that we publish. But to me, this idea of total disclosure seems incredibly obvious, factual and benign. Ulrike Meinhof's manifesto – that was crazy. She was so sensitive to things we hardly notice anymore. The crippling effects of consumer culture – there she was talking about the "masses" – and of professional competition – in which she was obviously talking about herself and her own world. Career is so ingrained now we don't even question it. Of course, Meinhof was mad. But so is Fanny Howe.

S: The Madness of Truth.

C: To think about anything for very long is delirium.

Part 2: Sylvère's Second Dream

(Next morning – Los Angeles California – 10:45 a.m.)

S: In the dream I had last night I was trying to hide a piece of paper from people who were hounding me. It was several layers thick, like parchment, a piece of text, thick with many layers. A thick piece of paper that I was wearing on me, and I was trying to protect it from people who wanted to grab it, but however hard I tried I could never make it disappear – it was bright red – and then they would always find it, and I had to fend them off. Then the paper turned into some sort of living material – not exactly meat or insect life, but made of layers too. And it was attacking me and I was trying to beat it and take pieces off and get rid of it but it would always grow back, and it was thick and slimy. I didn't have blood on my hands but I had this meaty feeling, that I was pounding on a piece of meat that wouldn't let itself be torn away. You put this book together. What do you think it's about?

C: What I like about the book is that it feels very seamless – that all the different parts of it are pieces of the same organism. In this sense, Baudrillard's hysteria about the end of politics and Louis Wolfson's numeric prophecies and Michelle Tea's descriptions of the wan goth kids of Copley Square and Ann Rower's druggy memories of Tim Leary circa 1961 are all part of the same thing. Eileen Myles asks if she's the only person in the room who can't afford to fix her teeth and Alain Joxe explains how genocidal skirmishes are structurally inbuilt to global capitalism. Every piece of writing in this book is totally polemical. It's action writing, totally self-aware that it is paradigm. In that sense, all the writing in this book embraces the philosophy of terrorism.

S: At first I didn't want to do the book because it seemed like a first class funeral. *Semiotext(e)* never published any manifestoes; therefore it's preposterous to think that there could be any kind of ending or conclusion.

C: It was nice this morning, working in the garden.

S: Yes, the roses… Pruning.

C: In the place where I grew up, there were these two older women living down the road. Claire and her aunt. I always saw them working in the garden. Claire's aunt was very old. She dressed entirely in black except for a straw hat. Which had a black veil. She was like an ancient beekeeper.

S: And?

C: That's how I pictured what we were doing. (Her eyes mist up.) It was so peaceful.

S: During WWII we had this long narrow garden in the distant suburbs of Paris. We were growing rutabagas – it was the only vegetable that was allowed, and every leaf was full of brown bugs that we had never seen before – they'd come along with the German army and were devouring every bit of food we had. But we had six beautiful rabbits – do you want to hear the whole thing? – We were fascinated by their teeth. I used to put my finger through the mesh of the cage. They were like lions. They snapped off the finger of the neighbor's little girl. Do you know what became of them? There was one I liked a lot called Blackie… he was black and velvety to touch and I thought his twitching nose was full of wisdom. The rabbits were our food reserve. Every bit of them was used, my father skinned them, their flesh turned black again in the sauce my mother made. We knew that Blackie would turn out that way.

C: So did you save him?

S: No. We couldn't. There was nothing else to eat. So one day my parents killed it, but my sister and I refused to touch it.

C: That's a sad story. But so is Nina Zivancevic's, about the war in Yugoslavia. (PAUSE) I think that we are approaching a Californization of *Semiotext(e)*. The best part of being in L.A. is when you can enter this really suspended kind of time – to just go with the emptiness and float through the day. The texts themselves are less important than the mesh effect that they create together.

S: It's like what the magazine was doing in New York in the '70s and early '80s –

C: Yes, it's more like an atmosphere of meaning than any particular meaning. Except there was this guerrilla fashion element to it then. Part of reading the magazine was always wondering where you stood in relation to the in-crowd. Now it's much more open.

S: That's because there's no more center, no more edge. But this book is like a homing head, finding issues that are urgent in the midst of this diffusion.

HATRED OF CAPITALISM

Eileen Myles
An American Poem

I was born in Boston in
I never wanted
this fact to be known, in
fact I've spent the better
half of my life
trying to sweep my early
years under the carpet
and have a life that
was clearly just mine
and independent of
the historic fate of
my family. Can you
imagine what it was
like to be one of them,
to be built like them,
to talk like them
to have the benefits
of being born into such
a wealthy and powerful
American family. I went
to the best schools,
had all kinds of tutors
and trainers, traveled
widely, met the famous,
the controversial, and
the not-so-admirable
and I knew from
a very early age that
if there were ever any
possibility of escaping
the collective fate of this famous
Boston family I would
take that route and
I have. I hopped
on an Amtrak to New

York in the early
'70s and I guess
you could say
my hidden years
began. I thought
Well I'll be a poet.
What could be more
foolish and obscure.
I became a lesbian.
Every woman in my
family looks like
a dyke but it's really
stepping off the flag
when you become one.
While holding this ignominious
pose I have seen and
I have learned and
I am beginning to think
there is no escaping
history. A woman I
am currently having
an affair with said
you know you look
like a Kennedy. I felt
the blood rising in my
cheeks. People have
always laughed at
my Boston accent
confusing "large" for
"lodge," "party"
for "potty." But
when this unsuspecting
woman invoked for
the first time my
family name
I knew the jig
was up. Yes, I am,
I am a Kennedy.
My attempts to remain

obscure have not served
me well. Starting as
a humble poet I
quickly climbed to the
top of my profession
assuming a position of
leadership and honor.
Is it right that a
woman should call
me out now. Yes,
I am a Kennedy.
And I await
your orders.
You are the New Americans.
The homeless are wandering
the streets of our nation's
greatest city. Homeless
men with AIDS are among
them. Is that right?
That there are no homes
for the homeless, that
there is no free medical
help for these men. *And women.*
That they get the message
– as they are dying –
that this is not their home?
And how are your
teeth today? Can
you afford to fix them?
How high is your rent?
If art is the highest
and most honest form
of communication of
our times and the young
artist is no longer able
to move here to speak
to her time...Yes, I could,
but that was 15 years ago
and remember – as I must

I am a Kennedy.
Shouldn't we all be Kennedys?
This nation's greatest city
is home of the business-
man and home of the
rich artist. People with
beautiful teeth who are not
on the streets. What shall
we do about this dilemma?
Listen, I have been educated.
I have learned about Western
Civilization. Do you know
what the message of Western
Civilization is? I am alone.
Am I alone tonight?
I don't think so. Am I
the only one with bleeding gums
tonight. Am I the only
homosexual in this room
tonight. Am I the only
one whose friends have
died, are dying now.
And my art can't
be supported until it is
gigantic, bigger than
everyone else's, confirming
the audience's feeling that they are
alone. That they alone
are good, deserved
to buy the tickets
to see this Art.
Are working,
are healthy, should
survive, and are
normal. Are you
normal tonight? Everyone
here, are we all normal.
It is not normal for
me to be a Kennedy.

But I am no longer
ashamed, no longer
alone. I am not
alone tonight because
we are all Kennedys.
And I am your President.

TERROR

Prisoner in the United States

Assata Shakur

This is the testimony of Assata Shakur, formerly JoAnne Chesimard Malik, who was arrested on the evening of May 2, 1973, along with Sundiata Acoli and Zayd Malik Shakur (who was killed by the New Jersey state police). Assata Shakur, who is now in exile, in Cuba, was a member of the Black Panther Party and of the Black Liberation Army. Here she gives testimony regarding her treatment after being captured by New Jersey state troopers.

Assata Shakur: On the night of May 2, I was shot twice by the New Jersey State Police. I was kept on the floor, kicked, pulled, dragged along by my hair. Finally, I was put into an ambulance, but the police would not let the ambulance leave. They kept asking the ambulance attendant: "Is she dead yet? Is she dead yet?" Finally, when it was clear that I wasn't going to die in the next five or ten minutes, they took me to the hospital. The police were jumping on me, beating me, choking me, doing everything that they could possibly do as soon as the doctors or nurses would go outside. I was half dead – hospital authorities had brought in a priest to give me the last rites – but the police would not stop torturing me. That went on until the next morning when I was taken to the intensive care unit. They had to calm down a little while I was there. Then they moved me to another room, which was the Johnson Suite, and they closed off the exit from the hallway. So they could virtually control all traffic in and out. It was just open season on me for about three or four days. They'd turned up the air conditioning so that I was freezing to death. My lungs were threatening to collapse. They were doing everything so that I would get pneumonia.

Q: Did the medical staff participate or acquiesce to this treatment while you were under their care?

Some of them did. The first night there was a doctor who was just as bad as the state troopers. He said: "Why did you shoot the trooper?" – He didn't know if I'd done it or not, but he just jumped on me. Some of the nurses were very supportive; they could really see the viciousness of the police. One of them gave me a call button, so that I could call whenever the state troopers came to my bed. That way I was able to avoid being further beaten up. They had my legs cuffed to the bed, even though I was half dead and my leg was swollen. Some of the nurses protested the way they had my foot cuffed. It was really bleeding and sticking in the flesh.

Is it your opinion that were it not for the medical staff, the police authorities would have murdered you in the hospital with the complicity and compliance of certain doctors?

That's definitely a possibility.

These members of the medical staff that showed human compassion towards you, were they Black or white, or both?

Black and white. The one who gave me the call button was a German nurse; she had a German accent. Some of the Black nurses sent me little packages of books which really saved my life, because that was one of the most difficult times. One was a book of Black poetry, the other was *Siddhartha* by Hermann Hesse, then a book about Black women in white America. It was like the most wonderful selection that they could have possibly given me. They gave me the poetry of our people, the tradition of our women, the relationship of human beings to nature and the search of human beings for freedom, for justice, for a world that isn't a brutal world. And those books – even through that experience – kind of just chilled me out, let me be in touch with my tradition, the beauty of my people, even though we've had to suffer such vicious oppression. Those people in that hospital didn't know who I was, but they understood what was happening to me; and it makes you think that no matter how brutal the police, the courts are, the people fight to keep their humanity, and can really see beyond that.

How long were you at the hospital and how long did your state of medical deterioration last after your capture?

I spent about two weeks at the Middlesex County Hospital. And then I spent another two weeks in the Roosevelt Hospital for the chronically ill. I had two bullet wounds – I still have one bullet in my chest. I was paralyzed in this arm. I had trouble breathing. And after I was released from the second hospital, it took me a couple of years to gain full use of my hand. I was not allowed physical therapy, or medical treatment in the hospital, we had to get a court order for simple things like a rubber ball so I could squeeze my hand and teach myself how to use it again. And the only kind of exercise that I was able to acquire was at the instructions of the nurses. I asked them, what can I do? I was acutely aware that the prison system would do everything possible to frustrate my getting well again. The nurses would give me a towel and even though I couldn't wring it up, they'd say: "Just try." So I would put my hand on top of it – and then the police would come and take the towel away, even though I was cuffed to the bed. I don't know what they thought I was going to do with the towel, but the towel wasn't the point. The point was just to do everything possible to make me suffer.

So is your experience that you were not given any recuperative or reha-bilitative therapy for the wounds that you suffered on May 2, 1973?

I was given some, but I mean the state, the police, the DA's office, the FBI, I believe, did everything possible to frustrate my recovery.

So you had to get medical therapy as a consequence of legal litigation?

My lawyers went to court and said, she has one arm that's paralyzed, but I never got physical therapy. We were able to get one team to come in and examine me on one occasion, that was it. The prison doctor would just take my arm and say: 'Oh, it's perfectly fine. You don't have a problem.' And his treatment for most things was laxatives.

After the hospitalization came to an end, were you taken to a detention center or a prison?

Yeah, I was taken to the Middlesex County workhouse. I was put in solitary. A cell which had a door of bars and outside was another big metal door. I was there from June until October–November, when I was taken to the Middlesex County Jail in New Brunswick, and put into a basement, in solitary again. It was a men's jail, and I was the only woman there. I was kept there until I was taken to New York to go on trial in December, 1973.

You were confined to your cell approximately how many hours a day?

Twenty-four hours a day.

Were you allowed contact visits?

The rules were that you could have contact visits with immediate family and lawyers, but the police kept entering our conversations. They would just ignore the fact that there were supposed to be client-lawyer privileges, or that it was a family visit. They would just be there and there was nothing we could do about it. Children were not even allowed to visit that prison and it was real sad. You'd just hear the children during the visiting hours screaming their parents' names, and they would be outside of the prison. You'd just hear these little voices, it was real painful.

Were you aware at the time that there is a law in the US that says that attorneys and clients have a right to confidentiality?

Yeah. My lawyer (and aunt) Evelyn constantly protested the conditions, but she was talking to deaf ears. She went to court I don't know how many times to have the lawyer-attorney visits respected, with the doors shut, but they were virtually in the room, and that room was bugged anyway.

What do you mean by the term "bugged"?

I mean that they had electronic listening devices where we would meet. The guards would come around and say "We know what you're saying." It was their way of saying: "We've got it on tape anyway. So what?"

In your view, did the combination of inadequate medical therapeutic attention and the lack of confidentiality with your attorney impede your ability to defend yourself against the main state charges that were subsequently brought against you?

Absolutely. My lawyers had to fight for such elementary things that they couldn't even deal with the case. The state resisted everything. Most of the energies they would normally be spending preparing for trial, they had to spend filing suits around the right for me to have a ball, to have medical attention, or even have food, which was the worst of any prison that I've ever been in. The women protested the food, it wasn't just me that they brought this food to, but they said that I was the cause of the protest, even though I was held in solitary confinement and could only speak to the women if I climbed up to the top of the bars and talked out of these little holes. Our whole attempt to prepare for the trial was frustrated on every level.

Did you suffer any disciplinary procedures as a consequence of that protest?

I was already in solitary, so the only thing they could do was just harass me, make my life more difficult.

Did the other women suffer any disciplinary procedure as a consequence of trying to communicate with you?

They were threatened in terms of their court cases; they were told that I was a terrorist... I was accused of killing a New Jersey state trooper and the police claimed that they had to keep me in solitary for my own protection. But the women didn't believe that. They did every little thing they could to make me feel human.

Could you tell us exactly what happened when you first went to court in your first trial? What were the charges that were brought against you and exactly how did the state deal with prosecuting you in this particular case?

The first trial that I participated in was the New Jersey trial. They put in a whole lot of other charges like armed robbery – I was supposed to have robbed the police of guns – and then assault, and a whole list of charges. But the main charges were murder of a New Jersey state policeman and wounding another one. We were on trial, we were in the jury selecting process.

When you say "we," could you state exactly who –

Sundiata Acoli and I were on trial together. We had the same charges and we decided that we would go on trial together. They didn't oppose that.

Had you recovered from your wounds at the time?

I was still wearing a brace for the broken clavicle, but the problem was mainly my right arm. I was basically paralyzed. And I was a wreck. I'd broken out in a rash, I was very thin… Anyway, we started the jury selection process. And in the middle of the trial it was stopped. It was postponed until January, 1974.

Why?

Because it was found that there was such a racist climate in the jury room that the trial could no longer proceed. There was like this lynch mob atmosphere, there was no way we could receive anything resembling a fair trial. So they gave us a change of venue to another county

– Morris County – where we were supposed to resume trial. Morris County just happened to be 99% white and one of the richest counties in the state of New Jersey, as a matter of fact, in the whole country.

What evidence was presented to indicate that there was a racist climate at that time?

There was no evidence presented, but the press had been trying me for years. I was turned into a monster. They pictured this vicious woman that goes around terrorizing police, this madwoman essentially... They had created this whole mythology in order to destroy me. They started building this whole campaign in the press 1970–71. The press were free to say anything and the police, the FBI, the CIA were the ones who were feeding the press information. No one ever asked me any questions or even attempted to deal with the fact that we were human beings, people who had a long history of struggle. It was just overwhelming, and people believed that.

You notice that there was a correlation between the information the police had in their possession and the information and the distortions in the press?

It wasn't information. They just fabricated things, and fed them to the press. They would accuse me of having I don't know how many pending charges, and none of that was true. Anybody reading the paper would think that we had been convicted of committing so many crimes all around the country and never was there a mention that we'd never been found guilty of any crime.

You said that the trial was suspended because you could not get an impartial jury panel. Did you have the opportunity to select a jury of your peers when the trial was recommenced?

No. The jury selection process was biased. Most of the Blacks who were prospective jurists were gotten rid of by the prosecution. Then, people who obviously were prejudiced, and obviously thought that I was guilty, were included in the jury. At the second trial in New Jersey there was a severance and I went to trial alone. The judge would say: "Well, can you put your opinion aside? Can you follow the law as I give it to you? Can you listen to my instructions and come to a verdict?" Even though a poll was taken that showed that 70% of the people of Middlesex County believed that I was guilty and had heard of the case through the media, the judge said it was a fair trial and there was no prejudice. I was tried and convicted by an all-white jury, a jury that was clearly prejudiced in favor of the prosecution. The jury was sequestered but the police and the jurors kept intermingling freely. The same thing happened in Sundiata's case. One of the Black jurors in his case tried to really come forth but they beat her down. There was a real investigation of the way in which the police interacted with the guards, the court officers interacted with the jurors while they were sequestered, and especially in cases where the defendant is charged with the killing of a police officer, that's a tool of influencing the jury.

In December of 1978 your attorney, along with other organizations and groups, filed a petition with the UN Commission on Human Rights, alleging a consistent pattern of gross violations of human rights in regard to prisoners in the U.S. Your case was one of the ones cited, and you were visited by a group of international jurists and attorneys. Could you tell us exactly what type of unit you were housed in and for how long and under what conditions?

Well, I spent two and a half years – maybe more – in these prisons. After I was convicted in 1977 I was taken to Quentin prison for women for about a week, and after that I was transferred to Yardsville, which is an all-men's prison. Not a jail, a prison. They gave me a booklet: "These are the rules for the New Women's Unit at Yardsville Prison." I was the only woman in the New Woman's Unit and they told me that I was going to be there for the rest of my life. They got a prison psychologist to testify that I was a hardened revolutionary and that no amount of time in solitary confinement would bother my mental health whatsoever. I was kept in this – it was like a cage – within a completely isolated section of the prison. There were two guards in front of the cell at all times, lights at all times.

Were these female guards?

No. Male and female guards. In front of my cell, writing down every-thing, you know: 'Subject is now eating. Subject is now on the toilet. Subject is now reading' – everything I did they wrote. I had no contact with the other prisoners, no access to the legal library, no access to any of the other educational facilities, no outside recreation whatsoever. No – my family visits were held in a filthy, nasty place – a search room for the normal prisoners. And so we had to sit in this filthy – and it was just unbearably filthy – room and have our visits, what few visits I was permitted to have. Lawyers' visits also took place in that room. The other thing I talked about to the international lawyers was the fact that I had been sent to Alderson, West Virginia, which is a prison within a prison. Although I had no federal charges, there's this agreement called the Interstate Contact Agreement, by which any person in order to settle their relationships with their family, with their community, can be shipped into the federal prison system anywhere in the country. Sundiata was sent to Marion prison, which is the worst concentration camp in the United States. Alderson was set up for the most "danger-ous" women in the U.S., a maximum of 20. Most of them were Manson family women, one had been accused of attempted assault against President Ford, and the rest of the women – the overwhelming majori-ty – were members of the Aryan Sisterhood, which is a fascist, Nazi organization. Even though the prisoner population in Alderson in gen-eral is overwhelmingly Black – Black, Latino, Asian – the control unit was all white, with the exception of me. I was there with thirteen or fifteen Nazis who wore swastikas embroidered on their jeans, who took pictures giving Hitler salutes. And I was there until the unit was closed down and I was shipped into the Hole…

What is the Hole?

The Hole is solitary confinement. It's punitive segregation. Even though I had not been accused of any disciplinary infraction the whole time that I was there, I was thrown into the Hole while they were deciding what to do with me. They didn't want me to be in the prison population, in any normal situation, so I had to stay in the Hole until they finally decided that they were going to ship me back to Quentin Prison. In Quentin Prison, immediately on my arrival, they closed the building that I was in, which meant that all of the women who worked in the prison, and were going to school or had jobs in the population lost their jobs and could only move around inside the maximum security building. All of the recreation programs women had been allowed to participate in – until I came – they lost all of that. And the prison administration would go around to the women, saying: "She's the reason that you've lost your job and are no longer able to get an education. She's the reason why you are confined to this building 24 hours a day." I could see the prison officials were trying to create a situation where the women would move on me. They had moved most of the women who had some kind of an insight as to what was going on to the other maximum security building, and had crowded the building where I was with women who were informers, who were tools of the administrations or women who were just mad or who were absolute fools.

So is it your view that the prison authorities tried to incline other inmates to physically attack you?

Oh yes. They would incite these women constantly, they had their people moved to that building especially for the purpose, women who had no long-term sentences, no reason to be in the building, were sent there for the sole purpose of stirring up trouble. It got to the point where the guards – Black guards – would say: "Don't go outside today 'cause they got something cooked up for you." I would always listen to what the guards had to say with a grain of salt, but in certain instances I found out that they were saying the truth.

According to the United States Constitution, everyone accused of a crime has the right to chose their own attorney, and if they do not have the funds to choose or to afford the attorney of their choice, they are then appointed an attorney by the court. This is the law of the land.

The records reflect in your case, however, that one of your attorneys was mysteriously killed during the course of one of your trials. Could you explain to us the trial you were attending, what happened, and what is known about that, how that impacted your ability to defend yourself?

This happened in trial in Jersey. There was a consistent attack on my lawyers. They were being threatened with contempt, with being thrown off the case – that's the first thing. Stanley Cohen, who was murdered, was one of the lawyers on that case. There is a myth that someone who's accused of a crime has a right to a lawyer. The reality of it is that most people who have no money get lawyers who have no interest in their case, do no investigation, no work whatsoever. In my case, the state had millions of dollars at their command to prosecute me and we had no money whatsoever. We needed experts to mount a defense, ballistics experts, because so much of the evidence – the so-called physical evidence – was manufactured. Things that appeared on discovery reports then disappeared, then appeared again, and it was obvious that all the evidence was tampered with. So we needed a forensic chemist, an investigator, ballistics experts, and we had absolutely no money. Finally, after the lawyers whooped and hollered, the judge gave an order granting some assistance in paying for the experts, even though it's very difficult to find a ballistics expert or a forensic expert who doesn't work for the police, especially if you're being accused of murdering a police officer. Just finding one was a task in and of itself. Stanley Cohen had made some initial contacts and initial agreements with an investigator, and was en route to being able to deal with some of these experts and expose some of this tampered evidence – and the next thing I knew, he was found dead in his apartment. The cause of his death has never been made public. The initial report said that he was a victim of trauma – but we never got the real cause of death, whether or not he was murdered. They finally said something about natural causes, but there never was a report of how he was killed. What we do know was that all of my legal records that were in his apartment were taken by the United States – no, by the New York Police Department – everything. They said that they took those – my legal records – as evidence. They didn't say evidence of what. Evelyn had to file a lawsuit to get those records back. Different records were missing; all the notes that referred to investigations of the case were never found. Then, immediately after Stanley Cohen's death, the judge retracted the orders saying that the state had to help us pay for these experts. The city's order said that we hadn't gotten these experts in time, and therefore the order was no longer good. William Kunstler was one of the lawyers on the case, and so was Lennox Hines; the next thing we knew, both of them were cited for contempt. The judge held a hearing to get Kunstler thrown off the case, because he was trying to raise money so we could pay the experts. Instead of even being able to prepare my defense, my lawyers were put in a position where they had to prepare their own defenses... And that went on through my whole time in prison. Evelyn Williams – who was also my aunt – was my lawyer. She was cited for contempt, she was smitten with it daily, she spent time in prison for contempt, for no reason at all. That happened to most of my lawyers, if not all of them: they were all threatened. Lou Meyers, a lawyer from Mississippi, said that he would rather try a million cases in Mississippi than try one in New Jersey, because New Jersey was the most racist place he'd ever been in. But it wasn't just New Jersey, it was New York, it was every place that I went to trial in. And it didn't just happen to me, it was something that was repeated across the board in all cases that concerned political prisoners; on every single case the lawyers were harassed, the prisoners received the worst treatment.

Was your family in any way harassed or intimidated by state authorities during this period?

Absolutely. First, let me say that the prison authorities try to make the visits as uncomfortable as possible. They build prisons in places where it's very hard to visit. Families have to spend hours in line, just waiting to get in, standing out in the cold. There are no facilities for them, often nothing to drink. When my daughter was tiny, my mother would bring her to visit me, and the guards would say: "She can't have milk. She can't have diapers." Just insane things to make life so much more difficult. My family was subjected to police harassment on every level. My mother had a heart attack because the police went to her job, they tried to storm the door. Surveillance cameras, phone bugs, devices, strange phone calls at all hours of the night playing forged recordings of my voice, all this stuff they suffered because they were my family. They couldn't just sit and have a conversation in the house, everything was being recorded. Part of the car's motor would fall off and they would take it to the garage and see that it had been mysteriously sawed; tires would be slashed. Letters, all kinds of letters, from police agents, threatening letters – it was just an onslaught of harassment, meant to break them down and destroy our family unity, trying to turn us against each other, trying to scare them to death so that they would be afraid even to have a relationship with me. But it didn't work. We survived it, and I think that our family is stronger as a result of that. We resisted together, and we struggled together, and that has made us – all of us – much more serious about who we are and about our love for each other.

Our Theatre of Cruelty
Jean Baudrillard

I. Mogadishu

In the terrorist act there is a simultaneous power of death and
simulation which it is intolerable to see confused with "the morbid taste
of death," and with the frenzy of the "morbid" and the "spectacular."
Dead or living, it is elsewhere that terrorism wins out. At least by this
single fact: it alone makes the event, and thus returns the whole "political" order to its nullity. And the media, all the while orchestrating the
victory of order, only makes evidence of the opposite reverberate: that
terrorism is burying the political order.

The media are terrorists in their own fashion, working continually
to produce (good) sense, but, at the same time, violently defeating it by
arousing everywhere a fascination without scruples, that is to say, a
paralysis of meaning, which retracts to a single scenario.

Terrorism is not violence in itself; it is the spectacle it unleashes that
is truly violent. It is our Theater of Cruelty, the only one that remains,
perhaps equal to that of Artaud or the Renaissance, and extraordinary
in that it brings together *the spectacular and the challenge at their highest points*. It is a model of simulation, a micro-model flashing within a
minimally real event inside a maximal echo chamber. Like a crystal
thrown into an unstable solution or an experimental matrix, terrorism
is an insoluble equation which makes all the variables suddenly appear.
Terrorism offers a flash, a scenario, a condensed narrative – opposing
the purest form of speculation against every event said to be real. It is
a ritual, opposing political and historic models in the purest symbolic
form of exchange.

Terror is a strange mix of the symbolic and the spectacular, of challenge and simulation. This paradoxical configuration is the only original

form of our time, and subversive because insoluble. There is neither victory nor defeat: no sense can be made of an event which is irremediably spectacular, or irremediably symbolic. Everything in terrorism is ambivalent and reversible: death, the media, violence, victory. Who plays into the other's hands? Death itself is undefinable. The death of the terrorists is equivalent to the death of the hostages. In spite of all efforts to set them into radical opposition, fascination allows no distinction to be made. Rightly so, because power makes no final distinction either, but settles its accounts with everyone, and buries Baader and Schuyler together at Stuttgart, unable to unravel these deaths and rediscover the fine dividing line, the distinctive and valid oppositions which are the secret of law and order. Nor is it possible to reclaim a positive use for media, or a transparence of repression; the repressive act traverses the same unforeseeable spiral as the terrorist act; no one knows where it will stop, nor all the setbacks and reversals that will ensue. There is no distinction possible between the spectacular and the symbolic, no distinction possible between the "crime" and the "repression." *It is this uncontrollable eruption of reversibility that is the true victory of terrorism.*

This victory lies not at all in the fact of imposing a negation and forcing a government to capitulate. Besides, the objective – usually to liberate imprisoned comrades – is typically a zero sum equation. The stakes are elsewhere. And if power wins out at the level of the objective, it loses at the level of the real stakes. It loses its political definition, and is forced to accept, all the while trying to thwart, this reversibility of all the actors in the same process. Terrorist, killers, hostages, leaders, spectators, public opinion – there is no more innocence in a system which has no meaning. No tragedy either (despite the Baader group's ideology, and the pedagogy of terrorists worldwide). The force of the terrorists comes precisely from the fact that they have no logic. The others do: it is quick, effective, flawless, without scruples: it is why they "win." If the terrorists had one, they would not make the errors that they do, but they would no longer be terrorists. To demand that they be at the same time illogical, which gives them their power, and logical tacticians, which would make them successful, is absurd – again a fantasy of synthesis, and of defense on our part, which allows us to recuperate in the fury of defeat.

Hence the stupidity and the obscenity of all that is reported about the terrorists: everywhere the wish to palm off meaning on them, to exterminate them with meaning, which is more effective than the bullets of specialized commandos (and all the while subjecting them elsewhere, in the prisons, to sensory deprivation). It is still this rage for meaning which makes us, with the best will in the world, treat them like idiots incapable of going all the way and blowing up the airplane and passengers, which makes us want them not to have "won."

Not only have they not won, but they have inordinately encouraged the sacred union of all the world forces of repression; they have reinforced the political order, etc. Let's go all the way – they have killed their Stammheim comrades, since if they had not launched and then botched this operation, the others would still be alive. But all this participates in the same conspiracy of meaning, which amounts to setting an action in contradiction with itself (here to ends that were not desired, or according to a logic which was not its own). Strangulation.

II. Stammheim

The insoluble polemic in the way in which Baader and his comrades died is itself obscene, and for the same reason: there is an equal obscenity in wanting to forcibly impose meaning on the hijackers' act and in wanting to restore Baader's death to the order of factual reality. Principal of meaning as principal of truth: there you have the real lifeblood of State terrorism.

Thus, the German government's strategy attains perfection in a single blow. Not only does it link – in an almost improvised manner – the bungled taking of hostages with the immediate liquidation of the prisoners who disturbed it; it does so in a manner (coarse, equivocal, incoherent) that traps everyone in a hysterical search for truth, which is the best way to abolish the symbolic futility of this death.

The hijackers made so many errors at Mogadishu that one can only think they were done "on purpose." They have finally attained their objective obliquely, which was the challenge of their own death, summing up the virtual one of all the hostages, and more radically still, that of the power which kills them. For it absolutely must be repeated that the stakes are not to beat power on its own ground, but to oppose another political order of force. One knows nothing about terrorism if one does not see that it is not a question of real violence, nor of opposing one violence to another (which, owing to their disproportion, is absurd. All *real* violence, like real order in general, is always on the side of power), but to oppose to the *full* violence and to the *full* order a clearly superior model of extermination and virulence operating through emptiness.

The secret is to oppose to the order of the real an absolutely imaginary realm, completely ineffectual at the level of reality, but whose implosive energy absorbs everything real and all the violence of real power which founders there. Such a model is no longer of the order of transgression: repression and transgression are of the old order of the law, of the order of a real *system* of expansion. In such a system, all that comes into contradiction with it, including the violence of its opposite, only makes its expansion accelerate. Here, the virulence comes from the implosion. And the death of the terrorists (or of the hostages) is of implosive order: the abolition of value, of meaning, of the *real* at a determined point. This point can be infinitesimal, and yet it provokes a suction, an absorption, a gigantic convection, as was seen at Mogadishu. Around this tiny point, the whole system of the real condenses, is immunized, and launches all its anti-bodies. It becomes so dense that it goes beyond its own laws of equilibrium and involutes in its own over-effectiveness. At bottom, the profound tactic of simulation (for the terrorist model is very much a matter of simulation, and not of real death) is to provoke an excess of reality, *and to make the system collapse under an excess of reality.*

Paradoxical sleep is the edge of sleep where one does not really sleep, but where one dreams. Paradoxical death is where the reality of death is suspended, this edge where it acquires the status of a challenge that is symbolic *before becoming real*, a residue, the real always being only the residual principal of death's degradation and what's left over.

If it is possible then to think that the hijackers have acted purposefully in order to meet their death, this paradoxical death which shines intensely for a moment before falling back up on the real, it is possible to think inversely that the German government itself did not commit so many errors in the Baader affair; that they moved towards a well-defined end, even without desiring it. The government was able to stage Baader's death neatly – he did not do it. Far from seeing it as a secondary episode, it must be seen as the *key* to the situation. By sowing this doubt, this deliberate ambiguity concerning the facts, the government insured that the truth about this death, and not the death itself, became fascinating. Everyone exhausted themselves in argument and attempts at clarification – clarifications reinforced by the theatricality of the event which acts as a gigantic dissuasion of the terrorists' execution – everyone, and above all the revolutionaries who wanted strongly to have it that Baader has been "assassinated." They too were vultures of the truth. What's the bloody difference, anyway – suicides or victims of liquidation? The difference, of course, is that if they were liquidated and it can be proven, then the masses guided by the truth of the facts, would know that the German State is fascist, and would mobilize in order to wreak revenge. What a load of rubbish. A death is romantic or it is not. And in the latter case, there is no need for revenge; it is of the imaginary order. What non-sense to fall back on the reality of a contract of revenge and equivalence! The avengers are worthy of the moralists: always evaluate the price, and have the just price paid. It matters little that the "reality" of this death (the truth about...) is stolen from you. Since it is not of the order of the real, therein lies its force. You are the one who depreciates it by wanting to institute it as fact, as capital with the value of death, and to exhaust it in death. Whereas this death at full price, not liquidated in the equivalence of meaning and vengeance, opens a cycle of vertigo in which the system itself can only come to be implicated in the end, or brutally, through its own death. Against this vertiginous death the system defends itself by setting in place an inverse cycle – a recycling of the truth against the insoluble cycle of death. Such is the inspired maneuver of the German government, which consists of delivering through its "calculated" errors an unfinished product, an unrecoverable truth. Thus everyone will exhaust themselves finishing the work, and going to the end of the truth. A subtle incitement to self-management. The government is content to produce an event involving death; others will put the finishing touches on the job. The truth. Even among those who revolt at Baader's death, no one sees through this trap, and all function with the same automatism at the edge of open complicity which all intelligent power contrives to spread around its decisions.

Apart from Baader's death, the flaws of Stammheim stem from a strategy of simulation by the German State, which alone would merit analysis and denunciation. An amoral strategy of sacred union against the terrorist violence, and much more profoundly, a sacred union in the production of truth, of the facts, of the real. Even if this truth explodes (if in fifteen years it is finally established that Baader was coldly liquidated), it will hardly be a scandal. No power will be frightened by it. If necessary, the crew of leaders will be changed. The price of the truth for power is superficial. On the other hand, the benefits of general mobilization, dissuasion, pacification and mental socialization obtained through this crystallization of the truth are immense. A smart operation, under which Baader's death threatens to be buried definitively.

Translated by John Johnston

Aliens and Anorexia
Chris Kraus

Countdown on the millennium clock at 34th Street and 7th Avenue in Manhattan, a grid of twitching light-dots advancing into numbers, ringed by brightly-colored logos of its sponsors burned into the plastichrome – TCBY Yogurt, Roy Rogers, Staples and Kentucky Fried Chicken – a neo-medieval message from our sponsors, instructing us that time is fluid but Capital is here to stay –

468 days, 11 hours, 43 minutes, 16 seconds to go

1.
New York City, Autumn 1978:

IT IS a large room on the second floor where Pisti and Eva live. Squat Theater, a Hungarian group of actors-artists-underground intellectuals whose work was banned in Budapest because it was "morally offensive, obscene" and did not "serve the objectives of the government's cultural policy" are now living in a building on West 23rd Street, New York City with their children. They need a place where they can live and work, where they can dissolve and realign the boundaries between their collective daily life and their performances, the inside of their theater/house, the passersby and traffic in the street. They spend months planning and discussing the details of all of their performances, but they do not rehearse.

In *Andy Warhol's Last Love*, Eva Buchmiller, a young woman with long hair in a short black slip sits in front of a bookcase at a table. She is channeling the voice of the dead Ulrike Meinhof through a set of headphones. She is smoking while she listens very hard:

...... zzzzz ......

This is Ulrike Meinhof speaking to the inhabitants of Earth. You must make your death public. On the night of May 9th 1976 in a special isolation cell of Stammheim Prison where I was confined without sentence by order of the Chief Prosecutor of the Federal Republic of Germany, as co-leader of the Red Army Fraction....

zzzzzzzzz

As the rope was tightening around my neck, moment of losing my mind, suddenly I lost my perception but regained all my consciousness and discernment. An Alien made love with me.

If it is true as certain as newspapers write, that traces of sperm were found on my dress, these could be traces of intercourse.

After making love, I could state that my consciousness went on functioning in a new and uninjured body.

Afterwards the Alien took me to a special planet which belongs to Andromedas, the society there treats time and space with intensity, gentleness, discipline and freedom. Over...

In this play, Andy Warhol and Ulrike Meinhof, two cultural icons who might seem literally to oppose each other, come together – They are a dialectical synthesis transposed to psychic states. Years later, Buchmiller wrote: "Ulrike Meinhof is a legend who turned politics into tragic poetry... According to the principles of pop culture, Andy Warhol is a clone of himself. Thus, he is as real as he can get. How did Andy Warhol meet with Ulrike Meinhof? By chance."

2.

WITHIN MOMENTS of her death in 1976, Ulrike Meinhof became an Alien. "It's only at the moment of death when an earthling can achieve the quality and intensity which Aliens start with." In the Squat Theater play, Andy Warhol arrives in the financial district of Manhattan riding a white horse. Meinhof comes back to meet him, inhabiting the host-body of a child. Zzzzzz. "You must," she says, "make your death public."

As channeled by the Squat Theater, the myth of Warhol and the myth of Meinhof meet in a performance. Instead of scripting it, "a potential field of action was staked out." This unpredictability made reality alive, and much more immanently theatrical than theater.

Long before the artist Gerhard Richter physicalized her mythic image in his blurry spectral paintings, Meinhof had recast her life as myth. How did she become one? While Andy Warhol, as Squat Theater says, "turned exhausted art into daily food and gained freedom in complete unity with the existing world." Meinhof lived in opposition. Eva Buchmiller sees her politics existing outside historical time, an act of "tragic poetry."

What moves me most about Meinhof's life is the way she underwent a public transformation. The way she left the conscience, conscience-driven world of academic public discourse far behind and entered, just before her death, a real of pure sensation. As Squat describes an actor's job, so she lived, "manifesting an existence that overrode its represen-tation."

Ulrike Meinhof crossed the line between activist and terrorist on May 14, 1970 when she helped Andreas Baader to escape from Tegel Prison. Posing as the TV journalist she often was, she set up an inter-view with him at the tony German Institute of Social Questions. When he arrived manacled between two prison guards she was waiting with her press card and gun. Then two girls with wigs and briefcases walked in on cue and started flirting with the guards, creating a distraction for the masked man who entered brandishing a gun. In a blur that lasted thirty seconds, Ulrike pushed one of the wall-length leaded windows open, grabbed Andreas' hand and jumped. They hit the ground and ran.

Until that time, Meinhof had been an increasingly militant but highly visible journalist and intellectual. Married briefly to Klaus Rohl, a mainstream communist official who later claimed to have taught her everything she knew. "Her love for communism and for me," he wrote later in a self-serving biography, "amounted to the same thing." At 18 she was considered brilliant, winning scholarships and prizes, courted by the leadership of Rohl's own party who saw a great political career in Meinhof's future.

At 27, she was editor-in-chief of *Konkret*, an influential political magazine. She and Rohl had twin daughters and a country house. She lectured, commented on politics for television, wrote. She was a token woman on every panel. And yet, she didn't like her life. "The relationship with Klaus, the house, the parties, all that is only partially fun; it provides me with a basis… to be a subversive element… It is even pleasing personally, but does not fill my need for warmth, solidarity, for belonging to a group," she wrote in her diary when she was 31 years old.

During Meinhof's difficult pregnancy, which caused her ceaseless, blinding headaches, Rohl took over her editorship at Konkret and turned it into a kind of German *Evergreen*: politics mixed in with arty pix of naked hippie girls, "a jerk-off rag," she called it. In 1968 she divorced him and led a widely publicized insurrection at the magazine.

And then she took a year off and spent it researching a television play called *Bambule*. She hung around the Eichenhof, a reform school in Berlin for illiterate, fucked up teenage girls. Meinhof had achieved her influence and success because she was never at a loss for words, but at that moment she fell in love with the confused logic of their voices. She found herself unable to objectify them; fought with the director; rebelled against the journalist's role.

In the script published years after her death in 1976, Meinhof lets her subjects speak in the stark and blunted rhythm of their own words about what keeps them in the streets. She introduces the story of Irena from the observer's stance: "Irena's history was a fairy tale, a joke. She ended up with the police involved, locked in solitary confinement…" And then Irena's voice takes over…

Erica and me used to be allowed out into the courtyard. They were hoping that we'd break something. But we didn't give them that satisfaction. Instead we stayed downstairs and plotted. Erica looked outside and she saw the teacher was gone and she said she wanted to split – and she asked, Did we want to help her? And we said Yeah, sure. So Erica went and got a ladder and she put it up against the wall but she fell and nearly broke her neck. Well, we started cursing.

So finally it was me who started. I climbed up onto the wall and started stacking stones to jump from. And then Erica did it too, she climbed the wall and started stacking stones, and as soon as Erica made up her mind to do it, she was gone!

I went back downstairs and they said to me, What've you been doing. And I said nothing. And they said Nothing? What does that mean, Nothing? Where's Erica? What're those stones? Well, I said. Then one word lead to another word and finally I owned up. And they asked if anyone else was involved, and I said NO! IT WAS JUST ME!

Well, here we go again – solitary confinement. And then they threatened to call the cops. Go ahead, I said, I don't give a shit. Well I didn't think that they'd really call the cops but they did and two cops came, and one of them kicked me, and the other one tied my hands behind my back and before you knew it, I was back in the hole...

And then Meinhof-the-journalist discovers the psychic mobility of friction. She flips. She empathizes, starts to speak from the position of the girls:

Girls end up in Eichenhof because there's no one to look after them. To have one: that means there's no bread and butter waiting for you when you come home from work, you have to fix it yourself. And so you walk around the streets, you spend a little money, you don't sleep at night, but above all it means having no one to turn to except yourself.

As a working journalist and intellectual, Meinhof felt a certain empathy but had no direct emotional connection to what frightened and seduced her most about these girls: the absence of ambition, the lack of plans, the floating stare of being lost and insignificant. Unlike her contemporary Alexander Kluge, who anthropologized the troubled teenager "Anita G." in his acclaimed movie *Yesterday's Girl*. Meinhof was willing to think about the distance that separated herself and her young subjects *as a subject.* Yet still, they were worlds apart.

Could Meinhof's entry into "armed struggle" really be a war of language? Direct action as escape from the self-conscious claustrophobia of arrogant, objectifying discourse. One year later she was friends with Gudrun Esselin, a member of the RAF, masterminding Andreas Baader's escape from Tegel Prison. Here is the text of the communiqué she wrote following their escape:

Our action of May 14 was exemplary because anti-imperialist struggle deals with the liberation of prisoners from prison, which the system has always signified for all exploited and oppressed groups of the people.

From the imprisonment of total alienation and self-alienation; from political and existential martial law, in which the people are forced to live within the grip of imperialism, consumer culture and controlling apparatuses of the ruling class.

Direct Action as a means of escaping fate. As every act of terrorism must be, the raid on the Social Institute was "exemplary" a metaphor exploding from the margins onto a much larger screen. Yet Meinhof herself still lived within the confines of discursive language. It was not 'til six years later, when she was incarcerated in a maximum security cell in Stammheim Prison, that she herself became "exemplary." That she became an Alien, i.e., someone who had changed.

Writing in a secret diary some weeks before her murder-suicide, she was speaking in the same stark cadences she'd once transcribed among the girls of Eichenhof:

Feeling your head exploding. Feeling your brain on the point of bursting to bits. Feeling your spine jammed up into your brain and feeling your brain like a dried fruit. Feeling continuously and unconsciously and like an electric wire. Feeling as if they've stolen the associations of your ideas. Feeling your cells move. You open your eyes. The cells move.

At 42, she'd finally come to occupy the same sensate psychic space she'd once longingly observed among incarcerated teenage girls.

Armed Anti-Imperialist Struggle

Ulrike Meinhof

West Germany: post-fascist state, consumers, culture, metropole-chauvinism, mass manipulation through media, psychological warfare, Social Democrats. The GUERILLA is a politico-militaristic organization operating within illegality. It struggles aligned with internationalism, the Internationale of the liberation movements waging war against imperialism in the third world and in the metropoles. These liberation movements are the armed avant-gardes of the world proletarian struggle.

Reality can only be perceived in a materialism related to struggle – class struggle – and war. Revolutionary action – no matter how it is brought about – will always be understood by the masses. Words are senseless, outrage is no weapon; the Guerilla takes action.

The Guerrilla has no real viewpoint, no basis from which to operate. Everything is constantly in motion, as is the struggle. Struggle comes out of motion, moving on. The struggle is moving on. All that matters is the aim. The Guerrilla perceives class struggle as the basic principle of history and class struggle as the reality in which proletarian politics will be realized.

Man and woman in the Guerrilla are the new people for a new society, of which the guerrilla is the "Breeding cell" because of its identity of power, subjectivity, a constant process of learning and action (as opposed to theory). Guerrilla stands for a collective process of learning with the aim to "collectivize" the individual so that he will keep up collective learning. Politics and strategy live within each individual of the Guerrilla.

(Speech of Ulrike Meinhof on Sept. 13, 1974, in Moabit prison, West Berlin, on the escape of Andreas Baader from prison.)

PURE WAR

Pandora's Box
From Inside and Outside Byzantium

Nina Zivancevic

A shiny bulletproof vest and a gun are placed on the table before me. Off the rack, as it were. Good-bye to my dearest Buddhist prayers and meditations – with luck in my next life I'll be reborn as a cockroach, though more likely I'll return as a stone. But no… how can I carry a gun? I can't even swat a fly. Then Jo says, "Take the gun, who knows what might happen, people are getting shot at." I am off to Bosnia, to the front, in the morning. What choice do I have? How much humiliation can one swallow, and how many products of ignorance? Of course I suffer my share of fears, but, still, I have to see for myself: who is responsible for this war, and who is guilty of these most incredible human crimes, crimes performed daily against a random sampling of other equally human beings in my motherland?

—

Today I received a letter. It is a press release, and, having worked as a journalist, I immediately doubt its validity. It is a compromised piece of nonsense, warped truth which cuts to the bone. It reads as follows:

"After World War II, a group of Vatican officials, under the direction of Pope Pius XII and Monsigneur Giovanni Monitini (later Pope Paul VI) coordinated a mass evacuation of notorious Nazi war criminals to the United States, Canada, Australia, and South America through a clandestine network named Operation Ratline. The operation headquarters of the Vatican was the Croatian College of San Gerolamo. The central figure was a Croatian priest, father Krunoslav Draganovic, who had been a secretary to the Catholic Bishop of Sarajevo, known as the Hangman-of-the-Serbs during the Ustashis' bloody massacres in Bosnia.

Father Draganovic assisted the Franciscans and the Jesuits, provided forged Red Cross passports to the Nazis, sheltered the Nazis in the Vatican, and escorted them in diplomatic vehicles to Genoa. There, another Nazi Priest, a former concentration camp official, Father Petranovic, arranged their voyage to the final destination. The Ratline network lasted for a decade, and conveyed tens of thousands of prominent Nazis, such as Adolf Eichmann, Josef Mengele, Klaus Barbie, Martin Bormann, Franz Stangle, Gustav Wagner, and Walter Raulf. Over 35,000 Croatian Ustashi criminals from the British zone in Austria were smuggled to safety. Croatia has been particularly favored by the Nazis for zealously solving the Jewish and Serbian problem, and by the Vatican for its role as a shield of Catholicism against the Eastern Orthodox Church. In the Jansenovac concentration camp, the Croats had butchered and mutilated 700,000 Serbs and 60,000 Jews. The primitive brutality of the Croats had appalled even the visiting Nazi officers. The Vatican Ratline rescued not only influential demons like Ante Pavelic, the head of the Croatian state, who had proudly displayed his official kegs full of Serbian eyes and other organs, and Andrija Artukovic, the Interior Minister and architect of Croatia's bloody genocide, but also thousands of deranged murderers like Ljubo Milos, known for the ritual slaughter of Jews while impersonating a physician in the Jasenovac infirmary…"

—

At this point I stopped reading and set the page aside. It occurred to me that I had heard these stories before. I recalled the eyes of my grandmother as she told me similar tales. I was only 8 years old and can't remember the details, but I can recall the weather, it was a lazy summer afternoon, and I was learning how to read. The book I was reading was *The Diary of Anne Frank* and my grandmother had come up to our old attic to bring me some cookies. "Granny, I am reading something quite terrible," and I told her that it was a story about a girl with such an ugly and boring childhood that she had to hide in her room all the time, and wasn't even able to go out to play with Nono – I called every toy and doll I had "Nono," after my most favorite Venetian doll. I asked my granny if she thought such a story was possible.

My grandmother, always a remarkably proud and composed woman, grew visibly upset. She sat down next to me and – I remember this vividly – almost dropped the macaroons. Her large brown eyes, so soft and watery, examined my face, then rested on the title of my book. She hesitated before answering my question. Unlike my other granny, my father's mother who was much friendlier, this granny spoke little and was careful with her words, so I was usually quite cautious about speaking to her. She had been a schoolteacher in her youth, and was always strict with us children. She would lecture us about rights and wrongs and rarely just let us play. But she didn't like lies, that I knew, and she always insisted on the importance of correct behavior.

I caught her unprepared – I could feel that – and she stuttered, which was truly strange to see because she was always so sure and precise. It was as if she had become a total stranger.

"This little girl had her childhood stolen from her," she spoke in a whisper. "Just as your mother did when she was a child."

I asked my grandmother why my mother had been deprived of her childhood.

"Because when she was your age," my granny told me, "she saw Ustashis slaughter her own grandmother before her eyes." She continued on with visible effort. "We lived in a very big house ten kilometers from Jasenovac, which was a place where many people were killed during the war. Jasenovac was something like hell, but only evil people go to hell, and in Jasenovac it was the evil people who tortured the good. Your mother's uncle died in Jasenovac, and the rest of your grandfather's family did as well."

"When I die," I asked her, "and if I was bad, would I go to Jasenovac too?"

I could see that my question disturbed her, and I felt guilty. She twisted her fingers, searching for the right answer, but I could tell that she couldn't think of one. Finally she stood up and forced out an answer – though short of breath, like a fish out of water – "No, my dear boubou, you will never have to go to Jasenovac. No one will ever have to go there again. Maybe it was just a bad dream I once had, and that your mother had too."

I wasn't satisfied by her answer, so an hour later I came downstairs to ask her again about her bad dream. She was in the living room in the middle of an intense conversation with my mother, and I overheard her say, "Why did you give her that horrible book to read? She's too young for it. It won't broaden her, it will damage her!"

"That book isn't nearly as horrible as the answers you gave to her questions," my mother admonished. "She has such a happy child-hood.... She may be sensitive, but she'll forget about all this as soon as something new comes along. Still, isn't it better for her to learn some things indirectly, rather that watching us struggle for the right answers?"

She was right, since I had already virtually forgotten about the book, though as usual I was determined to find the answers to my questions in my own way. Years later, I would only ask questions when I felt them to be absolutely necessary, only when I was unable to figure things out through direct experience.

—

One problem I have been unable to solve is why my mother has recently become so turbulent and paranoid. During the summer I come to visit her in Belgrade from my home in the United States, and each time she seems more lonely and aged, but never before has she seemed as upset as she does today. Is she getting enough to eat? Does she need more company when I am away? Aging can be lonely when the children move away and the relatives die; the elderly come to feel helpless. And the political turmoil that has devastated Yugoslavia has done little to soothe my mother's nervous mind.

She has become a victim of the television. She stares at it daily, absorbing the misinformation. The latest announcements issuing from that gruesome box: five Serbian villages in Lika were attacked by neo-fascist Croatian Ustashis. Another announcement: several people died in a fight last night, allegedly Serbs defending their property in a village near Gospic; the father of one of the dead was interviewed by a TV journalist who asked him how it all started. He said, "We were approached several times to sell our houses by a Croat named Katic, our neighbor who had just returned from Germany. My son, Marko, said we wouldn't sell since he had just finished fixing up the house, and after all it's our property, our family has lived on this land for 200 years. Katic came back again and asked us to reconsider his proposal. We again said no, but then he threatened us that if we didn't sell to him now we would be forced to one day soon. The next morning my daughter-in-law, Milija, found our cattle slaughtered in the barn. In animal blood they had written on the barn door, 'Sell or this will happen to you!' We couldn't understand, because we had always lived together peacefully, Serbs and Croats. But my son, God help his poor soul, always had a quick temper. He loved the cattle, they were like his other children. He had to take revenge so the village would not take him for a fool. One night he and Milija set fire to Katic's stable. I knew this wasn't smart, God help him, but he was so proud. Then he went to the inn and met Katic. They both already had too many drinks in them. What can I tell you? Katic cursed him for setting that fire, and Marko cursed Katic for his dead cattle. In no time they'd pulled out knives, and Katic mortally wounded my son, my only son. What am I to do, now, at my age? But my son will not go unavenged! I swear by my eyes that his cousins will find Katic, then let God help him too."

—

"Mother," I said, "you watch too much TV." She is silent, but I can tell that the story upset her. I want to help her somehow, I should get her out of the apartment more, invite her to visit me in New York. I finally convinced her to meet a friend and take a short walk outside, and find myself in the apartment alone. Looking for a document I need to renew my drivers license, I uncover my mothers diary. Usually I wouldn't be interested in it, but now she was so down and depressed, I thought I would probe the terrain, reading through it like a Freudian acupuncturist, trying to find the point that hurts most. With trepidation I read of her days scattered across pages covered with nearly identical statements. Oddly the statements do not address our family life or her admitted regret that I'm spending my life in a big city across the ocean. Her diary from August 3,1990 through February 1991 is a series of variations on a single phrase: "I am so afraid for the Serbs in Bosnia. If these provocations continue they will be butchered. *I remember everything.*"

—

My poor mother, still tortured by memories of another war. I grow furious at television, and how it coldly manipulates one's fears and anxieties. So many lies pour out of that box. The country had long been the victim of state controlled propaganda, so long the voice of the communist dictatorship that snaked all our people's traditional biases through that magic box and into every home in Belgrade. When my mother comes back from her walk she is smiling. "See mom, you should watch less TV, because it makes things look even worse than they are, if it doesn't make them appear unjustifiably better." Then I rest my case, only to return to it again two days later when I complain to my friend Lili about the twisted frame of my mother's mind.

"Lili, you don't watch much TV, do you?" My friend is a writer, an intellectual, and I am asking her a rhetorical question sure to be answered in the negative. Some friends I don't have to ask questions, I take their opinions for granted. Our long years of friendship assure me that I can rely on the movements of their minds as if they were my own. But to my surprise Lili begins to answer my question so carefully and tentatively that it hits like a slap in the face. Why be so careful? Had she lost her belief in our friendship, which until then had been anything but formal and tentative? Lili's blue eyes are pulled back wide as she strains to put something difficult into words. It felt as if when someone asked her "How do you do," she felt compelled to tell her whole life story.

"Well," she started cautiously, "you know me... I've never had the time or interest or energy to watch that box very closely. But recently, with all the bad news, you have to be informed. In fact," a bitter tone grew in her voice, "there are few people here, or anywhere in the country for that matter, who would say they're indifferent to what's happening. *Everyone* is involved, everybody has someone, a family member over there, somewhere in a different part of the country, in another republic."

I felt Lili and I had lifted the lid to Pandora's box, like the first time in high school when we went to see a porno film together, when we were on the verge of grasping something new and unknown, strange and invisible. Lili had peeped inside first, and so was a bit ahead of me this time around. I knew her well, and so did not have to feel ashamed of exposing my own ignorance to her. I knew she would be there for me, to answer my most ridiculous questions.

"Lili, I've been out of the country for so long. Please excuse my ignorance, but would you explain to me, slowly, what has been happening here?"

We've left the rhetorical questions behind and have entered the realm of the personal, contrary to my expectations. "Well," she again starts with reluctance, as if speaking were a form of torture, "you know that I'm about to be married, to a Croat." I was going to congratulate her, again, but she continued on without pausing, and so didn't give me the chance. "But my fiancée can't stand going to work after what happened in Croatia a few days ago." Now I restrain myself from asking questions, realizing that to do so would hurt her too much, and I was suddenly embarrassed by the depth of my ignorance.

—

What was it that happened in Croatia a few days ago, I asked myself, and then asked another close friend whose mother barely survived Auschwitz forty-five years before.

"The Croatian nationalists, the so-called neo-Nazis, were torturing Serbs in Osijek," he told me, "so the Yugoslav army was sent to quiet them down. The Croatian nationalists are also very well-equipped, and their General Tudjman led them into a huge battle with tanks and everything. The odd thing, though, was that the media always referred to the Yugoslav army as 'the Serbs,' as if it wasn't the national army and had Croats and Muslims in it as well. I thought this was the army of all the Yugoslav republics."

"What did you say the Croatian soldiers were dressed like?" I asked Leo.

"They're in black shirts with Nazi symbols on the sleeves, and they carry a checkered flag, like they did in the last world war. One of their generals had just published a book in which he claims that no Jews died in Jansenovac, can you imagine? But wait, what time is it? I want to catch the TV news. I heard they stopped a jumbo jet in Split this morning that was carrying weapons to Zimbabwe."

From Zimbabwe? Where are these arms going? And why? I watch the box carefully. After the "news" they show a documentary which, they say, was confiscated from inside Croatia – a classified film that depicts an incredible Croatian nationalist plot to lay siege on Serbian villages in Croatia. A tiny man with an angular face appears to say, "Here, use this knife. And remember, once you enter a house no one can be spared, not even the children. Don't spare them because they wouldn't spare you, would they?" They salute each other in Nazi fashion, as in Hitler's day. This film, they claim, was shot two years ago.

—

The film appalls me, as the possibility that men were trained to wield such destruction over the course of years seeps into my consciousness. I make a copy of the documentary on a VCR, eager to show it to my friends in the United States, but when I return home to New York what I find in the media is reporting of a completely different sort. In the American papers I read of how the Yugoslav army, headed by the Serbian Milosevic, spares not a bullet when it comes to torturing the Croatian people. The papers report how the Serbians are only after Croatian territory while they claim to be protecting the Serbs of Croatia from attack. Then I read that the national army of Yugoslavia was bombing Debrovnik, the pearl of the Adriatic. Dubrovnik was always a gem. Neither Serbian nor Croatian, it remained independent of nationality, like myself, for more than 500 years. A friend of mine, an art critic of renown and a famous esthete, tells me, "I feel so sorry for Dubrovnik." I tell him that I feel more sorry for the people, those on both "sides" who are butchered, slaughtered, every day. I read in the newspapers that the Yugoslav army under Serbian control is actively exterminating the Croats. CNN broadcasts live images of the horror show called

Vukovar, a city which is under siege and where the Yugoslav army is bombing the populace. Images of massacred faces on TV, and the reporter says, "Here the people are all Croatians. No, excuse me, it seems there are some Serbs in there as well." I see them all, recognize their nationalist uniforms, and grow pale.

It seems so strange, I think. *The media is warping the news,* but why? Later I hear that as many Serbs as Croats died in Vukovar, that before the army marched in and destroyed the city forever, the Croats massacred the Serbs who lived there, in an act of vengeance. Before the war Vukovar's population was evenly split between Serbs and Croats.

—

The war makes me ill and unable to write. I call my family in Belgrade and my mother tells me she's okay. I know she is lying – if things were better she'd complain about the poor food and the rotten weather, as she always has. My father is more honest with me. He's old now, nearly 82, and has survived many wars – the Turkish, the Balkan, The First World and the Second World Wars. This is his fifth. He tells me calmly, "I will stay here in my garden. Let them run me over with a tank."

—

Now my mother never goes out of her apartment. She is afraid that as soon as she leaves a family of refuges will occupy it in her absence. Thousands of people sleep on the streets of the city, or in hallways, basements, train stations. There is no food for them, nor money, nor clothes. The Red Cross can't give nearly enough to make a difference. As we march in to the fall of 1991, people and villages and cities all disappear engulfed by the front lines of the war. Young people everywhere leave the country to evade the draft. My good friend, one of the best writers of our generation, leaves Belgrade with a hundred dollars in his pocket and flees to Amsterdam where he hopes to find work as a dishwasher. The Belgrade pharmacies are without medications, everything has gone to the soldiers. The killing continues unabated. The American media never gets exact dates, places, or names of those killed in the attacks, but prefers murky references to destruction. Politicians meet to jabber at each other in the Hague. Western Europe doesn't act, only whispers insults from the sidelines, denouncing Serbia for its aggression. In the *New York Times* you will never read a word about the truly guilty, the generals who profit from this welfare, the arms merchants whose pockets bulge from international indifference, the intelligence agencies of the world that thrive on conflict, the already dead whose corpses fuel the passion of the dead-to-come.

—

The war grows worse each day. My nephews escape to Frankfurt where my brother now has to support them, plus his family. Almost no news appears in the American press. I grow tired, tired of being ill-informed, and after ten years away I decided to go back to my country. I call my mother, and she begs me to stay in New York. "Your mother knows, and she loves you best." I'm outraged and can't speak. I cry softly, in whispers, and then cannot cry. Some friends, mostly poets, understand my feelings. "If you're tired of the lies you hear in America, then why not come here?"

—

Arriving in Paris I learn that a brother of my friend Lili was killed in a battle near Vojvodina. I would cry but I've run out of tears. I buy a copy of the Belgrade daily, *Politika*, and sit with a friend from Macedonia on a Parisian metro and read the paper. It is full of photos of young men, all between 18 and 25 years old, all of them killed at the front. Now I am crying , my friend and I sobbing aloud, and the French and Arabs in the train watch us with a mixture of amazement and indif

In *Le Monde* we read that more Yugoslav refugees are in France today than during any war in this century. The Yugoslav situation has become worse than Lebanon's.

I look up some old friends, journalists. One is a senior editor at *L'Express*, and he complains to me that he has in his hands extensive documentation of war crimes in Yugoslavia but no one, including his own magazine, will print it. He asks me if I would translate it into English. With the documents are photographs of hundreds of Yugoslav children brutally murdered in villages from all over the country. The documents detail the facts about massacres of Serbs in Glina, then at the Gracanica bridge. There are murky stories about prisoners and death camps. Looking through those photographs I realize that no language would ever be adequate to convey the horror – how will I be able to write poetry again?

—

It is late December and I'm at my desk with a high fever, nearly 104. It's the week of Christmas, and I'm translating my friend's document on Yugoslav was crimes into English. I'm driven to work on by the thought that the world must be informed about the unutterable madness that has taken the lives of these people whom I love. Or don't love. Should it matter? But even the generals of this war lack the basic compassion you would expect from a human being. How is it that entire populations are driven to stand against one another and commit these despicable acts against each other? Every lesson of the Holocaust has gone unlearned, and it leaves me drained and sad.

—

New Year's Eve. A friend calls from Berlin. "Nina, don't be so sad tonight. Think of Lao Tzu."

Lao Tzu says, "In victory there is no beauty. He who calls it beautiful delights in slaughter."

—

But then think of how the Chinese have treated the Tibetans this century!

—

It's the first day of 1992, late morning. I am still feverish, and have made little progress on the translation. I feel changed, suffering through an experience from which I will never recover. To telephone my family requires all the strength I can gather, and to ask them how they are raises the greatest fears. I translate an apparently endless list of those killed or missing during the siege of Vukovar. But the work goes slowly. I vomit every five minutes, almost once after every five names.

Milic Radovan, male, born 1962, killed.

Lidija Prokic, female, born 1970, missing.

Miloje Prokic, male, born 1945, killed.

Vasilije Prokic, male, born 1965, killed.

Anastasija Prokic, female, born 1962, killed.

Whole families slaughtered, wounded or disappeared. I vomit, then return to my computer.

Lale Bojic, male, born 1933, missing.

Mika Stojanovic, male born ___, missing.

Darka Stojanovic, female, born 1925, killed.

Ruza Stojanovic, female, born 1912, killed.

This last one has the same name as my grandma, and was born the same year. I vomit again. How can I continue with this translation – though I do. Who else will translate this horror? How else will it get published – though no one who reads it will believe it. Who thought Dr. Mengele was still alive and well and so impressively productive?

—

I finish the translation and bring it to my friend at *L'Express*, hoping it may shed light on the murky situation in my country. Will the world finally act once it's learned of these atrocities, of the decapitated children, of their mothers and fathers crazed with hatred and driven to endless cycles of violence? The world, I'm afraid, will respond just as my French friends have responded when I mentioned such things to them – with casual indifference. A nod of a head during a conversation, then on to another subject. It makes my blood boil. I should calm myself, keep a cool head. I criticize myself and my generation of writers, artists, so-called intellectuals, but don't understand why we have achieved such a monstrous, cumulative failure. I think of Brecht and Thomas Mann, and of their courage in opposing the rise of Hitler. And I think of our responsibility as artists to instill people with skepticism toward violence, a devotion to tolerance, to the basic principles of pacifism – was it that we didn't work hard enough, or that no one was there to hear us? I think of my miss spent efforts to place art reviews in newspapers and magazines – what was the point?

While walking to *L'Express* I pass by the Grand Palais where they've mounted a retrospective to Theodor Gericault, and as if under a spell I mechanically enter the gallery, even though I have no interest in his paintings. I see his huge canvases of landscapes and Algerian battle-fields, and I cringe and run out of the building thinking, so what brilliant critical observations can I make about *that*?

—

Later at the café with an older French journalist we share a bottle of inevitable red wine. "You must be going through hell because of what's happening to your country," he says. I stare absently at my wine glass.

"I hate Europe. What can I tell you? Europe is incapable of learning from its own history. By now you'd think that this continent would have learned it's lesson about war." We leave the café and walk together to Trocadero, to the Palais Chaillot, to observe a panel of a writer's conference addressing "The Situation in the Former Yugoslavia."

The panel begins in an amiable fashion. A number of writers, including my personal heroes Peter Handke and Arrabal, speak meaning and with intelligence, and I start to feel as if I am not necessarily absolutely alone in a mad world. Then a renowned French philosopher, coincidentally a Jew, is given the microphone and is about to speak, when a team of police suddenly enter the hall and form an aisle through the middle of the crowd to make way for the surprise appearance of the French President! The President takes the microphone, clears his throat, apologizes for interrupting the conference and launches into a speech. Loudly, clearly, he tells the audience how he was a witness to the end of the war in 1945, when unjust borders were forced upon

Central Europe, and that these borders, he says, are the cause of the conflicts today. First we must have new borders, he declaimed, then we will have the peace, as all European countries great and small will take part in the new common market that promises ever-growing prosperity for everyone.

It crosses my mind that he might be less sure of himself if Corsica chose to separate from France. I feel a bitter taste in my mouth. A Canadian friend took me by the arm and we left the room together.

—

We walked to a demonstration that was happening near Nation Square. 25,000 people had come to express outrage at the division of the former Yugoslavia. They spoke of German conspiracies and the rise of neo-fascism in Europe. They mourned the passing of their country, Yugoslavia, which had ceased to exist. They had come from mixed families, had mixed marriages. Many were guest workers, some had been sending money back to their families for twenty years so they could to build a house in their homeland, a homeland they could no longer return to.

In the crowd I met an old Slovene and his Serbian wife who curse the war. He showed me his hands, damaged by years of construction work, and said, "For ten years we worked to build on a piece of land that I now can't bring my family to. They won't let my wife into the country."

There was nothing I could say to him, my nerves had worn thin, and I returned home. I got a phone call from Marseilles inviting me to participate in a writer's conference where I was to read the poetry I could no longer write.

—

At the conference I was asked whether all Yugoslav writers were now forced to live in exile. I answered that I was far more concerned about the people who were not writers who were forced into exile. Writers are familiar with the conditions of exile; exile is not foreign to writers, they often choose to live that way. Exile can be one's state of mind even while living in one's own homeland. I've chosen to live in many different countries over the years because I've always felt closer to mankind *per se* than to any nation in particular, even my own. Until recently it had seemed banal to say that every person is entitled to think and breathe under the same sky, but as our imperfect human race has difficulty recalling its own history, we're now obligated to state the obvious over and over again.

—

When I returned from the writer's conference I learned from my journalist friend that none of the facts I had translated into English have been printed in any newspapers of the world.

—

As I write, the war continues, and no one will venture to guess when it may end. Words fail and reason is useless. Hope too has disappeared, as has poetry. And so I have decided to go to the front in Bosnia, where human life is worth less than a cigarette, in an effort to bear witness, and maybe to catch sight of the invisible, to understand a fragment of the incomprehensible, which spits boldly in the face of all that we dream is the essence of the truly human.

The Empire of Disorder

Alain Joxe

The division of the world into two camps, which no longer interests anyone today, had two advantages. The first was to posit the existence of Humanity in eschatological terms. An entire generation of strategists forced itself to think about the end of the world in order to avoid it. The second was the institutionalization, through this binary division, of the somewhat occult separation of the world between rich and poor countries. This aspect should not be forgotten: there was at the time a semi-alliance between Communist countries – semi-poor themselves – and underdeveloped Third World countries. Today, the becoming-Third World of former Communist nations has succeeded the communization of Third World countries, revealing the existence of a comparable level of development in cultural spaces as diverse as Latin America and the Russian Empire. For a historian of the long-term, it is as if these two late semi-colonial Roman Empires, each with its own history of slavery, the Russian and the Spanish Empires, that spread the wings of their two-headed eagle to the East and West respectively, were now brought together in a common fate after a century of differences. With each empire like the Ottoman Sultanate leaving behind *balkanized* confederations to the South of the overdeveloped Euro-American center.

Europe remained a constellation of nation-states during the Cold War; the contract of the Euro-American alliance was aimed at maintaining this level of sovereignty, to avoid transforming the alliance into a military empire opposed to the Soviet Empire. This agreement disappeared with the disappearance of the enemy. The United States was able to unify the transatlantic West through the military alliance of the Cold War, NATO, and through the economic homogenization motivated by its hegemony over the free market norms that systematically weaken state prerogatives in favor of private enterprise and the central imperial system. This evolution pushed the world towards increased economic inequality within each society and towards accelerated impoverishment of considerable masses of the world population on a global scale.

1. The Two Strategic Options of the Imperial System: Contained Genocide and Satellite Control

The "moral and political" question that could be proposed today at the Academy of Moral and Political Sciences would be the following:

- Is genocidal war necessary for the organization of human society? (Like the "pro-Serbian" European defenders of appeasement seem to think, those who dragged their feet so that ethnic cleansing would simplify the landscape.)

- Or can everything be controlled by means of targeted, ubiquitous threats in real time, accompanied by a moral discourse, made possible by a few technically spectacular missile attacks (Iraq, Kosovo)? (Like the futurist, computer-satellite experts of the "Revolution in Military Affairs" in the United States seem to think.)

Post-Cold War strategists seem to hesitate between these two options: Huntington, proclaiming the *clash* between civilizations-religions and Anthony Lake, who has introduced the paradigm of market and democratic *enlargement* under global surveillance (following the *containment* of the Iron Curtain and dissuasive nuclear stockpiling). These are the options defined and used during the recent administration, by "world powers", of the Gulf War, the Bosnian War, the war in Kosovo as well as the "peace processes" and their accompanying massacres that have filled the news.

Strategic Classifications of Genocide

Those who react strongly whenever this word is uttered consider that it can only be applied to the Nazi crimes of the Holocaust or the most extreme massacres in quantity and cruelty, without considering the current legal definition:

Genocide or the threat of genocide is today, as it has always been, the concrete and violent form of the strategic process of *community separation,* dividing the human species against itself through hatred or vendettas in order to dominate it. But there is genocide and there is genocide. Although it is true that certain States have organized genocides recently, in Serbia and Croatia under Mr. Milosevic and Mr. Tudjman, for example, they are no longer the same as the genocide orchestrated by Hitler to prepare a core of international imperial conquerors made up of a "master race" biologically selected through a mythical defense of ethnic cleansing. Nor are they like those committed during British decolonization to clearly mark the departure of imperial forces from Ireland, India, Palestine or South Africa while leaving behind instruments of indirect domination. Recent genocides have been carried out to *reestablish archaic divisions* in the face of the *negation of specificity,* national specificity, brought about by the unstoppable advance of the globalization of speculative capital markets. I am a small communist bureaucracy: what should I do if the central power collapses? Become a little nationalist bureaucracy by means of a little genocide. A small project, but a real threat.

This psychotic version of *resistance through isolation,* brought about by secession through threat of genocide, has appeared in both former communist countries (Yugoslavia, Russia, Azerbaijan-Armenia) and in former Third World countries (Rwanda, etc.). It is even simmering in the pots of the extreme-right National Front party in France, great admirers of the Chetniks and Ustachis. It is a means of resisting globalized capitalism through fantasy. In fact, in certain cases, it is *in the interest* of the multinational forces that organize the market to see local identities and regional vendettas develop in the clouded minds of impoverished peoples, leading them to self-destruction through the resurrection – or pure "invention" – of traditional divisions.

Genocides have not only appeared in their etymological form – ethnic and local mass murder (Rwanda, Bosnia) – but also in the more general form foreseen in the legal definition of genocide as "so-called religious assassination" (Algeria, Yugoslavia, Afghanistan, Sudan) or "political assassinations" of leftist citizens or those who support anti-oligarchic peasant guerillas (Columbia, Mexico) or even social assassinations (social cleansing = social *limpieza*), the murder of outcasts, the homeless, street children, drug addicts, prostitutes (Colombia, Brazil). The concept of auto-massacre in times of crisis, that in Cambodia describes the mass murders carried out against the community itself in the name of ideological purity, leads to a zone of horror where genocidal logic becomes definitively "pathological," even though the precise political pathology has yet to be defined. One possible definition: "an excessive political cruelty that comes to have a negative effect on the preservation of the power it is supposed to uphold."

The Origins of Genocide

Numerous studies show that the local genocidal wars of the contemporary world are not the product of a spontaneous mass social movement. The legal definition of genocide, that genocide corresponds to a *calculated* massacre *organized by a decision-making political institution*, also describes this reality, or rather four levels of strategic reality that are essentially local rationalizations:

1. *Economic and Logistical Strategy*: Even the massacre of defenseless civilians is expensive; the money to finance massacre-wars, maintain groups of assassins and acquire weapons and munitions are all paid for by "invisible" sources that often include drug trafficking (Colombia, Lebanon, all the wars in Yugoslavia, Africa, Afghanistan-Pakistan). This is almost always the case. It should be pointed out everywhere it occurs because it is one of the dimensions of the transnationalization of financial capital. "Delinquent" financing takes the same shape as "normal" financing, even if it does not always use the banking circuit. It uses State hostility to illicit trafficking to its advantage as a means of increasing prices, and is therefore a factor in accelerating profits and State corruption. Through this dialectic, the narco-economy contributes in its own way to the war carried out on the global level against the former glory of already formed Nation-States.

2. *Social Strategy*: Identity massacres provoke massive refugee flight and, by this means, contribute to local land interests (by freeing land that can be seized to increase farm size or establish a certain form of colonization or by taking land for urban real estate speculation as in Algeria, Colombia, Brazil, etc.). These microstrategies concerning land

are the result of the degradation of the State or of a very archaic definition of oligarchic class interests and lead to a sort of socio-economic disaster: the massive influx of rural populations into the city, a population movement that contributes to no political or social rationale except the lowering of wages for unskilled workers in urban areas. This objective itself is no longer rational in the current stage of the process. The current stage is the "final moment" for a certain number of Third World countries to avoid a situation where an increase in the rural exodus with no redistribution of resources among the urban population would make the establishment of a peaceful urban population impossible, with consequences on a global level.

3. *Political Strategy*: The development of "barbarian militias" is the local product of the *decomposition* of the State and its exclusive hold on the use of force and widespread corruption. This development is also often part of the attempt to *rebuild* a more narrow state power, based on violent geographic divisions or the foundation of a racist internal regime, the domination of one ethnic group over another, an apartheid strategy, one that allows more or less violent forms of semi-colonialism and/or demographic elimination (former Yugoslavia, Cyprus, Rwanda, Kosovo, Kurdistan).

Contradiction: a Universal Empire that no longer has an exterior cannot use this solely local political strategy. If the United States wants a world empire, it will have to proclaim an Edict of Caracalla one day, granting American citizenship to all inhabitants of the empire. But to do so, it would have to reinstate slavery to create a "universal exterior" within the empire. It's hard to imagine.

4. *Military Strategy*: In cases of local genocide, there is always an organic relationship between certain branches of the regular State army and the paramilitary groups that launch the genocidal act and legitimize it to the point of engaging the death impulses of entire populations. The legitimization of massacre by a politico-military authority, either as part of the State in crisis or part of the emerging State, is always possible and proves most often to be the case (Turkey against the Armenians, Serbia, Croatia, Colombia, Rwanda, Algeria). In other words, genocide is empirically associated with every attempt to found or re-found a State. It is one of the ways to establish the famous "monopoly of the use

of legitimate armed violence."

I purposefully avoided classifying Israel in one of the preceding paragraphs, since it would be impossible to accuse Israel of employing a genocidal strategy. The slow repression and Bantu-type treatment that have accompanied Israeli recognition of the Palestinian identity are, however, part of an extremely alarming *sui generis* process, one that is exacerbated by support from long-term American policy. This process could eventually pass for one of the possible solutions of the United States – Third World relationship if it had a purely socio-political definition: colonization, reducing the first inhabitants to the status of citizens with no political rights of a state with no sovereign rights.

Does the formation of a World State require the multiplication of massacres, violations of human rights and new kinds of submission? Which ones?

The Cold War and the bilateral nuclear arms race avoided this type of foundation while at the same time *imitating* it through nuclear strategies. This particular genocidal imitation has disappeared since the collapse of the Soviet Union. Today, the United States, one could say to its credit, formally attempts *to avoid founding their global economic empire on global genocide*, but it has not sought to prevent the multiplication of partial genocides or to control the causes of these barbarian phenomena, since they allow it to base its legitimate monopoly on military intervention on its role as an anti-genocide fire-fighter.

This technical-military and legal definition of monopoly allows a "marshalling of forces." It corresponds to American socio-economic and strategic interests as a major commercial and financial power. But it does not propose to take socio-economic charge of the conquered peoples (like the colonial empires of yesteryear claimed to provide) and keeps the American Empire from having to define a clear political project.

Micro-genocide versus Macro-strategy

Genocide as an instrument of dividing and decomposing States is only useful for the system of global domination in certain cases and in the defense of well-established beliefs:

- Based on a conventional neo-Darwinist ideology, massacre is acceptable if it involves poor countries with no real interest in terms of resources, in which auto-massacres are the most economical way of eliminating a "disposable" society (to translate the Colombian expression deshechables that assimilates part of a population with disposable products like razors that can only be used once).

- Based on a pragmatic economic empiricism: if massacre allows the surgical separation of a useful region (with its mines, petroleum, irrigation, urban centers) from a useless one, so that in the sphere of the "Market civilization" only the profitable segments of social and geographic space remain, leaving the rest to fall in the dustbin of history.

In general, however, from the perspective of modern economic systems, these divisions should not reach down to a minute or spiteful scale, which would produce regional or local sub-systems that are hostile to the growing market. *Lebanonization* has been used to describe this irrecoverable division. *Bosniazation* calls to mind a division of equal finesse. We will soon talk of *Palestinization* if the Israeli project of treating Palestinians like Bantus continues after Netanyahu.

The impasse created by the Dalton Accords or the Oslo Agreements that were not applied to the reunification of Bosnia or of Israel-Palestine has up until now been representative of the contradiction between the goals and means engaged in American diplomacy, and Europe is still incapable of producing an alternative global project. If Europe, or even the "West," has to admit the constant presence of a bloody massacre on the Southern flank of its enlargement project, then both democracy and the market have failed.

Air & Satellite Domination

A first recourse to control genocides would be the strategy of an air-satellite menace. This strategy reflects the global technological dominance characteristic of the United States and financial capital at the material and logistical level: the threat of modern air intervention from the highest levels is enough. Why does this solution seem to be successful?

In each of the two domains, the "techno-strategic" nature of the means of control is key. Domination through precise targeting in real time thanks to technology from the computer revolution and satellite observation is merely a working hypothesis that must still prove its capacity for success. Techno-strategic domination failed in Israel, where American "precise targeting" (despite the loudly trumpeted deployment of Patriot missiles during the Gulf War), did not succeed in convincing Netanyahu to submit to the general control of the Protector or to apply the Oslo peace accords. The American Imperium recently had to take the archaic, if not to say Ottoman or Austro-Hungarian, form of direct control of the Israeli-Palestinian security sector by sending in the CIA. This direct seizure of power did not, however, succeed in accelerating negotiations under Ehud Barak.

The threat of air strikes seemed to work in Bosnia in 1995, after the unpunished genocide of Srebrenica, tempering the Serb militias and forcing Karadzic and Milosevic to back down. But it only worked in appearance, as revealed by the return to free massacres in Kosovo in the Spring of 1998 and the insufficiency of the first strike threat, which lead to the October agreements, their violation and the Rambouillet ultimatum. The culmination of the air-satellite strategy in 1999 with NATO strikes in Serbia will be the object of more precise study at a later point. The "school" of enlargement that is the guiding spirit behind aero-technological leadership, is idealist, or at least it has a very different ideal than the one defended by the self-serving, realistic, laissez-faire proponents of genocide who weakly or regrettably dominate the halls of international institutions. Enlargement idealism is based on a progressive, typically Yankee belief in the possibility of dominating vast geographical spaces through constant control, in real time, with a global threat of death or even with a threat of non-lethal "global" air strikes, which are much more precise than a nuclear bomb. The world leader and its satellites (both literal and figurative) are obliged to maintain the monopoly on this method of intervention. The goal is to turn the spaces threatened from above into elements that can be easily integrated into unified markets by rendering illegitimate, illicit and dangerous any use of force within them that might disturb the networks, stocks, logistical platforms and delocalized stock markets and auctions that shape human society into markets, and therefore sources of profit.

A leader obsessed with aerial domination wants peace to reign on the ground and despises the little customs borders and regional, neighborhood or archaic identity vendettas that are Neolithic, bloody and absurd, and that keep capital from circulating. But this leader also realizes that, more and more, questions on the ground are only solved by the presence of occupation troops on the ground with a properly political mission, a situation that is contrary to the recent ideal that states that a leader should not waste resources acting as regent for real societies with real inhabitants. The preferred solution of the United States was to delegate the work to archaic mercenaries, auxiliary allies, who do not have access to the noble level of air-satellite options and *cyberwar*. This would explain the presence, not only of French and British soldiers, but also Egyptians and Argentinans in the FROPRONU and SFOR, as well as the insistence on Russian and Ukrainian involvement in maintaining order.

2. Ethical Consequences of the Strategic Couple [Genocide/Air Control] Five Principles of Prudence

To arrive at this two option system, neo-realist/idealist, without creating pangs of conscience, a number of *prudent ethical principles* are indispensable for the reflection behind Euro-American dominance, and serve as a basis for a laissez-faire philosophy moderated by air threats. The five principles in this list are by no means exhaustive, but are proposed as a critical tool. They imply the destruction of all moral and political sciences.

1. *End of historical responsibility as a sequential analysis of responsibility.*

No longer make any distinction between aggressors and victims of aggression in the legal treatment of the state agents of irregular wars. This principle replaces chronic memory, sequential consciousness with a numbed consciousness of the instant. Example of application: Bosnia. *The end of history.*

2. End of the theoretical construction of social agents in conflict.

Do not attempt to identify, at the level of diagnosis and democratic assessment of the *human* causes, in other words in determining the responsibilities for a conflict, the agents or common interests *constructed* by sociological, anthropological or qualitative economic analysis (class, political interests, beliefs, local economic concerns, Mafia, petroleum); on the contrary, always accept the types of *self-definition provided by the violent agents themselves* (Serbs, Croats, Muslims; Tutsis and Hutus in Rwanda; the Guerilla, Army, Paramilitaries in Colombia; the Military and Muslim Fundamentalists in Algeria).

This operation is a sort of militarist lobotomy because it means replacing the identification of political and social interests with armed groups. When transferred to the main element of democratic commentary, or televised political analysis, this commonplace negation of the social sciences as a search for causes through reference to the social practice of the threat of death becomes an involuntary element of the fascization of mentalities.

The end of sociology.

3. End of the distinction between aggressive and defensive violence.

The problem is to condemn (and punish) the *symptoms of violence* alone and no longer determine responsibility for violence. Violence is in fact *always reciprocal* when resistance is possible (unless those who are attacked are required not to counterattack). Through the process of "anti-violent" ethical evaluation, "both parties" can be condemned, aggressors and victims of aggression alike, as violent, and each can be threatened with a superior form of violence. In practice, this leads to favoring the aggressor, who is always the strongest at the start, and therefore *penalizing the victims of aggression in the name of a condemnation of violence.*

The end of the Clausewitzian distinction between aggression and defense.

4. *End of the distinction between executioners and victims in the selective use of repression.*

This proposition is merely a corollary of the previous statements and does not even succeed in raising a scandal to the extent that the preceding "absence of analyses" allows for the statement that "in any case there are executioners and victims in each camp." It provides an ethical basis for the Obligation for each "party," executioners and victims, to negotiate for peace under the threat of violent "techno-strategic" intervention (military) or geo-economic intervention (embargo) or both.

It also signs the final blow to the idea of *justice*, whose death is masked, however, by the persistence of a certain type of *equity* in the indifferent distribution of threats by the dominant leader.

The end of justice.

5. *Apotheosis of post factum judicial treatment – the end of preventive or dissuasive or operational strategies against crimes against humanity.*

This final ethical precaution, a corollary of the previous statements, provides for the rehabilitation of the notion of justice in the long term after its violation in the neighboring space of the preventive moment: only fight genocide legally and *after* the crimes are committed, never politically and militarily *before*, or in flagrante delicto, *during* the crime. *The end of preventive politics.*

What must be noted here is that without a preventive policy, there can be no deterrent or operational strategies.

Reciprocally, only an operational strategy can serve as the basis for the threats of a deterrent strategy, and only a deterrent strategy can serve as the basis for the political-military interaction of a preventive policy.

The end of justice through the weakening of the distinction between executioners and victims while crimes are being committed is masked by the apotheosis of the judicial treatment of crimes against humanity. This evolution makes the end of preventive strategies morally tolerable. Providing assistance to people in danger seems to be gaining ground, but it is actually losing ground, since rescue operations are hindered and neutralized by the declaration of a new judicial tradition: punishment of future criminal heads of State, after the fact.

These five principles, coherent when taken together, imply the end of History, Sociology, Strategy, Justice, Prevention, not to mention candid and honest morality. Western diplomats, through the consensus implicit in practice, have recently adopted these principles.

I am convinced that this is a provisional situation arising from the disturbance caused by the crisis of sovereignty. But it must be said that the Bosnian experience provided a new clean conscience for our representatives who content themselves with remarking that traditional diplomacy is incapable of dealing with situations arising from the decomposition of established nation-states.

These five implicit principles are truly mind-boggling, since they take us back to the time before Nuremberg, before the UN, before the League of Nations, perhaps even before the Congress of Vienna, the treaties of Westphalia, the Council of Trent. They essentially permit *waiting and non-intervention* and therefore serve the "clean-handed idealists" with their satellite techno-strategies just as much as the "realists in favor of the freedom to massacre" and their motto: "let the strongest win."

3. The Religion of Non-Violence, Subverted by the Empire of Disorder

In order to remain a just, but victorious, military power, American leadership prefers not to intervene in ground combat and wants to command while remaining at the virtual level of a strike threat that could be called "celestial." Rather than seeking to take sides and as a result win a local victory, this strike threat must remain a pure peace-making act punishing reciprocal violence.

Next to this *divine* strategy, there is its necessary accomplice: the *human* strategy of the genocidal "realists." The solution to a problem, for this school, always comes from simplifying the problem (as in mathematical equations); simplifying a problem avoids having to work at the level of complex causes, since resolving a problem through its causes is a *preventive* approach. Prevention is no longer necessary once a war has already begun. Since war in itself is a traditional operation of simplification in the face of complex political problems, the onset of a genocide is welcomed by realists who see it as an attempt by at least one adversary to implant a strategy for simplifying the problem. When the time comes to negotiate, separation of the enemies is carried out by those who began the genocide and by the flight of those threatened with genocide that leads to a distillation (called "ethnic cleansing").

The pragmatic realist therefore has the tendency to *wait*, not for the genocide to reach the "final solution," but for it to arrive at an acceptable geographic redistribution, allowing the adversaries to be separated in defined territories. The fact that the separation is brought about by terror and that the terror is the product of a large quantity of crimes against humanity must be considered by the pragmatist to be inevitable.

Moreover, while the traditional Empire, in its principles, put an end to low level genocidal disorders through an obligation to abide by *imperial peace*, the American Empire only proposes to watch and limit them through *peace processes* without end and to stagnate conflicts in complex, inviolable legal configurations that make permanent military mediation necessary: in this way, a new type of protection takes shape, like the Bosnian constitution produced in Dayton. Combined with the theological condemnation of local violence, realist management of genocide gives shape to an Empire of Disorder that accepts a high level of latent violence.

Algeria
Kathy Acker

A SERIES OF INVOCATIONS
BECAUSE NOTHING ELSE WORKS

THE LAND IN ALGERIA IS PINK
LIFE IN THIS AMERICA STINKS

CUNT
IN 1979, RIGHT BEFORE THE ALGERIAN REVOLUTION
BEGINS, THE CITY IS COLD AND DANK...

1
THE STUD ENEMY

I am fucking you and you are coming you have a hard time coming you breathe hard you have periods when you strain to come then your cock withers you strain to come again. I hear you I see you I don't feel I am doing anything to help you the rhythm is so steady I come jagged to your steady rhythm my coming is insignificant compared to your building. You gasp. You are three laps away. Oh I am coming again. My coming is always so unexpected. I want you to come. I want you to come. I want you. I want you. When you come I never come you are unable to move it is always so unexpected.

I leave Kader because I live in New York City and Kader lives in Toronto. In New York I feel I'm a jagged part skin walking down the street. I feel part of my being no longer is. That is disgusting. That is an outrage.

I have to leave the man I love because I have no money and he has no money. I want to bust up the government to destroy every government that's telling me what to do, controlling the me that I most want to be me, bust up the society that causes government, the money that denies feeling and irrationality I hate.

Separation from Kader makes me have to fill that separation with nothing, makes me grab at everyone, makes me hate everyone for me every single thing is equal to every other single thing: I have to get to you. I have to get to you.

I HATE equals I LOVE YOU.

Here in New York, every morning I wake up, I don't want to be awake. I have to persuade myself to wake up. I have to use my will to get food in my mouth because my heart sees no reason for anything. I don't feel unhappy. I don't think my life's repulsive even though I have no money for food I have to beg friends for food. I don't care about poverty. I want.

Kader and I write each other a lot. I write Kader I'm a terrorist which is obviously a lie. Kader writes me he's waiting on a subway platform when the subway comes he doesn't know whether to throw himself under it or walk into it when he gets home he sticks a knife into his own hand beats his head against the wall. I write we're not going to see each other again because we live in separate cities and we have no hope of attaining money. Kader writes me if he doesn't see me soon he'll go crazy.

The Algerian revolution began on May 8, 1945, in Setif, a largely Muslim town 80 miles west of Constantine. The town inhabitants were preparing to celebrate the Nazi capitulation to Western European forces of the previous night. The Algerians had always passively resented their French occupants. The newly formed nationalist movement Parti du Peuple Algerien (P.P.A.) was the first occasion for direct Algerian anger. Right before the anti-Nazi celebration, the French sent the leader of the P.P.A, Messali Hadj, to jail. The Muslim population of Setif wanted the anti-Nazi celebration to become a strong suggestion that the French leave Algeria to the Algerians.

Actually there was no such important rational plan. All people are hungry, wanting. Hungry people do not act by rational plans, but by instinct. During the anti-Nazi celebration, a French policeman saw a beautiful Algerian boy, got a hard-on, couldn't tell what he should do. The Algerians were carrying their green-and-white national flag and banners saying "Long Live Messali" "Free Messali" "For The Liberation Of The People, Long Live Free And Independent Algeria!" Instead of fucking him up the ass, the cop shot the beautiful Algerian boy in the stomach. People act in accordance with the energy levels of their situations. The Muslims jumped the Europeans. Anger was out on the streets.

The next week the Europeans murdered 45,000 Muslims.

Over the phone I tell Kader to come to New York. He phones me he's planning to come he doesn't have any money he needs to find free rides each way and some free money. We're both feeling desperate.

Kader says he'll come to New York he'll borrow the money. I tell him if he can't get hold of the money, he's not old enough to have me. I'm forgetting who Kader is. My forgetting gets me scared cause I'm desperate to have someone else in my life.

I decide as if the decision is no part of me I stick with Kader. I ask him when are you coming to New York? Kader says he'll be here in three days because he's been able to borrow the money. I love him. I don't want him to come here, break into my isolation. My body desperately wants a cock inside her.

Before and after Setif, the French colonists were controlling more and more of Algeria and decimating more and more Algerians. By 1954 an average European in Algeria owned ten times the land an average Algerian owned and earned 25 times as much moola. The French pumped the Algerians full of penicillin and other antibiotics so the Algerians would have more kids. All these kids had no way to eat so they'd do anything for money. They were dispossessed de-everything-ed. The French Arab Culture ministers told the Arabs they'd have to stop speaking and writing their language, Arabic. They told the Arab women their Arab men had made them into slaves.

Over half-a-million Algerian Muslims a year fled to France to the garbaged cities in which they worked for French bosses for almost nothing though to them it was a lot because in Algeria the average Muslim worker earned twenty-two cents a day if he was lucky one-ninth of the population was unemployed and earned nothing.

I, Omar, live alone in a room. I almost never leave my room. I am lonely out of my mind sometimes. A lot of this time I worry a lot about money because for the last three months I have owned about ten dollars a week I am two months behind on rent I hate all other people; I am unable to fuck I am horny; I see nobody I am scared I am in danger kill kill; I am unable to kill my grandmother who is rich many people kill many people in wars I hate myself because I do not kill; because I do not walk out of my room.

Whenever a cock enters me every night three nights in a row, I ask myself regardless of who the cock belongs to should I let my SELF depend on this person or should I remain a closed entity. I say: I'm beginning to love you I don't want to see you again. The man thinks I'm crazy so he wants nothing to do with me.

THE IMPORTANCE OF SEX
BECAUSE IT BREAKS THE RATIONAL MIND.

The French police fastened the gégène's (an army signals magneto) electrodes to the Algerian rebel's ears and fingers. A flash of lightning exploded next to the man's ears he felt his heart racing in his breast The cops turned up the electricity. Instead of those sharp and rapid spasms, the Algerian felt more pain, convulsed muscles, longer spasms. The cop placed the electrodes in his mouth. The currents plastered his jaws against the electrodes. Images of fire luminous geometric nightmares burned across his glued eyelids. While the Algerian longed for water, they dumped his head into a bucket of ice-cold liquid until he had to breathe the liquid. They did this again and again. They did this again and again. A fist big as an ox's ball slammed into his head. The screams of other prisoners were all around him. He no longer knew he was in pain, pain was wrong, living wasn't a constant fire of torture and disgust. The moment before the Algerian went crazy and accepted horror as usual, his greatest fear and torment was this consciousness that he, the Algerian, is about to go crazy, has to give up his mind which is anger and accept the horrible inequality, the French way of living he is fighting against.

THE PROBLEM OF WE THE COLONIZED

All those people of whom we are afraid, who crush the jealous emerald of our dreams, who twist the fragile curve of our smiles, all those people we face, who ask us no questions, but to whom we put strange ones:

Who are they?

What can our enthusiasm and devotion and madness achieve if everyday reality is now a tissue of lies, a tissue of cowardice, a tissue of contempt for human mentality?

The degree of alienation of the people who gave me this world seems frightening to me. Alien to alienation, we now have to live depersonalized or....

Right now there is no difference between a legal and a criminal act. Lawlessness, inequality for the sake of desire, multi-daily murders of human beings have been raised to the status of legislated middle-class principles.

This social structure negates our beings, makes us who are without into nothings. If we hope: if we talk of or search for love, this hope is not an open door to the future, but the illogical maintenance of a subjective attitude in organized contradiction with reality.

Beneath the lousy material way we live, beneath our petty crimes, we want to eat food without roach-eggs and we want to love people. I think a society that drives its members to desperate solutions is a non-viable society, a society to be replaced.

HOW CAN I WHO AM DISINHERITED ACT?

I have to make Kader here even if he isn't here. I talk to Kader on the streets. I write down the conversations I have with Kader over the phone. I use Kader for everything. I can't write down what I think I should be writing Kader's thoughts keep interrupting me. I have to fuck I have to fuck I have to fuck I.

I think that for a kid American family life is so bad (cause the parents, taking shit from their parents, bosses, the media, etc., have only their kid to dump on), that all a kid can do these days by the time he has his first chance to try to control a little of his life is find some decent parents so maybe he can grow up. Each young person is desperately trying to find a parent. Since there are no adults now, there are no other relationships.

Kader is in New York now. I don't feel anything for him.

After the French murdered 45,000 Muslims, they seized and imprisoned the rest of the rebel leaders. But the Algerian people didn't stop being angry. The young Algerian boys who were growing up knew smatterings of Marxist revolutionary techniques. They didn't care for liberal sentiments or revolutionary discussions. They weren't interested in groups. They enjoyed hating. They liked to fight. They respected violence.

2
CUNT

All Algerian women wear the veil. This large square cloth that covers the whole face and body makes the woman anonymous. There is no such thing as a woman. Henceforth a woman is A CUNT. A CUNT can see. It cannot be seen. A CUNT does not yield itself it does not offer itself it does not give itself. The Frenchmen who say they want cunt find real CUNTS frustrating.

This is the way THE CUNT my mother committed suicide:

THE CUNT ate at the most expensive restaurants in New York City. It purchased five copies of every expensive piece of clothing it liked. It bought needlepoint designs at $300 a piece. It rode in taxis and hired limousines. THE CUNT ran through $300,000 of its husband's life insurance money and the money THE CUNT its mother gave it in two years. The closer THE CUNT came to no money, the more frenzily it spent. It stole money and jewelry from THE CUNT its mother. It ran out of jewelry it could steal from THE CUNT its mother. So it began to buy $50 apiece hangers and $20 a pair socks from Bloomingdales so it could spend more and more money.

THE CUNT was the one who came the closest to successful suicide by blowing money.

THE CUNT was left with no money and no source of money. Its

apartment in which it had lived for thirty years was about to be taken away from it because it hadn't paid rent in three months. Since its friends were close to a CUNT who had lots of money like them, it was about to have no friends. It had never worked for money. It had no idea how to live in this world.

Its empty hole was arising.

THE CUNT'S THE CUNT mother had made two million by marrying a rich man when it was thirty years old. On Monday THE CUNT asked THE CUNT its mother for money. THE CUNT mother refused. Now THE CUNT had driven itself as close to suicide by money as it could get. Money is simply rejection.

THE ACTUAL SUICIDE:

On Thursday, THE CUNT dressed itself in its new navy blue suit THE CUNT packed another suit, a skirt, a sweater, a pair of black patent leather shoes, a nightie, a bathrobe, two pairs of nylon underpants, a pair of sheer panty hose, a bra, and a small overnight case containing cigarettes, reading glasses, a red lip-stick, bobby pins, and three bottles of the diet pills and Librium THE CUNT had been eating since its dead husband's first heart attack eight years ago in a large cloth green-and-black plaid valise. THE CUNT opened the gray metal safety vault stored under the shoe shelf. It put all the papers except for bills, my adoption papers, and its medical insurance back in the vault.

THE CUNT transported the valise, the vault, and its brown poodle Mistaflur to the New York Hilton Hotel. When the New York Hilton Hotel refused to accept its expired Master Charge card, THE CUNT slipped them a bad check. THE CUNT told the New York Hilton Hotel it wasn't sure how many nights it planned to stay there; it would pay in advance for two nights. At noon THE CUNT walked the half block to THE CUNT its mother's hotel. It balanced THE CUNT its mother's bankbooks. THE CUNT was speedier and more agitated than usual.

The next day THE CUNT boarded its poodle at Dr. Wolbom's on 51st street off Third Avenue. THE CUNT told THE CUNT receptionist it'd pick up Mistaflur on the Tuesday after the upcoming Christmas.

THE CUNT had no one no thing. THE CUNT had no more time no

more space. But THE CUNT had itself. In the hotel room THE CUNT ate down all its Librium and died.

SUICIDE AND SELF-DESTRUCTION
IS THE FIRST WAY THE SHITTED-ON START SHOWING
ANGER AGAINST THE SHITTERS.

The Culprit ·
Georges Bataille

Is God merely a man for who death, or rather, thinking about death, is just one prodigious pastime?

Wrong way to talk? Perhaps.

Perhaps, more accurately, just one way to laugh. But can't we once and for all reconcile language and speech? By speech, I mean that speech without traps which doesn't flee in the face of the totality of its own consequences.

This narrative is a burst of cunning and thus lively laughter. The laughter of a man who forced himself to live shut-up within the perspective of death. He did this under favorable circumstances, but with great difficulty, and in the end, he failed. For life, a most intense, and often, most heartrending life, brought him back immediately.

This narrative evolved out of the 1939 declaration of war. It is independent of the author's life. In fact, the author put together this story from pieces of the "journal" which he kept despite himself from the day war broke out. Forty-two years old at this point, the author had never before kept a diary. But faced with the written pages, he soon realized that he had never written anything so much a part of him and so fully expressive of himself. He has only to remove those passages concerning the third person: in particular, those passages concerning Laure's death, to which Michel Leiris refers in *Rules of the Game.* This story is violently dominated by tears; it is violently dominated by death.

Today, the author was struck by the fact that the culprit is dominated by tears and death at the same time that it is dominated by the representation of God. [...]

September 14, 1939

Yesterday, I went to Laure's grave; as soon as I left the house, I
noticed how dark the night was, and I wondered If I could ever find
my way along the road. It was so black that I felt my throat tighten: I
couldn't think of anything else. So I found it impossible to go into
the state of near-ecstasy that normally overcomes me as I follow the
same path. After a long while, near the middle of the way, more and
more lost, I remembered the ascent up Etna and I was dumbfounded.
Everything then has been just as dark and charged with cunning terror
the night Laure and I climbed the face of Etna.

Mount Etna overflowed with meaning for us; we had given up a
trip to Greece to make the climb. What we had already paid for the
crossing had to be refunded. At dawn, we finally reached the edge of
the immense and bottomless crater. We were exhausted and in a way
taken aback by the overly strange, overly disastrous solitude. It was
heartrending to lean over that gaping crevice, that starry void that we
breathed in. The portrait of cinders and flames that Andre Masson
painted after we described that scene to him was near to Laure when
she died; it is still in my room. In the middle of our descent, after we
had entered an infernally hot area, we could still feel the far away
presence of the volcano's crater at the other end of the long valley of
lava. We couldn't imagine a spot where the terrible instability of things
was more evident. All of a sudden, Laure was gripped by such extreme
anguish that she insanely and blindly began to run. The terror and desolation that we had encountered has bewildered her.

Yesterday, I continued my climb up the hill towards her grave, troubled by a memory so full of nocturnal terror, but at the same time, so
full of subterranean glory, an already shattered nocturnal glory inaccessible to real men, accessible only to shadows, shivering in the cold.
By the time I reached the cemetery, I felt delirious. I was afraid of her.
I felt that if she appeared to me, I would scream. Terrified, despite the
extreme darkness, I was able to make out the graves, the crosses and
the tombstones. They emerged from the darkness as faintly pale forms.
I could also make out two glowing lines of verse. But Laure's grave was
completely covered by vegetation and, for some reason, was the only

absolutely black stretch of ground. Standing in front of her grave, I was so overcome with pain and sorrow that I held myself in my own arms without knowing why; at this very moment, I felt as if I had somehow split in two and was strangling her. My hands became lost around my body and I felt as if I were touching her, perceiving her fragrance. Suddenly, a terrible softness gripped me just like when we were close before; just like when the obstacles separating two people disappear. Then, when I realized that I would soon come back to myself, to the old self, restricted by my cumbersome needs, I began to tremble and ask her pardon. I wept bitterly, not knowing what to do because I knew I would lose her again. I was unbearably ashamed of what I would become, of the person I am now as I write this, or even worse. I was sure of only one thing: the perception of those lost to us who have broken their attachments to the customary confines of activity is in no way limited.

What I felt yesterday was no more burning. No more true or full of meaning than any other experience of the unintelligible, no matter how vague or impersonal. One's being burns with the desire to become pure through and throughout the night. It burns even brighter as love shows itself capable of crumbling the prison walls around each of us. But what could be more grand than the breach through which two beings might recognize each other without succumbing to the vulgarity and platitudes of infinity? (He who at least loves beyond the grave, for also he escapes the vulgarity of daily life but never the too-tenuous ties to Laure, even if they had been more completely severed by her. Sorrow, horror, tears, madness, surfeit, fever and finally death: these are the daily bread that Laure shared with me. This bread lingers as the memory of a dreadful and immense shadow. As the dimensions of a love eager to exceed the limits of all things; and yet, how many times when we were together did we achieve unachievable happiness, starlit nights, flowing streams? In the forest at nightfall, she would walk silently at my side, I would look at her without knowing it. Was I ever more certain of what life brings to us in response to the most unfathomable movements of the heart? I watched my destiny approaching in the darkness next to me. No words could ever express how much I was aware of her. Nor can I express just how beautiful she was; her imperfect beauty was the fluid image of an ardent and uncertain destiny. The flashing transparence of similar nights is equally indescribable.) At least he who loves beyond the grave has the right to free the love within himself beyond human confines, the right to give as much meaning to his love as he would to almost anything else.

I feel it necessary to include this passage from Laure's letter to Jean Gremillon of September (or October) of 1937, after our return from Italy:

"Georges and I climbed Etna. It was terrifying. I would like to talk with you about it, but I can't without a great deal of uneasiness; I compare everything I do to this memory, so it is easier for me to just grit my teeth…so hard – hard enough to break my jaws."

I copied these sentences down but I don't know anymore if there is any truth to them. I don't even look at them any more, because I simply can't unless I set out to achieve the barely achievable, and I have the strength to do this only rarely.

September 19, 1939

This is not a feeling that I alone experience. A nervousness that can only lead to a cataclysm has been growing now for over a month…

September 20, 1939

…But now I sense a new nervous condition. For days now it has been getting worse. This morning I managed to escape it somehow. This morning I found myself in an angelic harmony with reality that was the most… This morning, in this room that I must soon leave, here where everything was accomplished, all of the shutters were wide open. The sky was slightly hazy, but there were no clouds, and the plants in the window hardly moved. Surrounded by grand old trees, the only house to afford Laure some rest before she died, a brief respite. The nearby forest, her grave, the crow and the desert…so many curses, so much miraculous darkness. But this morning, a sun attenuated by a luminous haze and soon, the final departure. The secret transparence of the light, of chaos and of death, all the majesty of receding life, my fortuitous sensibility, my perversions. I will never abandon these things of which I am made, confusing myself with the immense sorrow of a fractured world, a world fractured by ill temper, by the crowd's sordid rage, by misery cringing before fate. I love who I am so much! But I've remained faithful to death (like a faithful lover). [...]

Laure's presence, as soft as an axe flashing in the night, springs up all of a sudden "like a thief in the night" and spreads a chilling embrace as deep and airy as a night wind. But I must make a concentrated effort to leave this presence; it demands that I leave just as forcibly. [...]

I was equally terrified because Laure's face vaguely resembled the horrible tragic face of that man Oedipus, empty, half crazed. The resemblance grew throughout her long period of suffering while fever wore her down. Perhaps the most disturbing were her fits of anger and hatred for me. I tried to flee what I saw there. I fled my father. (Twenty-five years ago, I abandoned him to fate during the German invasion, while I fled with my mother. He stayed behind in Rheims, attended by the maid. He was blind and paralyzed and he continually experienced great pain.) I fled Laure. (I fled her in a moral sense. I often faced her in terror, although I was by her side until the very end; I could never have given any less of myself. But as she approached the terrible end, I began to take refuge in a sickly torpor. Sometimes I drank, sometimes I just wasn't there.) [...]

The natural condition of simplicity is action. But in order to act, one must follow a cruel imperative to ignore all of the apparent contradictions. How can I possibly act if the imperatives which control me are Laure's sudden panic and suffering as well as that night of painful and sorrowful cries when my father appeared before me. [...]

September 30, 1939

Among all the pieces I've written for publication in a wide range of periodicals, only one, entitled *The Sacred* and published in *Cahiers d'art*, portrays with any real clarity that particular resolution which motivates me now. Although the piece is far behind me now, its "communication" is no more clumsily distanced or uneasy than in most of what I have published since. In any case, the demonstrative side of the case of the test did reach some of those for whom it was really intended. I believe that the remaining ignorance and uncertainty doesn't matter. We cannot possibly limit hope now. Men whose lives seem necessarily like a long storm – who can be saved only by a bolt of lightning – wait for something no less delirious than sacred.

When a really essential chance comes about, it shouldn't be attributed to the written word. When sentences impart a meaning, it is only because they unite some other things which were previously searching for each other. Sentences that scream continuously die from their own outburst. We must erase what has been written by placing it in the shadow of the reality which it expresses. This honesty is nowhere more pertinent than in that particular article.

~~I wrote it last year, from August through November, I agreed to do it with Duthuit, the special editor of the *Cahiers d'art* issue in which it was to appear. I should also mention one essential detail about the surrounding circumstances~~

Essentially, I feel I must describe one of the situations surrounding the writing of the article. During the last few days of Laure's sickness, during the afternoon of November 2, I had come to the passage in the article where I was describing the identity of the "Graal" which we are always seeking as religion's goal. I ended with this sentence: "Chistianity has substantialized the sacred, in which in which we currently recognize that the burning existence of religion, is perhaps the most elusive product of human interaction. The sacred is nothing more than a privileged moment of unity in communion, a convulsive moment full of what is normally smothered." I immediately added a note in the margins to clearly indicate, at least to myself, the meaning of these last few lines: "identification with love."

I wrote these words in the margins, as I often do, with the intention of coming back to them later in the article. I didn't. In addition, I read Laure's manuscripts before I continued writing.

I remembered looking up at this moment and seeing a thin ray of incredibly beautiful sunlight playing over the golden-red leaves of the trees about a hundred feet from my window. I tried to continue writing, but I could barely manage another two sentences. Then the moment came when I was finally allowed to see Laure again in her room. As I drew near to her, I immediately realized that her condition had worsened. I tried speaking to her, but she did not respond. She spoke continually, absorbed within a vast delirium. She no longer saw me nor recognized my presence. I understood that it was all over, that I could never speak to her again, that this was how she would die in a few hours, that we would never speak to each other again. The nurse whispered to me that it was all over. I broke out into tears; she no longer understood me. The pitiless world collapsed all around me. I was so overcome that I was unable to keep her mother and sisters from invading the house and her room.

She suffered for four days. For four days she remained absent, talking to this or that person according to some unpredictable whim. At times she grew tense, only to quickly relapse into lethargy. She understood nothing. Sometimes, briefly, her phrases made sense; she would ask me to look in her bag or among her papers for something she urgently needed. I showed her everything there but I couldn't find what she wanted. For the first time, I came across a sheet of paper, blank except for the heading "The Sacred", which I showed to her. I had the feeling she would speak to me again. After she died, I had the opportunity to read the papers she had left behind. I know that she had written, but she had never asked me to read any of it. I would never have thought I would find among all of her abandoned works an answer to precisely that question cowering in me like a starving animal.

I stopped looking for what she wanted. "Time" was ready to "cut her down"; it did and I stood watching what was happening, heavy with life, and yet powerless to understand anything more than her death. I won't say how she died although I feel most "horribly" the need to describe it.

When it was all over, I found myself sifting through her papers, reading pages that I had noticed for the first time during the period just before her death. When I read what she had written, I experienced one of the most violent emotions of my life, but I was never more deeply nor brutally affected than when I read the last sentence of a passage on the sacred. I had never expressed to her that paradoxical idea that the sacred is communication. I myself discovered the notion only once I had put it into words, a few moments before I noticed that Laure was about to die without a doubt. Nothing I had ever said to her came close to expressing this idea. The whole question was so important to me that I remember how and when everything happened. What's more, we almost never carried on "intellectual conversations." Once she even blamed me for not taking her seriously. The truth is, I disdained the inevitable impudence of "intellectual conversations."

Finally, towards the bottom of the page, I found the following sentences in Laure's scrawl:

"A poetic work is sacred to the extent that it is the creation of a topical event, 'communication' experienced as nudity. It is self-rape, denuding, communicating to others a reason to live, for this reason to live 'displaces itself.'" Exactly what I had written in my article, since my notion of "unity in communication" figures implicitly in Laure's ideas.

Let me interrupt this narrative for a moment to describe a captivating image that just came to my mind, an image that encompasses an entire vision, an image at best of an ecstatic outburst, of an "angel," as far away and as imperceptible as the horizon, piercing through the cloudy thickness of the night but never appearing as more than a strangely interior glow. It appears like the unfathomable vacillations of a streak of lightning. The angel raises up before itself a lance of crystal that shatters in the silence. [...]

October 2, 1939

Maybe the angel is the "movement of the worlds."

I love her neither as an angel nor as a recognizable divinity; the vision of the shattered crystal frees the screaming love within me that makes me want to die.

I know that this desire to die resides on the impossible edges of being, but I can speak of nothing else since I discovered those two sentences that link Laure's life and mine through the earth covering her coffin. Moreover, these very sentences exist nowhere else but at this very point.

Laure and I often thought that the wall between us was crumbling. The same words and the same desires went through our minds at the same time. Laure was repulsed because she often felt a sense of loss, a negation of herself. I can't remember any of these coincidences, but I do know that none of them ever had the extraordinary significance of these two sentences on "communication."

I find it very difficult to express just exactly what the parallel passages mean. I feel obliged to try, but first, I must describe all of the disparate elements that make up their meaning.

~~I will describe only one more thing today: the nearly simultaneous publication of these two texts obliges me to say to those who suffer from the same thirst as Laure and I that...~~

At the onset of the war when I began writing, I wanted to bring myself to this point. This was the only way I could do it, and I knew it for a long time. I decided to do what I'm doing now several weeks before the war broke out. But I haven't finished; I've hardly begun. Faced with what I still want to say, my "tongue is tied."

On the other hand, what's happening to me today is so very inexpressible and as foreign to what is real as a dream. Without almost animal austerity, nothing of myself can emerge from this fairy tale. This fragile illusion disappears at the sign of the slightest hesitation, the slightest break in attention.

Except when I was near Laure, I have never felt such gentle purity, such silent simplicity, and yet, this time, it is only a flickering in the void as if a nocturnal butterfly, unaware of its ethereal beauty, had come to rest on the head of a sleeping man.

October 3, 1939

It is becoming more difficult for me to continue. I must be entering that "kingdom" where even the kings are at a loss. And not only that: but from within this "kingdom" I have to speak without stuttering. In fact, I have to find words which go straight to the heart. The mission I must fulfill is as far away as possible from the obscure need I feel to lose myself. I am entering a desert of total solitude whose emptiness Laure, now dead, only magnifies.

About a year ago, I found a ray of magical sunlight on the threshold of that desert, struggling to pierce through the November fog, through the rotten undergrowth. Through the unreal ruins, this ray of sunlight revealed before me an old pane of glass in the window of an abandoned cottage. At this moment, I felt ecstatically lost, at the desolate edge of everything human. I had just wandered through a forest after having left Laure's body to the gravediggers. I walked along a protruding wall of brick until I discovered a musty pane of glass, covered on the outside with a century of dust. If some vision of decay or waste had appeared to me in this abandoned place, I would have taken it as an accurate image of my own misfortune. I was wandering aimlessly, feeling that I myself had been deserted. I was ready to wait an infinity for the world of my desolation to open up before me, splendid but insufferable. I waited and I trembled. What I saw through the window where my wandering had brought me was on the contrary the very image of life in its most lucid whimsies. There, a few feet away, behind the window, was a collection of brightly-colored, exotic birds. I couldn't imagine anything more sweet behind the dust, the dead branches and the upturned stones than these silent birds, forgotten by their master who had long since departed. It was obvious that nothing had been touched since some long ago death. Under the dust, papers were spread about in the desk as if in preparation for a visit. I noticed a photograph of the owner not far from the window. He had white hair and a look that seemed to me to be one of good will and angelic nobility. He wore the clothes of the middle class, or more exactly, of the learned class of the second empire.

At this moment, from the depths of my misery, I nevertheless felt that Laure had not abandoned me and that her incredible softness continued to come through to me despite death as it had even when she was extremely angry and violent towards me (I cannot recall those moments without a feeling of horror).

October 4, 1939

Today is the first real day of autumn or winter. It is cold and gray. And, I'm thrown back to the desert world of last fall. Once again, I feel frozen and numb, far from shore and no less a stranger to myself than anyone lost at sea. Once again, I am gripped by a kind of monotonous and absent ecstasy. I clench my teeth as I did last year. Suddenly, the distance between my life and Laure's death vanishes.

When I walk through the streets of Rheims, I discover anew a truth that keeps me from sleeping. This peculiar and painful contraction of my entire life that is so clearly linked to Laure's death and the lingering sadness of autumn is the only way I can "crucify" myself.

On September 28, I wrote: "I realize that if I want to overcome my erotic habits, I must invent a new way of crucifying myself. It must be as intoxicating as alcohol." What I now perceive frightens me. [...]

October 11, 1939

During Laure's last hours, while I was wandering around our dilapidated yard amidst the dead leaves and withered shrubs, I found one of the most beautiful flowers I have ever seen. It was a rose, "the color of autumn," belly opened. Despite my frame of mind, I picked it and brought it to Laure. She was lost within herself, lost within an indefinite delirium. But when I gave her the rose, she came out of her strange state long enough to smile at me and say, "It's beautiful." This was one of her last coherent sentences. Then, she brought the rose to her lips and kissed it with a delirious passion as if she wanted to hold in everything that was escaping her. This lasted but a moment; she flung the rose like a child throwing down its toys and once again, she was a stranger to all who approached her, breathing convulsively.

October 12, 1939

Yesterday, in the office of one of my co-workers, while he was on the telephone, I was overcome with anguish. Imperceptibly, I retreated within myself, my gaze fixed on Laure's deathbed (the one in which I now sleep every night). Laure and the bed were within my heart; in fact, my heart was Laure stretched out on the bed. Within the darkness of this thoracic cage, Laure died just as she was lifting one of a bunch of roses spread out before her. She was holding it as if exhausted, and cried out in a voice almost absent and infinitely painful: "The rose!" I think these were her last words. There in that office and later that evening, the uplifted rose and the cry remained in my heart for a long time. Perhaps Laure's voice wasn't pained, perhaps it was simply heart-rending. I remembered what I had felt that morning: "Take a flower and look at it until harmony..." That was a vision, an internal vision maintained by a silently experienced need. It wasn't a random thought. [...]

October 21, 1939

I sent a letter today breaking off relations with some people whom I should never have trusted to begin with. Too often, I have second thoughts about my decisions. ~~Often, I criticized Laure's violent cursing although I bore it with no little pain, clinging to this suffering as to a chance to live. Now, knowing what I have lived through and what I love, I realize that I would have lost everything without my inexplicable patience. But those who have worn out my patience have completely destroyed the rapport I had with them.~~ [...]
What surrounds me now could all disappear in a few hours. At least, I could bodily leave this dream place. But a beautiful need has been inscribed within me as it was within Laure's destiny. A need to move around in a world full of secret meanings, where I cannot look at a window, a tree or a cabinet door without a great deal of anguish. Neither of us did anything (or very little) to organize the world around ourselves. It simply appeared in place as the fog lifted little by little. It depended on disaster no more than it did on dreams, because a man who desires beauty for what it is will never enter into the world. Insanity, asceticism, hatred, anguish and the domination of fear are all necessary: one must have so much love that even on its threshold,

death appears ludicrous. A window, a tree, a cabinet door, are nothing if they cannot bear witness to movement and to heart-rending destruction. [...]

November 7, 1939

Laure died one year ago today.

I received the following letter from Michel Leiris last Sunday. He has never before expressed himself like this.

Colomb-Bechare: October 29, 1939

Dear Georges,

Here we are, close to that moment of the year when we can look back and consider, sometimes with terror, all that has happened in one year.

I don't want to insist on any one thing (any insistence would be a sacrilige in this case); rather, I want to tell you that sometimes, when I'm in a melancholic mood, I automatically return to certain memories which, everything considered, are more reason to hope than despair.

What unites us with just a few individuals cannot be the extent of all humanly valuable things, of all things capable of surviving any and all vicissitudes.

I'm using rather solemn language. Here – far from my usual practice – language which makes me a little ashamed, out of modesty perhaps, or out of human respect (sacrificing once more my mania to reduce everything). I hope you will forgive me and understand despite my words all that I would like to say to you as spontaneously as an expression of grief or a burst of laughter. [...]

Michel

I just came out of the Helder Theatre where I saw *Wuthering Heights*: Heathcliff living with Cathy's ghost as I wanted to live with Laure's ghost. Last Saturday, in La Vaissent, I dreamed about Wuthering Heights, I even dreamed about it in Ferlouc. I suppose this peregrination from house to house in the mountains was necessary for me to forget my dislike for "comedy," but that is my current explanation. After all, I'm beginning to feel more and more ignorant.

I have stopped thinking insistently about Laure. The thought of Denise, alive, possesses me entirely. In the middle of all this chaos, I am alive. Inebriated by this weighty purity of Denise, more beautiful than I could have ever imagined (but beautiful, it seems to me, as an animal is beautiful). To not love Denise this way, to not feel this death like uneasiness in my heart would be to betray everything. It is as inconceivable as a plant that has stopped budding and growing. [...]

In December of 1937, we asked Maurice Heine to drive us to the spot that Sade had chosen for his own burial. "He shall be sown over the acorns..." Consumed by oak roots, disintegrating to nothingness in the earth beneath a thicket of bushes... It was snowing that day, and we lost our way in the forest. The wind was savage. After we returned, Laure and I prepared a dinner for Ivanov and Odolevtsova. As we had expected, dinner was no less savage than the wind. Odolevtsova undressed and began vomiting.

In March of 1938, we went back to the same spot with Michel Leiris and Zette. Heine didn't go with us. On this occasion at Eperon, Laure saw the last film of her life, "The One Way Trip" (a 1932 film by Tay Garnett), which she had never seen before. She walked all day as if death weren't wearing her away. And we arrived in broad daylight at the edge of the pond Sade had chosen. The Germans had just taken Vienna and the air already smelled of war. That evening, Laure thought about taking Leiris and Zette for a walk along a path we both liked. We wanted to invite them to have dinner with us, but no sooner had we returned than Laure began to feel the first effects of the illness which would eventually cause her death. She had a high fever and went to bed, unaware that she would probably never get up again. After she saw Sade's "grave," Laure went out only once. At the end of August, I took her by car to our Saint-Germain house in the forest. She fell once, in front of a tree that had been struck by lightning. On the way there, we traveled over the Montaigu plains whose hills and fields greatly delighted Laure. But no sooner had we entered the forest than she saw two dead crows, hanging from the branches of a tree...

> *I would have wanted him to always*
> *accompany me*
> *and precede me*
> *Like a knight and his herald.*
> [*The Crow*. From *The Writings of Laure*]

We were not far from the house. I saw the two crows a few days later, when I passed by the same spot. I told her; she shivered and choked on her words so badly that I was frightened. I understood only after her death that she had considered the dead birds as a sign. But by then Laure was nothing more than an inert body. I had just looked through her manuscripts and one of the first I had read was *The Crow*.

June 3, 1940

Paris was just bombed and someone told me that a bomb had fallen on the Boileau Street Clinic where Laure had spent two months before our trip to Saint-Germain on July 15, 1938, where she eventually died. I don't know if anything was destroyed. Will Saint-Germain crumble to the ground, too? In a letter to Leiris, Laure herself wrote that the house which she disdainfully called "the Nunnery" would certainly come to a disastrous end. I'm writing this now as everything is tending towards the "sonorous, absurd and violent chaos" she foresaw as the fate of the world. Let me add: on the threshold of glory, I found death masquerading as nudity, complete with garters and black silk stockings. Whoever met anything more human, whoever tolerated a more tolerable fury? Yet this fury took me by the hand and led me into hell.

I have just told you about my life: death had taken the name Laure. For those whom I love, I am a provocation. I can't stand to see them forget how much good fortune they would have if they only would play.

Laure used to play. I played with Laure. Now I can no longer rest because I won. All I can do is play again, re-animate this really insane fate...

Laure played and won. Laure died.

Soon, said Laure, I'll miss the sun.

Translated by Tom Gora

"The Writing, Always the Writing"
Interview: Hélène Cixous

Partie.

I departed from Algeria. I am a part of Algeria. I am still part of Algeria. I am detained in Algeria by the dead who clutch the fringes of my memory. By the innumerable unknown Algerian dead. By the body of my father whose dust returned to the North African dust, my father from Oran much more anciently and entirely African than I, and no doubt even more autochthonous than we knew when he was alive. Algeria is my forbidden mother. I was born from her womb but I knew from my first words that we were destined for separation. I am bound to her by feelings of mourning. It's an original and painless grief. I was born into this separation and I always made the most of it. I have never lost it having never thought of it as mine. I have always felt for her a detached love. It's perhaps from her, who knows, for having always been a departed part of her, that I got the experience of love without clutching, delicate love, without a movement of appropriation. I was four years old, I knew that the day would come when I'd have to leave, it was inscribed and necessary. While living in Oran, in Algiers, my mind was elsewhere, in the North. The body in Oran. I lived each detail each mark, each rhythm of my native City with passion. I contemplated it and I took it in as one looks at one's dear mother's face in the window of the train on the station platform. I saw Oran. Oran has always existed as an epiphany. Like a minor character, but one who had always already been transported by Accident above the theater, I saw everyone around me in the Oranian scene as if I were ejected into the air. (Compare the experience of Nils Holgerson.) In this way I grasped very early the strange mythical structure of the Oranian topology. Hard to imagine a more metaphorical geography.

Although I could not name it at the time, my neighborhood had the configuration of an epic theater. I was sitting to the right on the second balcony, and I saw the events of the century summed up on the Place d'Armes: I saw the parades of Maréchal Pétain. The entry of the forces françaises libres. De Gaulle. The American landing. All these fateful scenes whose action reshaped the history of the world were perfectly readable for me. On one hand I saw the shining world of the Allies on the rise. But on the other I saw the other world, forgotten by the victories, going down my somber street. I never knew the naíve joy of a clear conscience. What's more, the tobacco shop bazaar that my grandfather opened on the corner formed by two streets of the Place d'Armes was called The Two Worlds. There is no mistake about it. My life has always been in the angle of the angle, angled, on the corner between two worlds. The boutique still exists long after the deaths and the departures. Some Algerian friends just told me that there, at The Two Worlds, for the last fifteen years Mr. Alloula met with his friends from the Theater of Oran, all democrats and artists, before being murdered yesterday. Standing at the corner of the two worlds, I saw what I still see, conjunction, discord, anachrony, all the conditions for tragedy.

I knew the impatiences and the impotence of mothers or prophets: I prayed that the war of liberation would flare up. I want freedom for the other, without which my own freedom is nothing, but I cannot give it to him: it is you my child, you my sister who must take it. Freedom given: freedom taken back. I departed from Algeria. All that I am and all that I have done starts in Algeria.

I have said elsewhere (in *My Algeriance*) that when I departed, it was a pure departure: without return and without arrival; I departed. Gesture of weaning. Behind me my mother stays in Algeria, and my father is dead. I had not counted on going to a country either chosen or desired. I went to France without thinking about it: I went to non-Algeria. So that when I arrived in France, I did not find myself there, I did not arrive there. What is more I have never managed to arrive in France. I have traveled in the language with visas borrowed from Montaigne or Stendhal. I did not exchange one country for another. I did not lose Algeria: I did not replace her. If I had arrived somewhere, if I had become someone, if I had taken the name of a country, she would have slipped in the past. I did not have the need for a country, I had already entered the borderless country of texts. But to have the experience of not-arriving where you sojourn was unexpected. First a fright, then an exaltation. Some people have a desire to belong. Clarice Lispector responded to the accidental arrival of her family in Brazil with a gesture of active adoption of the country and the language that had happened her way. I have never wanted, never been able to want to "belong" to France. A complex, overdetermined, dated History.

There are many Frances, of course, one on the right, one on the left, one pro-Dreyfus, one anti-Dreyfus, one France that swore she would gladly take in, another France that expels, drives out, hunts down, hands over, betrays. One is no more France than the other. I have non-French nationality. The impossibility of an identification and any settling down is my historical luck. Elsewhere is my nomad home. I am not the only one of my kind.

There are non-French people born of that Algeria kept impossible, with whom I speak non-French. I have in common with J. Derrida a freed language, that does not become fixed.

My books do not settle down. I like books that slip away, the escapees.

Algeria is not in my texts, neither in person nor in plot. There could never have been "the Arab." An instinctual respect has always kept me from claiming a share of the inheritance that was due to the Algerians, or to exercise the right to write about a land that had not had the time to get its breath back: I did not know its past when I lived there, I was only the witness to a violent present that made of my existence a time of anguish and anger. As a child I was exposed, eyes peeled, ears open, what was not said with words, the rage, the humiliation, the truth of the exploitation, the hatred, the resentment, was said with looks, with intonations, with cries moans and silences. I saw everything and heard everything and I wept. Most "French people" had secreted that wax in their eyes and ears that allows oppressors to live happily amongst the tortured.

Not to write about Algeria, not before she was resuscitated from among the dead, not before the Algerians had written their Algeria, was my loving farewell to this country.

Algeria was beautiful, musical, perfumed, desirable. With emotion, with regret, but without resentment or bitterness, I did not taste of its dances and festivals. But it is always the Algeria in me that has danced, and Algeria the woman is the first woman I ever loved.

I would like to talk about hatred, in Algeria, about a certain quality of hatred that united us, a composite of hope and despair, I would like to talk about love, because there was love, and about outlawed love, about the hunting of love, about the obligation to reluctantly respect the stiffening of the other obliged to remain faithful to the spirit of separation. At that time I preferred Corneille to Racine. Corneille was the ferocity of self against oneself: for honor.

There was a great deal of honor. Out of the spirit of honor I let myself be hated by my Algerian neighbors. We were locked more than once in hand-to-hand combat, in the avid embrace of separation. I departed out of impossible love. In Algeria, Romeo and Juliet would have had to separate for at least fifty years, not to obey their families, but in order to wait for the passing of the incredible disjunction of times that made relations fated between those who, much later, in another life would embrace each other.

I thought: we will never meet while I'm alive. I will never again see Beauty. Well, I was mistaken about the date. Algeria returned to me in 1995, covered with blood, but smiling beneath the tears. She called me my daughter my sister.

Interviewed by Rosalind C. Morris
Translated by Keith Cohen and Eric Nowitz

POLITICS, DOMESTICITY AND FLIGHT

Why Theory?
Jean Baudrillard

To be the reflection of the real, or to enter into a relation of critical negativity with the real, cannot be theory's goal. This was the pious vow of a perpetuated era of Enlightenment, and to this day it determines the intellectual moral standing. But today this appealing dialectic seems unsettled. What good is theory? If the world is hardly compatible with the concept of the real which we impose upon it, the function of theory is certainly not to reconcile, but on the contrary, to seduce, to wrest things from their condition, to force them into an over-existence which is incompatible with the real. Theory pays dearly for this in a prophetic autodestruction. Even if it speaks of surpassing the economic, theory itself can not be an economy of discourse. To speak about excess and sacrifice, it must become excessive and sacrificial. It must become simulation if it speaks about simulation, and deploy the same strategy as its object. If it speaks about seduction, theory must become seducer, and deploy the same stratagems. If it no longer aspires to a discourse of truth, theory must assume the form of a world from which truth has withdrawn. And thus it becomes its very object.

The status of theory can not be anything but a challenge to the real. Or rather, the relation is one of respective challenge. For the real itself is doubtless only a challenge to theory. It is not an objective state of things, but a radical limit of analysis beyond which nothing any longer obeys, or about which nothing more can be said. Theory is also made solely to disobey the real, of which it is the inaccessible limit. The impossibility of reconciling theory with the real is a consequence of the impossibility of reconciling the subject with its own ends. All attempts at reconciliation are illusory and doomed to failure.

It is not enough for theory to describe and analyze, it must itself be an event in the universe it describes. To do so theory must partake of and become the acceleration of this logic. It must tear itself from all referents and take its pride only in the future. Theory must operate on time at the cost of a deliberate distortion of present reality. In this one must pursue the model of history, which has separated so many things from their nature and mythical origin in order to reverse them in time. Today they must be wrested from their history and end, so they may recapture their enigma, their reversible path, their destiny.

Theory must anticipate its own destiny, because for every thought one must expect a strange tomorrow. Theory is, at any rate, destined to be diverted and manipulated. It is better for theory to divert itself, than to be diverted from itself. If it aspires to any *effets de vérité* it must eclipse them through its own movement. This is why writing exists. If thought does not anticipate this deviation in its own writing, the world will do so through vulgarization, the spectacle or through repetition. If truth does not dissimulate itself, the world will conjure it away by diverse means, by a kind of objective irony, or vengeance.

Once again, what is the point of saying that the world *is* ecstatic, that it *is* ironic, that the world *is* objective? It is those things, that's that. What is the point of saying that it is not? It is so anyway. What is the point of not saying it at all? All theory can do is defy the world to be more: more objective, more ironic, more seductive, more real or unreal. What else? It has meaning only in terms of this exorcism. It thus takes on the power of a fatal sign, even more inexorable than reality, which can perhaps protect us from this inexorable reality, this objectivity, from this brilliance of the world, whose indifference would enrage us if we were lucid.

Let us be Stoics: if the world is fatal, let us be more fatal. If it is indifferent, let us be more indifferent. We must conquer the world and seduce it through an indifference that is at least equal to the world's.

To counter the acceleration of networks and circuits, the world will seek slowness, inertia. In the same movement, however, it will seek something more rapid than communication: the challenge, the duel. On the one side, inertia and silence. On the other, challenge and the duel. The fatal, the obscene, the reversible, the symbolic, are not concepts, since nothing distinguishes the hypotheses from the assertion. The enunciation of the fatal is also fatal, or it is nothing at all. In this sense it is a discourse where truth is withdrawn (just as one pulls a chair out from under a person about to sit down).

The Angel
David Rattray

July 2, 1961, en route from Oaxaca to Pochutla. It's now more than a week since we drove from Saint Louis out to Texas. We left the Buick in El Paso, with arrangements for its eventual recovery, crossed the border and caught a southbound bus out of Juarez. We have been up on amphetamine much of the time. We look like escapees from a reform school.

In Oaxaca we examined a map with elevation lines like spider webs. I noticed quite a few peaks above 3,000 meters – in other words, 9,000 feet. Looking at the Pacific coast, we had to choose between Puerto Escondido (Hidden Port) and Puerto Angel (Angel Port). I liked Hidden Port where you vanish. Van insisted on Angel Port: "We'll get our wings."

The mountains between Oaxaca and the coast are cold and steep. The one-lane highway never stops climbing, a ribbon of mud strung between curtains of silver fog and sleet. An hour ago, hail was beating against the rusty frame of this bus. We huddled together, sweating and shivering and grinding our teeth from too much dexedrine. A handful of our fellow-passengers are Indians; the rest are Spanish, a dozen in all. There are also a goat and several crates of chickens. The storm passed, and the inside of the bus flooded with moonlight. I could see the driver's face in the rear-view mirror, black-mustached under a quasi-military cap.

Van's mind is like an all-night movie house. I sleep, then wake up, the bus standing still. Van tells me there was a couple fucking in the back seat. The driver and his Cuban assistant joked about the floor show. We just reached the head of the pass. From here on, until we reach the coast tomorrow morning, it's downhill. We step out into a cold wet cloud, Van humming *Round About Midnight*.

The cloud flowing round us, we piss. Lit up by the bus headlights on the rockface, there is a shrine the size of a bird house with a statue of the Virgin Mary: Ntra. Sra. de la Soledad. The floor of the inside of the shrine is bright red, its walls cobalt blue, suggesting a point where Heaven touches a blood-soaked hilltop.

The mountain is sopping wet and makes the same sound all mountains make when the sounds of forests, streams, and waterfalls are far below.

The cloud parted. We plunged in brightest moonlight, covered with mist droplets as if with tiny diamonds. We could see fifty miles of mountains stretching westward from the glistening sheet of mud at our feet.

We went to the refreshment shack at the roadside and bought some mezcal. Does it contain peyote? We cracked jokes about gruesome accidents on mountain roads.

At dawn we reached Candelarias, on a plateau at the head of the foothills leading down to the coastal plain, a village of mudbrick houses with palmleaf roofs. It is the relay station for the last leg of the journey to Pochutla. The relief driver who should have been waiting was not there. Our driver announced there would be a stop of several hours in Candelarias. We could sleep for free on the terrace outside the café.

The sun rose through the treetops, a warm red disk. The café owner offered straw mats for those who bought food and drink. Hungover and shaky, we got glazed donuts and some café con leche, then went for a walk in the still-cool morning.

On either side, the dirt path was overspread with lush vegetation, leaftops powdered with dust. Van estimated we were looking at no less than fifty different narcotic plants. We peered at them, trying vainly to guess which were the ones.

Little Rootie Tootie is also a favorite of Van's. He once tinkered with it for hours on my piano, expanding it into a cadenza from a Romantic concerto, then rendering it a la Satie, and at last filling it out Cecil Taylor fashion. He assured me the history of music was in that one tune. There was a bar with a piano in Saint Louis where Van was improvising one afternoon last winter. A black musician came in and laughingly told him he had "a deep streak of coon."

July 4, on the beach outside Puerto Angel, in a shack rented from the local police commander. Steaming under the sun, the jungle that starts just behind this place is full of birds, yellow, orange, green, singing, screaming, screeching mostly, sailing among the floppy leaves of nameless trees, tearing through holes in the treetops and out into the sky. Victory rolls, Immelmanns, loop the loops. That's some crazy flying, Van comments.

From his verandah in Pochutla when we made the rental agreement for the shack, the commander was taking pot shots at small crocodiles in the adjacent ravine. He collects pistols and has a library of Spanish classics, as well as Greek and Latin authors, Church fathers, and many books on philosophy and the history of religions, magic, and the occult.

The Pacific: a warm bathtub filled with an infinity of parasitic and carnivorous beings. One does not feel like stout Cortez. The barracuda are too close. I wade in in the underpants I've had on for the past few days. This will wash them out. Tepid water disgusts me. Van plunges in, wearing nothing but his sunglasses. He says he loves water like this. After splashing about for a few moments we emerge, unrefreshed, in steaming sun. In this light Van's hair looks burnt-gold, curling like Alexander the Great's. There could be a hint of Africa in his cheekbones. His lips contribute to this impression; his body is lean to the point of emaciation, with a thin, vertical scar over the solar plexus, from the operation last year.

Paroxysmal nocturnal hemoglobinuria is a chronic, invariably fatal disease. The splenectomy was a shot in the dark before they knew what he had. Now the diagnosis of P.N.H. has been established, it turns out the operation was a serious error. He is likely to die any time now. On the other hand, he might hang on for years.

July 5. Puerto Angel is such a small place, one meets the aliens immediately. Outsiders are not particularly unwelcome here, but not all that welcome, either. Yesterday we made friends with Chino, a Colombian sailor, age twenty-nine. His English is perfect. He lived in the States. Van says it's obvious Chino is on the lam.

July 6. Leslie Fiedler has an essay in which he pulls together a half dozen instances in American literature of men swimming together and demonstrates that it is really a homoerotic fantasy more or less unconsciously sublimated. This flashed into my mind yesterday, as Van and I paddled in the lukewarm Pacific between stingrays and a bright miasma abuzz with horseflies and mosquitoes. There I was, swimming in an ocean I'd never seen until that day, with my best friend, the two of us like an updated Thomas Eakins. Are we men or boys? I don't know. We do swim a lot.

Last summer, shortly after he recovered from the splenectomy, Van and I made a trip to the White Mountains. We hiked over summits and ridges above timberline, slept in lean-to shelters and cabins. In my mind's eye I remember seeing him jumping up and down in an icy pool in the heat of the midday sun, bathing.

Van talks of blood. Having a blood disease makes him think about it all the time. He quotes Artaud: "To be somebody, you need blood..."

By the time a person turns into "somebody" via a method of analysis whereby one is reduced step by step to a submolecular level, the process is complete. Like a viable work of art, this life continues to evolve in the minds of those touched by it. At an unforeseeable moment, the person living it vanishes.

We have rigged up tents of mosquito netting inside this shack. "Shack" is a grandiose term. It has a roof of palmleaves supported by four posts with a couple of hammocks slung between. There is one wall. The floor is pounded dirt. We have a couple of kerosene lamps borrowed from the commander. I wonder if we will leave here alive.

My mother's friends in East Hampton shop around for a doctor with the perfect bedside manner. Don Giovanni ran through his thousand and three. As a child I was forever daydreaming about Atlantis. According to Van, the kingdom of heaven is here and now, no place else. He quotes the Gospel of Thomas. I on the other hand always want to be elsewhere, someplace like Mu.

Van is concerned about my drinking. It's a strange thing for him to be worrying about, considering the company he kept in Saint Louis. My eyebrows shot up the other day on the mountain pass, when I saw the serape-draped roadside vendor in a round-crowned Indian hat pouring mezcal into empty Coca Cola bottles through a funnel and found out the price was about a dime for a pint. Van noticed my reaction. I expected some kind of comment. Instead he got drunk with me.

July 7. We made friends with the prisoners in the Pochutla market-place. We went in from here on the dawn bus and found them in front of the jail, playing basketball. They get out twice a day, morning and afternoon. We shot a few baskets with them. Soon it will be a habit. Yesterday afternoon we swam out to a rock in the bay near our beach. Sitting on the rock, we saw a barracuda swim past a couple of times. We raced each other ashore.

Whenever we order something to eat at the cafe on the beach, a little Indian girl waits on us. Van says he would like to take her back to the States.

Van has a blazer from Saint Louis that shimmers like a rainbow. He wore it to Pochutla one day and the commander, joking, called it his coat of many colors. Around here Van wears his torn chinos and, when going to the port, puts on an old black teeshirt and tennis sneakers.

We got shaves and haircuts in Pochutla. In the barber shop I read a picture magazine article on Willi, the yodeling parrot. His first owner was a Hitler Youth leader. They are shown skiing in the Tyrol in the summer of 1938. They taught him to scream, "Sieg Heil!" In 1941 he was part of a revue given for Hitler at Berchtesgaden. Today, Willi belongs to a flea circus on tour in the Middle East.

Our general plan is to live here and write books. Puerto Angel's relation to Pochutla is that of Piraeus relative to Athens. Every now and then, the government announces a plan to transform Pochutla and Puerto Angel into something big, because a lot of coffee and other produce move out of here, in spite of the fact that loading is all done by rafts, in the absence of any docks. This year they resurrected the project. The only evidence of anything actually happening is the presence of a German engineer, engaged to survey the possibilities for a real port. No one has any idea what they may be.

Evenings, the cafe on the beach can have its charm. Watching the shadows of the hammocks slung next to the door jump back and forth to the flickering of a kerosene lamp, I recreate the scene as an engraving in a *Harper's Monthly Magazine* of the 1870s. In my mind's eye I picture a title like "Tramping in the By-Ways of Oaxaca." In this light the engineer sitting alone at his table on the other side of the cafe has a pre-Raphaelite bohemian look. Van grows ever more enthralled with the little Indian girl. She is the owner's niece.

As I pause from writing, I can look straight up into the Milky Way. When I climb into the hammock, my feet will point west, toward the Pacific. Van says poetic license is freedom to do exactly what you feel like doing from one minute to the next.

Some things repeat themselves and have to be turned off. Lost continents. A belle époque. I'm twenty-five. This is my belle époque. I am losing out on it. The idea of loss keeps bobbing up to the surface. I don't like putting it in words, even mentally, much less on paper, because saying it makes it come true. I concentrate on the idea of finding, or invention. I draw a blank on that, too. I asked Van if invention wasn't an illusion.

In reply, he said something about alchemy and the concept of the philosopher's stone as a scorned, or unnoticed, beautiful thing that is there in the dust by the roadside, free for the taking. "Just something like a dime you find on the sidewalk, when a dime is what you need."

He said he liked the idea of metamorphosis because change is the law of life and permanence suggests spiritual if not physical death, both of which are also strongly suggested by the idea of closeness with another person: "No one can ever come close to touching another person. Heaven help them if they try."

We saw what looked like a bright star moving across the twilit sky. Van informed me it was Sputnik.

July 8. Van gets skinnier and skinnier, yet it's impossible to think of him as being sick with a fatal illness. I doubt that any of the locals suspect. As we stepped out of the commander's doorway earlier today, I got a glimpse of him framed in pale afternoon sky, the rainbow-striped blazer hung loose about his shoulders, arms out because of the heat, his brown neck and thin shoulders forming an improbably jaunty angle, an effect completed by pegged slacks of olive-colored silk and a brand-new pair of dark brown ankle-strapped Argentino boots.

July 10. Last night Van and I were on the beach looking at a couple of racked-up fishing dugouts that had been parked in the sand. Men, women, and children were coming and going. At sunset, with mealtime impending, there is always much activity on the beach. People here eat seafood caught by themselves or their relatives every day of the week and sell the rest in Pochutla.

You don't need to be an expert to recognize what part of the world this racial type came from. I picture their ancestors trekking from Asia.

One of the dugouts has captured Van's fancy. He thinks it seaworthy. We want to find out whose it is, and whether we could rent it.

Van got diarrhea yesterday. I'm a little off myself. It may be getting time to start taking the Enteroviaform. Dysentery is supposedly endemic here.

I hate the cafe because they play the radio so loud, mostly commercials, a half-hour at a time, and then one ear-splitting love song after another, in which the key word is *corazon*. We can hear the songs deep into the night all the way over here at the shack, half a mile away across the water.

There was a movie on the beach last night. They stretched a bedsheet between two poles. A schoolteacher from Pochutla who has been chatting with me about Lumumba and Fidel manned the projector. For the equivalent of a nickel apiece we rented folding seats from the cafe. It was a double feature. First, a film starring Cantinflas, who looks like many of the guys around here. It was pretty much incomprehensible to us, save for the commedia dell'arte hamming that by itself was worth the price of admission. The second show was an Alan Ladd war movie I had never seen, with flickering Spanish subtitles and a damaged sound track. Small boys were crawling in the sand at our feet.

Pochutla Casino bar, Wednesday, July 12. Yesterday we fasted. The shits have gone away for the time being. Van went fishing with Chino today, in a boat Chino has the use of. Later they picked me up at Chino's place en route to Pochutla in a pickup truck belonging to the cafe owner, loaded with fish. I just came downstairs from fucking a half-Indian, half-Spanish prostitute named Chica in one of the rooms here. Van is still upstairs with the other one, Anita. Chica appears to be in her mid-twenties, my age. Her face is that of an intelligent but perverse child. This was my first experience with a prostitute in America. Van and Anita were still giggling in the next room when Chica and I came down to the bar a few minutes ago. Chino is visiting a woman somewhere else and supposed to come back here in an hour. I am sitting alone with a mezcal and a Carta Blanca. This expedition is costing us somewhere between $5 and $10 (U.S.) apiece. It was Chino's idea. We had no inkling of this place's existence, but when Chino told us about it, we were eager to make the scene. I don't believe Van has ever been inside a bordello in his life, but he sauntered in as if he owned the place. There was no sign of any pimps or bouncers. A crone with bleached hair in a bolero outfit who tends the bar here was the one who collected our money. Chino advised us to tip each of the women $5 (Mexican).

When Van and Chino went out fishing this morning, Chino gave me the keys and told me to go into his storeroom where I would find a bag of marijuana. He asked me to make up a few joints. He says smoking makes driving an adventure; you see more interesting things along the way.

Chino's house is at the other end of Puerto Angel from our shack, next to the Pochutla road, which is the only road leading out of Puerto Angel. The house is built into the side of a small cliff. Its front porch, or sleeping balcony, stands up on stilts. From it one sees the beach and ocean at a distance of maybe 150 yards. Several coconut palms shade the porch and a small front yard. The cliff is overgrown with vines, and there are plenty of birds in the trees overhead. Today they were sitting quietly, because it was raining.

There is a screen of netting round the porch. The house was unlocked. Going in alone, I felt like an intruder. I would make a poor burglar. Both the *Gita* and Bessie Smith advise: Do Your Duty. Another's duty, the *Gita* adds, no matter how well you may do it, will make you insane.

The first thing I saw was a hammock and a Sterno stove on the floor in one corner. The wall was decorated with religious pictures. Candles were set up in front of them on tin cans. These in turn were placed on a red silk cloth, next to a dream book with Art Nouveau lettering on the cover.

In the other corner there was a little alcove with mirror and wash-stand, a bar of soap and a straight razor.

I unlocked the storeroom door. The room is built into the hillside. It's cool and dark. I lit the kerosene lamp hanging in the doorway. Chino's cat was there, crouching in front of a cracked spot at the angle of the wall and the floor, seemingly poised to spring.

I located the marijuana. There was a table and chair. I set the lamp on the table and poured out some of the grass to roll. The cat remained motionless. I noticed, on the floor at my feet, a dead rat, or rather, half a dead rat. The cat had eaten the head and shoulders and part of the legs, but left the rest. Now he was waiting for another, perhaps one that would taste better.

The rat's viscera had begun to dry, taking on the look of a piece of old kidney. I was struck by the absence of flies. The netting works. But the room was a mess, with empty Carta Blanca and Coke bottles and stubbed-out cigarettes on the floor.

The cat sprang. There wasn't even a flurry. He might as well have blown the rat's head off with a gun.

I rolled four, five joints. The cat looked up at me, the prey dangling wetly from his mouth.

I heard steps in the front door and recognized Van's light-footed stride. "Everything under control?" He pushed the door open and took in the scene: me, the marijuana, the cat, the two rats.

"A stricken field," he commented, making a face. The cat slipped by him with a little bound, the rat still dangling. We stepped into a drizzly fog, the same fog and drizzle we have had since yesterday.

I got in the truck next to Chino, giving Van the window place, and showed Chino the jays I had rolled. "Perfecto." As the truck jolted forward, I glimpsed the cat staring at us, its eyes green jewels.

Puerto Angel, July 13. Although Van never mentions P.N.H., he fears he may get a relapse of the "disgusting condition" here. The phrase is a reference to Burroughs: "I am not innarested in your disgusting condition." When someone questioned Van about it, he said it was too disgusting to discuss, and "since I'm not innarested, why should you care?"

We consider the difference between *neether* and *nyther*. Both of us *neether* people, we despise twits that say *nyther*. My grandpa used to say *envellup* for "envelope." Noah Webster probably said it that way, too. I hate linguistic change. Van welcomes it. In an *American Legion Magazine* found in a hospital waiting room he once read the following poem:

Whence all these new faces?
Whither are they going?
Indiscriminate mixing of alien races
May yet prove America's undoing.

"Who's the poet talking about?" he asked, poker-faced.

I said I couldn't begin to guess. "He's talking about us," Van laughed. "The man is an American Indian."

It has been two weeks since we got here. The commander has grown steadily more familiar. Something is happening, Van says. Just tune in on it, you'll pick up.

It began one afternoon when the commander, in a fit of bonhomie, got out a prize possession he keeps in his safe, a jade statuette of a seated jaguar-masked figure that he informed us was a representation of its original owner, an ancient Mixtec prince, or, rather, his heavenly double.

"It's mirrors that are recent," Van pointed out. "Twins have always been around."

"Have you seen the mirrors here?" the commander rejoined. "The black ones? Thomas was Christ's twin."

"Every time I see double," Van replied, "I get the feeling I am peeling off layers."

"*With my eyes of light I see my Twin,*" the commander quoted.

"The last words of Mani," Van put in.

"Spoken while being flayed alive by the King of Persia," the commander added.

As the two of them volleyed back and forth, I sat at a stereopticon viewer that the commander had affably insisted on getting out for me. Replacing the cards one by one in the device's sliding frame, I inspected a series of 3-D images of trussed-up persons being dismembered inch by inch with machetes during the repression of a turn-of-the-century uprising not far from here.

"My father's time," the commander explained.

As I gazed, fascinated, the commander invited us to join him later for dinner at the Casino. Taking leave of the commander for the time being, Van and I issued forth. A letter awaited at the post office, from my mother. She sails next month for Southampton on the *France*. After sleepless nights worrying that I might come to harm in the wilds of southern Mexico, those deck chairs will be heaven, unless they get torpedoed by a Russian submarine. She is dieting to prepare for ship-board dinners. The wicked French make it easy for one to break all the rules without a moment of regret.

Arriving at the Casino, we noticed that Chica and Anita were not present. It turns out the commander owns the place.

The color scheme is red and yellow. Yellow bar, barstools, chairs, tables. Red walls, ceilings, floors, ashtrays. Tibetan colors, Van pointed out. We found the commander enthroned amid half a dozen girls, in an alcove surrounded with potted palms, drinking beer. In the middle of the table was a blood-red bowl filled with flowers. Bullfight music blared from a jukebox. Chatting with the madam-cum-bartender in her bolero outfit, the commander had the air of a queer Oriental potentate. Did Solomon in all his splendor know glories such as these? Address-ing us with courtly formality in the presence of his satellites, the commander wanted to know if we were happy out there in Puerto Angel, did we need anything, would we mind if he came calling some day soon? So he is definitely going to be coming over here this afternoon, or possibly tomorrow. He will bring Chica and Anita, Van tells me.

The dysentery is coming on, no way to stop it. Van jokes about running down the beach and shitting green. There is a low fever and a feeling of tiredness, whether hung over or not. Three tablets of LSD sit in my knapsack like a time bomb. There is a small cemetery a hundred yards east of the shack. People were standing around in there with lit candles yesterday morning when both of us were too sick to move. An English-man who lived for a time on the beach here a few years ago is buried nearby, whether inside the cemetery or outside of it was not made clear.

July 15. Van envies Beckford for writing *Vathek* at one sitting. In 1782, when Beckford did that, facility was at a premium. To be any good, a work of art had to be "easy." Beckford took piano from that paragon of ease, Mozart, and was twenty when he composed *Vathek.*

I have been up for the past couple of days on speed, outlining a story. based on our coming here. I wrote a bit, then drew a blank. To finish it would be too easy. Van says coming here means arriving at the edge of America, the jumping-off place. I don't want to jump in the ocean, thank you. One of my ancestors did just that. She walked into the water at Amagansett beach one night in the 1840s. All they ever found was footprints down to the surf line. For me, coming here was more like jumping through an invisible hoop that is in the air, and if you go through just right, you are on the other side. Also, there is something special about the mountains and the wilderness to the south of here.

For instance, 120 years ago a Danish botanist named Liebman was in that very wilderness collecting specimens and came upon a village of blond Indians speaking old-fashioned Danish. He later looked into records at Pochutla and learned that a Danish pirate ship was wrecked off Huatulco in 1600, or thereabouts. Survivors made their way up the coast. Their descendants were still speaking Danish in the vicinity of Pochutla within living memory, Mexico's secret Vikings. The commander's father was on friendly terms with them.

My contemporaries in East Hampton call me Moon. How are they hangin', Moon? The nickname goes back to a day in 1944 when I electrified the schoolyard by pointing at the moon in the mid-afternoon sky and shrieking "Moon! Moon!" I induced a crowd of other children to scream and point the same way. We pranced, screeching at the top of our lungs, back into the schoolhouse. This went on for weeks. Many who saw it never forgot.

Soon after, I began my first writing project. A chum named Frankie showed me a children's book, *Many Moons,* from the local library. We did a stage adaptation. I wrote the script, and Frankie directed. My whole reason for doing it was to play the role of the black-caped, elegantly Luciferian villain.

Frankie and I squabbled over the parts in a version to be played by just the two of us. Frankie said I wanted all the best ones. He called me a show-off.

Our thoughts were diverted from the theater when we found a huge Victorian baby carriage in the barn, a natural for the nacelle and landing carriage of an 1899 model Clement Ader "Avion." All it needed to become airborne was an engine hooked up to an aerial screw, I explained, plus a pair of batlike wings and a tail. This could all be easily put together at the garage, Halsey's, where Frankie's dad was a mechanic.

"David," Frankie said (he never called me Moon), "that carriage is a stagecoach."

Years later, I learned the moon was a hieroglyph of exile, separation, separateness, a way-station for souls descending from the stars into the bodies of "all creatures here below" (in the words of a hymn we sang in church Sunday mornings). Ultimately, it stood for the presence of the Deity withdrawn from the world.

I called the hermits in my story "girovagos" because they were wanderers (vagos) who gyrated through both mundane and mystic spheres. They were also citizens of a secret utopia.

July 16, the commander's visit. Today was a turning-point. I think we are going to have to leave soon.

There is a crummy shell of a building, on a bluff over the water midway between our shack and the port, belonging to the commander. He is reviving a plan to fix it up and open a casino here in Puerto Angel. Wait till they start building the new port, he exclaims. In his enthusiasm the commander refers to the old concrete ruin as The Angel. You fellows have got to come out to The Angel with me this afternoon. It's fascinating. The path is overgrown. My mozo is going up right now with a machete.

The commander's valet was off and running. Van gazed after him from behind horn-rimmed wraparounds. The commander had brought Chica and Anita from the Pochutla Casino, as well as a bottle of tequila. We had been shitting our guts out of late. I hoped the strong drink would give some relief. We stood round the jeep, clinking glasses. "To the Angel!" The tequila burned going down. My head swam. We gazed at the lagoon shimmering in wet heat half a mile out over the bay.

"Yesterday an Indian was half killed by a barracuda over there," the commander mused. "Incidentally, I read an article about an experimental product, LSD. Are you familiar with it? Writers I would expect to keep up with such things. You must have looked into it. I wouldn't be surprised if you had brought some with you here. If so, could I ask you as a favor to part with some of it? I have an experiment in mind. A single dose would do."

"As a matter of fact," Van answered, and I didn't believe I was hearing him say this, "we are able to oblige. It is a tiny amount, but that is all that's necessary."

The commander enacted a pantomime of delight, his hands and eyes upturned as though thanking Heaven.

Had someone gone through our things? Did Van tell him? I was scared. I spoke, for the first time since we had toasted The Angel, "I'll get it out for you before you go back to Pochutla."

"Oh, no, thank you," said the commander. "I'd prefer to look at it immediately, if you wouldn't mind. I was asking the doctor only yesterday. He knows very little but thinks it may be related to some of the substances Indians use. He has noticed people in the marketplace at times when they come down from the hills, places you wouldn't imagine exist in this day and age, with something very odd about their eyes and the way they move. He'd like to check. I was thinking, as a favor, don't you know, why not provide a subject?"

The valet was returning, trotting along the road, his shouldered machete gleaming in the sun.

Van went into the shack and returned with one of the tablets, setting it on the red oilcloth in front of the commander. The commander filled a glass, then rolled up his sleeves. I noticed marks that had to be needlemarks on the veins of his forearms.

"Should it be dissolved or just washed down?" the commander asked.

"Washed down is okay," Van replied.

"All right, my boy," said the commander, "here's your drink and here is a special vitamin for your head." He patted the mozo on the head, then shouted, "Yes, your head, your head," slapping it from side to side, "tu cabeza, your pretty little head, tu cabezita, chico!"

Like a Bedouin storyteller unfolding a tale in which the hero is carried by a bird to a city of greater than material splendors, the commander raised one hand to point to the clouds over the mountains thirty miles to the east. "You will walk on those clouds over there."

The commander's lower lip was edged with a hint of froth at one corner of his mouth. The skin over his cheekbones stretched smooth and taut, his eyes were pinned. The mozo knelt at his feet, hands clasped, eyes imploring, gasping as the commander continued. The machete was out of reach, in back of the jeep. The mozo stood up with a shriek. The commander knocked him down and pinned him in the sand, whooping delightedly. The mozo was unable to move. Chica pried his jaws apart, jamming his cheeks between the molars. The mozo was stubborn. Anita held his head still, whispering endearments. Chica located a gap in his teeth and pushed.

Van stood there looking imperturbable behind his dark glasses. The commander gazed up at me. I knew what I was supposed to do. I picked up the tablet and dropped it into the mozo's bleeding mouth. He tried to spit it out, an impossibility because his mouth was being held open. The commander looked up again. The glass of tequila. I stared at the orange tablet. It was stuck to his tongue, which for the moment had stopped lolling around inside his mouth. The tablet was dissolving. His tongue was coated white. The tablet formed a little patch, magenta on white, slashed with a vivid streak extending from it like a comet's tail. I could count each individual taste bud on the tongue's pink-and-white stippled surface. The bright orange reached me out of the midst of it like the fiery wheels Ezekiel saw bursting out of the cloud. The tongue started moving. Amazing how much the human tongue resembles the tongue of any other animal.

The commander was gazing insistently into my eyes. The drink. Get the drink and pour it down his throat. I'd forgotten about that. I turned to Van. He hadn't moved. Behind the dark glasses he was staring, too. The valet was struggling now. I reached for the glass and poured its contents in his mouth. The mouth was bleeding quite a lot by this time. What was left of the tablet vanished down his gullet. They clapped his mouth shut and held it tight. He gulped, trying to vomit. After a while he lay still. Chica ran to the jeep and returned with two lengths of rope.

We tied the mozo and carried him to the back of the jeep. Anita wiped his face, licking a corner of her handkerchief and dabbing the cut on his lip. She wiped the tears from his cheeks, kissing him, "We love you, honey, we wouldn't do you any harm."

"Maulhalten!" said the commander. He turned to me, "That's what the German fellow says when he has heard enough girl-talk."

"Maulhalten!" he repeated, imitating the engineer. Anita looked down at the still-tearful valet. She kissed his eyes and patted him. We all went down to the water's edge and washed the blood off our hands. Women are sentimental, the commander said. Yes, Van agreed, they are. The commander poured a final round before setting out for the Angel. He said he intended to turn our friend over to the doctor as soon as they returned. As we filed through the path hacked out of the thick undergrowth by the mozo an hour earlier, the commander questioned Van about symptoms, duration of intoxication, and possible after-effects.

Anita and Chica followed the two of them; I brought up the rear, cradling the tequila bottle in my arm. I wondered how I could ever have been attracted to Chica. Her cream-colored jacket sagged to one side from the salt cellar and lemon she had picked up from the back of the jeep when we stowed the mozo. She wasn't wearing it when she helped subdue him. The commander paused to roll down his sleeves. As always, he was wearing a white shirt. Van and I were in tee-shirts, slapping bugs. We climbed round another little bend in the path, then after a quick scramble past some freshly mutilated undergrowth, we were there, on top. The commander stretched his arm in a seigneurial gesture. We seemed to have moved outside the mosquito zone. Gulls were going crazy in the sky between us and the bay.

Since the advent of concrete, one abandoned semi-finished resort hotel is more or less identical with another, making due allowances for size. I've seen them in several parts of the world, and they're all alike. The Angel was no exception, only it was smaller and tackier than most.

The sudden change in perspective, together with the first breath of somewhat cooler air in days, brought about a sudden, if only momentary, clearing of the wind. In this interval of lucidity, it occurred to me that our journey to the edge of the world was just a copy of something we had been reading and seeing movies about ever since childhood.

The white adventurer who goes to an exotic land, usually some tropical hellhole with dark-skinned people and a cast of characters evolving from G.A. Henty and the Tom Swift books through Bowles, B. Traven, and on to Burroughs, in search of buried treasure, gold, diamonds, drugs, the secret of life, what have you. After many adventures, the hero grabs the goods and hightails it home. Many fail (*The Treasure of Sierra Madre*, for instance, or Rimbaud's attempt to get rich off gun-running and the slave trade), but others make a go of it. Would we want to be among the successful ones? I rather doubt it. Van actually sympathizes with the locals. I don't all that much myself, in spite of admiration for Castro and others like him, but that kind of reading predisposes me to look on our whole enterprise, Van's and mine, as a cliché in the collective fantasy life of the imperialist nation we hail from. Only a couple of years ago in Paris, I even toyed with the idea of renouncing my nationality in order to become a naturalized French citizen. This was when my fellow-students and I actually believed it possible to turn the struggle against De Gaulle and his generals into a revolutionary civil war, and what a joke that was! This is an even bigger one. Thanks to our books, Van and I have gravitated toward the kind of people and situations we read about, and now we are in the middle of the same sort of mess in real life, only there is no story-line, no coherence to it, it's just a mess. The commander is a lunatic. I am quite sure he could kill us on a whim and never give a thought to the consequences; but I think behind all his funny ways he's too conventional, too much of a mediocrity to dream of doing such a thing. In real life the commander is more like a figment of a Hollywood imagination than he would be if we saw him in one of the thrillers they project on a bedsheet one the beach here Sunday nights...

The Last Vehicle
Paul Virilio

Tomorrow learning space will be just as useful as learning to drive a car.
—Wernher von Braun

In Tokyo there is a new indoor swimming pool equipped with a basin of intensely undulating water in which the swimmers remain in one place. The turbulence prevents any attempt to move forward, and the swimmers must try to advance just to hold their position. Like a kind of home-trainer or conveyor belt on which one moves against the motion of the belt, the dynamics of the currents in this Japanese pool have the sole function of forcing the racing swimmers to struggle with the energy passing through the space of their confluence, an energy that takes the place of the dimensions of an Olympic pool just as the belts of the home trainer replace stadium race tracks.

In such cases the person working out thus becomes less a moving body than an island, a pole of inertia. Like in a theater set, everything is focused on the stage; everything occurs in the special instant of an act, an inordinate instant offering a substitute for expanses and long stretches of time. Not so much a golf course as a video performance, not so much an oval track as a running simulator: space no longer expands. Inertia replaces the continual change of place.

One observes a similar trend in museographic presentation. Being too vast, the most spacious exhibitions have recently been subject to temporal reduction in inverse proportion to their overall dimensions. Twice the amount of space to cover means twice as little time to spend in any one place.

The acceleration of the visit is conditioned by the area of the exhibition. Too much space, too little time, and the museum welters in useless expanse that can no longer be furnished with works of art. In any case, probably because of this situation, the art works tend to make a show of themselves, to pour themselves into these vast and utterly uninviting surfaces, just like the grand perspectives of the classical period.

Whereas our monuments were once erected to commemorate significant works that can still be viewed for long periods by visitors interested in the past, they are presently simply ignored in the excessive zeal of the viewer, this "amateur" who seems to have to be forced to fixate for more than only a moment. The more impressive the size of the volumes presented, the quicker he tries to escape.

We are speaking of the monument of a moment in which the work tends to disappear without a trace, more than its self-exposure. The contemporary museum vainly attempts to assemble and present these works, these pieces that one ordinarily views only from a distance, in the atelier, the workplace, in these laboratories of a heightened perception that is never the perception of the passer-by, this passing viewer distracted by his exertion. With regard to this perspective of retention, of the restriction of the time to pass through, of passing by, we should point to another project. It presents a miniaturized reconstitution of the state of Israel where "in complete safety and with a minimum of physical movement, visitors can marvel at the exact copy of the Holocaust museum, a small section of the wailing wall, and the miniaturized reconstitution of the Sea of Galilee created with a few cubic meters of water from the original." The directors of this institution could well seize the opportunity to exhibit electronic components. Products could be sited in Douarnenez, on Tristan da Cunha when these islands are finally ceded by France to Israel.

Even if this utopia never really comes to be, it reveals in exemplary fashion this *tellurian contraction*, this sudden "overexposure" now befalling the expansion of territories, the surfaces of the vastest objects, as well as the nature of our latest displacement. It's a displacement in place, the advent of an inertia that is what has always been as the "still-frame" in film, as far as the landscape through which we walk is concerned. Also the advent of a final generation of vehicles, of means of communication over distances no longer associated with the revolution of transport – as if the conquest of space ultimately only confirmed the conquest of mere *images* of space. In fact, if the end of the nineteenth and the beginning of the twentieth century marked the advent of automotive vehicles, the dynamic vehicles of the railroad, the street, and then the air, then the end of this century seems to herald the next vehicle, the audiovisual, a final mutation: the static vehicle, stand-in for the change of physical location, an extension of domestic inertia, a vehicle that should finally bring about the victory of the sedentary, this time an ultimate sedentary.

The transparency of space, of the horizon of our travels, of our racing, should then be followed by this *cathodic transparency*, which is simply the final realization of the discovery of glass some four-thousand years ago, of iron two-thousand years ago, and of that "glass showcase," that puzzling object that has constituted the history of urban architecture from the Middle Ages down to our own times or, more precisely, down to the most recent realization of the *electronic glass case*, the final horizon of travel of which the most developed model is the "flight simulator."

This is also made obvious by the latest developments in amusement parks, those laboratories of physical sensations with their slides, catapults, and centrifuges, referencing training models for flight personnel and astronauts. In the opinion of the very people responsible, even vicarious pleasure is becoming a collective experimentation with mere mental and imaginary sensations.

In the previous century the leisure park became the theater of physiological sensations to a working population for which many different physical activities were no longer available. Thereafter, the leisure park prepared to become the scene of mere optical illusions, the place for a generalization of simulation, fictitious movements that can create in each person an electronic hallucination or frenzy – a "loss of sight" following upon the loss of physical activity in the nineteenth century. Though analogous to the unusual dizzying calling of the gymnast, it is nevertheless true that the "panoramas," "dioramas," and other cinematographies smoothed the way toward the "panorama," to "Geode," a hemispheric movie anticipated by Grimoin-Sanson's "balloon cinerama." These are all old forms of our present audiovisual vehicles, whose more precise forerunners were the American *Hale's Tours*. A few of these were actually funded by the railroad companies between 1898 and 1908. Remember that these films, which were shot on a panoramic platform either from a locomotive engine or from the rear of the train, were ultimately shown to the public in halls that were exact imitations of the railroad cars of that epoch. Some of these short films were made by Billy Bitzer, the future cameraman for D.W.Griffith.

At this point, however, we must return to the origins of kinematic illusion, to the Lumiere brothers, to the 1895 film "L'entrée d'un train en gare de La Ciotat," and above all to the spring of 1896, when the very first traveling shot was invented by Eugene Promio.

> It was in Italy that I first had the idea of shooting panoramic film. When I arrived in Venice and took a boat from the train station to the hotel, on the Grand Canal, saw the banks recede from the skiff, I thought *if the immovable camera allowed moving objects to be reproduced, then one could perhaps also invert this statement and should try to use the mobile camera to reproduce immovable objects.* So I shot a reel of film, which I sent to Lyon with a request to hear what Louis Lumiere thought of this experiment. The answer was encouraging.

To comprehend the significance of this introduction of the "mobile camera" or, to put it another way, the first static vehicle, we must again look back at the course of history. Disregarding for the moment Nadar's "aerostatic negatives" (1858), which were indeed the origin of cinematic weightlessness, one must wait until 1910 to find the first "aeronautic film," taken on board a Farman airplane. The now traditional "moving camera," which was mounted on tracks and which is inseparable from the contemporary cinema, came about four years later during the shooting of *Cabiria* by Giovanni Pastrone. For memory's sake, let us also mention the trains of AGIT PROP between 1918 and 1925 and the use of train travel in the work of Dziga Vertov. He joins Moscow's film committee in the spring of 1918, waiting until 1923 to promote the founding of a "cinematographic automobile department" that would provide cars if urgently needed to film important events. These cars are thus predecessors of the mobile video productions of television. With this use of transport, this conjoining of the automotive and the audiovisual, our perception of the world inevitably changes. The optical and the cinematic blend. Albert Einstein's theory, subsequently to be called the Special Theory of Relativity, appears in 1905. It will be followed about ten years later by the General Theory of Relativity. To make themselves more understandable, both take recourse in metaphors of the train, streetcar, and elevator, vehicles of a theory of physics that owes them everything, or, as far as people will see, almost everything. The revolution of transport will coincide with a characteristic change in the meaning of arrival, with a progressive negation of the time interval, the accelerated retention of the duration of passage that holds arrival and depart. Spatial distance collapses suddenly into mere temporal distance. The longest journeys become scarcely more than simple intermissions.

But if, as already shown, the nineteenth century and a large part of the twentieth experienced the rise of the automotive vehicle in all its forms, its eventual mutation is by no means completed. As before, except now more rapidly, it will speed the transition from the itinerancy of nomadic life to inertia, to a society ultimately sedentary.

Contrary to all appearances, the audiovisual vehicle has triumphed since the 1930s with radio, television, radar, sonar, and emerging electronic optics. First during the war, then after, despite the massive development of the private car, during peace, during this "nuclear peace" which will experience the *information revolution*, the telematic informatics so tightly linked to the various policies of military and economic deterrence. Since the 1960's to 1970, what really counts does not occur through the customary communication channels of a given geographic region, (hence the deregulation of rates, the deregulation of transport in general), but rather through ether, the electronic ether of telecommunications.

From now on everything will happen without our even moving, without our even having to set out. The initially confined rise of the dynamic, first simply mobile, then automotive, vehicle is quickly followed by the generalized rise of pictures and sounds in the static vehicles of the audiovisual. Polar inertia is setting in. The second screen that can be switched suddenly on substitutes itself for the very long time intervals of displacement. After the ascendance of *distance/time* over space in the nineteenth century, comes now the ascendance of the *distance/speed* of the electronic picture factories: *the statue follows upon the continual stopping and standing still.*

—

According to Ernst Mach, the universe is mysteriously present in all places and at all times in the world. If every mobile (or automotive) vehicle conveys a special vision, a perception of the world that is only an artifact of the speed at which it is displaced within its terrestrial, aquatic, or aerial milieu, then, vice versa, each of these visions, these optical or acoustical images of the perceived world, represents a "vehicle," a communication vector inseparable from the speed of its transmission. All this since the telescopic instant of the image's rectification in the passive lenses of Galileo's telescope, down to our modern "means of telecommunications," our active optics of videoinformatics.

The dynamic vehicle can thus no longer be clearly distinguished from the static vehicle, the automotive no longer from the audiovisual. The new priority of arrival over departure, over all forms of departure and, accordingly, over all forms of travel and trajectories, realizes a mysterious conspiracy – inertia of the moment, of every place and every instant of the present world, ultimately allying itself closely to the principle of inseparability, thereby completing the indeterminateness posed by quantum theory.

Even when one witnesses current attempts to conjoin technologies systematically, the installation of video landscape in the elevators of Japanese skyscrapers or the showing of feature films during commercial air travel, this momentary link will still only inevitably lead to the elimination of the least efficient vector of the speed of dispersion. The racing progress of contemporary high-speed trains, super-sonic aircraft, as well as the deregulation effecting both, shows cleaner than any other preview that the threatened vector, the threatened vehicle, is really that of terrestrial, aquatic, and aerial automotility.

The era of intensive time is thus no longer the era of means of physical transport. Unlike earlier, extensive time, it is a time solely of telecommunications, in other words, of walking in place and domestic inertia. Recent developments in both the automobile and formula-I racing prove the point. Since the high performance of the audiovisual cannot seriously be improved upon, people go about altering the performance of the racing car, the rules of racing, the weight of the vehicles and the fuel reserves. They even go so far as to reduce the power of the engines, which is really the limit! Finally, the dynamic land vehicle the most symptomatic of this sporting involution is the dragster (and the hot rod), who's motto could be: "How can I get nowhere, or at least as close to it as possible (400, 200 yards), but with ever-increasing speed?"

This intensive and extreme competition may eventually have to join finish line and starting line together in order to pull even with the analogous feat of live television broadcasting. As far as the domestic car is concerned, this development is the same in every respect, for the peculiar self-sufficiency of the automobile is evolving increasingly into a separate sort of property. Whence this move, this duplication of accessories, furniture, the hi-fi chain, radio telephone, telex, and videomobile turning the means of long-haul transport into a means of transport in place, into a vehicle of ecstasy, music and speed.

If automotive vehicles, that is, all air, land, and sea vehicles, are today also less "riding animals" than *frames* in the optician's sense, it is because the self-propelled vehicle is becoming less and less a vector of change in physical location than a means of representation, the channel for an increasingly rapid opticalization of the surrounding space. The more or less distant vision of our travels thereby gradually recedes behind the arrival at the destination, into a general arrival of images, of information that henceforth stands for our constant change of location. That is why a secret correspondence between the static structural design of the residential dwelling and the medially conveyed inertia of the audiovisual vehicle is established with the emergence of the *intelligent dwelling* – what am I saying? – with the emergence of the intelligent and interactive city, the teleport instead of the port, the train station and the international airport.

To a journalist's question about her address, a well-known actress responded: "I live everywhere!" Tomorrow, with the aesthetics and logic forcing the disappearance of the architectonic, we will live everywhere. That is a promise. Like the animals of the "video zoo," we will all be present only by virtue of a single image on a single screen, here and there, yesterday and the day before, images recorded at places of no importance, excessive suburbs of a cinematic development finally taking audiovisual speed, as it relates to the interior design of our dwellings, and placing it on the same footing as the automotive speed that has long transformed the architecture of our cities and the layout of our countries.

"Immobility simulators" will then replace the flight simulators. Behind our cathode glass cases we become the teleactors and tele-actresses of an animated theater. Recent developments in sound and light shows already herald this transformation, though they're repeatedly used by people ranging from Andre Malraux and Lyotard to Jack Lang on the pretext of saving our monuments.

It is thus our common destiny to *become film*. Especially when the man responsible for the *Cinescenie du Puy-du-Fou*, Philippe de Villiers, has become secretary for culture and communication and announced his intent to institute "scenic walks through areas being preserved as historical sites" in order to enhance the attractiveness of our monu-ments and compete with the imported "Disneyland" near Paris or "Wonderworld" near London.

In the footsteps of the theatrical scenography of the agora, forum, and church square as traditional sites of urban history there now fol-lows *cinescenography*, the sequenced mutation of a community, region, or monument in which the participating population momentarily changes into actors of a history intended to be revived. It does not mat-ter whether it is the war in Vendee with Philippe de Villiers or of the centuries-old services of the city of Lyon with Jean-Michel Jarre. The previous minister of culture paid tribute to this phenomenon by tapping the budget for funds (earmarked "Salamandar") to finance the produc-tion of an interactive videotape of a tour through the chateaux of the Loire. It is "Light and Sound" at home, and it turns visitors from a bygone age of tourism into video visitors, "tele-lovers of old stones," whose record collections and discotheques have now not only Mozart and Verdi but Cheverny and Chambord as well.

—

As noted in the poem "La Ralentie," by Henri Michaux, "One does not dream anymore; one is dreamed of, silence." The inversion begins. The film runs in reverse. Water flows back into the bottle. We walk backwards, but faster and faster. The involution leading to inertia accelerates. Up to our desire, which ossifies in the increasingly distinct medial distancing. After the whores of Amsterdam in the display windows, after the striptease of the 1950s and the peepshow of the 1970s, we arrive now at videopornography. The list of mortal sins in the Rue Saint-Denis is reduced to the names of the new image technologies, BETACAM, VHS, and VIDEO 2000, in the expectation of erotic automatism, or the vision machine.

Military confrontation is similarly transformed. After the home trainer for the pilots in World War I, the swivel chair for training pilots in World War II, and NASA's centrifuge for future astronauts, which is a reality test for the inability to become accustomed to weightlessness, we now witness the development of increasingly sophisticated and powerful simulators of supersonic flight. Projection domes up to nine yards in diameter and more; a geode for a single man. The most developed will have a field of vision of up to almost three-hundred degrees because the pilot's helmet will contain an optical system for expanding the retina. To enhance realism further, the trainee will don inflatable overalls that simulate the acceleration pressure related to the earth's gravity.

The essential is yet to come, though. Tests are being run on a simulation system derived from the oculometer that will finally liberate us from the spheric video screen. Images from aerial combat will be projected directly into the pilot's eyeballs with the aid of a helmet fitted with optic fibers. This phenomenon of hallucination approaches the psychedelic drug. In other words, this practice material denotes the future disappearance of every scene, every video screen, to the advantage of a single "seat" [siege], in this case, though, a *trap* [siege/piege] for an individual whose perception is programmed in advance by the capabilities of a computer's motor of inference. Before this future model of a static vehicle is invented, I think it would be appropriate to reconsider the concept of energy and the engine. Even though physicists still distinguish between two aspects of energetics – potential and kinetic energy, with the latter setting off motion – one should, eighty years after the invention of the moving camera, perhaps add a third, the *kinematic* energy resulting from the effect that motion and its more or less great velocity has on ocular, optic, and optoelectronic perception.

Today's simulation industry seems like a realization of this energy source. The computational speed of computers now approximates a final type of engine: the cinematic engine.

But the essential would not yet be said without a return to the primacy of arrival (which is momentary) over departure. If the profundity of time is greater today than that of space, then it means that notions of time have changed considerably. Here, as elsewhere in our daily and banal life, we are passing from the extensive time of history to the intensive time of momentariness without history – with the aid of contemporary technologies. These automotive, audiovisual and informatic technologies all operate on the same restriction, the same contraction of duration. This earthly contradiction questions not only the extension of the nations but also the architecture of the house and its furniture.

If time is history, then velocity is only its hallucination. It ruins any expansion, extension, and any chronology. This spatial and temporal hallucination, an apparent result of the intensive development of cinematic energy – of which the audiovisual vehicle would be the corresponding engine today, just as the mobile vehicle and, later, the automotive vehicle was for kinetic energy yesterday – ultimately displaces the energies of the same name that were invented in the previous century.

Let us not trust it. The third dimension is no longer the measure of expansion; relief, no longer the reality. From now on reality is concealed in the flatness of pictures, in the transference of representation. It conditions the return to the house's state of siege, to the cadaver-like inertia of the interactive dwelling, this residential cell that has left the extension of the habitat behind and whose most important piece of furniture is the *seat* [siege], the ergonomic armchair of the handicapped's motor, and – who knows? – the *bed*, a canopy bed for the infirm voyeur, a divan for being dreamt of without dreaming, a bench for being circulated without circulating.

For the Birds
John Cage

Charles: Do you concede the possibility of a "concrete solfège"?

Cage: What do you mean by that?

In the '50s, Pierre Schaeffer classified sounds according to a certain number of taxonomic requirements, capable of authorizing a reading, a deciphering of the most diverse sound areas; all of which was to lead to a less "surrealistic," more organic means of composition.

With such an effort at organization, I'm afraid we are falling back into outdated processes. After all, the very idea of a solfège of noises contains the word "solfège" doesn't it? And what could be more worn than that?

Then according to you, solfège amounts to a compromising holdover from the 18th and 19th centuries?

More or less. You see, what's bothered me all along about Schaeffer's work is his penchant for relations, and especially for relations between sounds. He had machines at his disposal, and he incessantly tried to use them in a way that would render relationships between noises and tonality. That was always his problem: for example, with his twelve speed recorder, how could he possibly have anything but a system based on twelve sounds? Even if he did proclaim that he didn't want it! The same problem arises with solfège; though a mental tool rather than a machine, its results amount to the same. It leads us fatally back to sounds, in the "musical" sense of the word, that is, to noises that must go with certain noises and not with others. I was attempting the opposite: not the repetition of some overly-common, almost habitual situation that would remain unchanged without our feeling the need to intervene, but an entirely novel situation in which any sound or noise might occur with or near any other.

What you call an "experimental" situation?

Right, one in which nothing is pre-determined, in which there are neither obligations nor prohibitions, in which nothing is foreseeable.

A situation of anarchy?

Of course! Thoreau pretty much described it when he replaced Jefferson's maxim, *"The best government is that government which governs least,"* with his own "That government is best which governs not at all!"

You would place Schaeffer on the side of the government?

I think that he and I don't see eye to eye on the difference between the number two and the number one. While I have always tried to think the plurality of the number one, *for Schaeffer plurality begins with two.*

Do you mean with two we remain at the level of objectal relations?

For clarity's sake, let's return to the example of "experimental" music. Music was long thought to exist first in the spirit of people – and in particular of composers – who wrote it and were supposed to hear it before it became audible. I believe the opposite, that we hear nothing *in advance.* Solfège is precisely the discipline which allows a sound to be heard before its emission…

Then you are a perfectly "concrete" musician!

Yes! What makes sounds "abstract" is when, instead of listening to them for themselves, we're content to listen to their relations. As I've said before, it would be just as worthwhile to express a musical idea with lights…

Doesn't your hostility to the notion of relation stem from a certain type of American philosophy? For example, William James' critique of relations. And yet James did not hold that critique to the end. He concluded by recognizing that relations themselves were "wholes" or "units." For him, relations exist as well in experience.

I am well aware that things interpenetrate, but I think that they interpenetrate more richly, and with a greater complexity, when I don't establish any relation. At that moment they meet, they compose the number one. But, at the same time, they don't form an obstruction. They are themselves. They are. And inasmuch as each is one in itself, there is a plurality in the number one.

But how can you abstain from all relational activity? Doesn't perception mean to forge relations?

I can accept the relation among a diversity of elements, as when we gaze at the stars and discover a group of stars which we baptize "Ursa Major." Then, I create an object. I have nothing more to do with the thing itself, designed as it is of elements and separate parts. I have before me, at my disposal, a fixed object that I could vary or play with precisely because I know beforehand that I will find it identical to itself at the end. In this, I obey that which Schönberg expressed: variation is one form, one extreme case of repetition. But, I can also break out of this cycle of variation and repetition. For that, I must return to reality, to the thing itself, to this constellation which is not really altogether a constellation. It is not yet an object! The constellation becomes an object by virtue of the relationship I place upon the parts. But I can refrain from positing this relationship; I can consider the stars as separate but proximate, *almost* gathered into a unique constellation.

I'm beginning to understand your choice, for the orchestral piece Atlas Eclipticalis, *of the astronomical maps which dictated the very topography of your score.*

When you mention a topography, you turn a network of chance operations into an object.

*But I have no choice! If I am to escape the exact cause-and-effect
relationships, then I must change my scales: I will have to deal with
clouds, with tendencies and with laws of statistical distribution.*

Yes, if you're a physicist. But the chance of modern physics, that of
random operations, corresponds to an equal distribution of events. The
chance to which I appeal, that of chance operations, is different: it pre-
supposes an unequal distribution of elements. That's what the Chinese
book of oracles, the *I Ching*, tells us, or the astronomical maps used for
Atlas Eclipticalis. I don't hold with the physical object of statistical
interest.

*Ultimately your indeterminacy is an extremely fragile, precarious
reality...*

Yes, even in my pieces one can find logic! But that requires will and
even willingness. The problem was already formulated by Duchamp.
He says essentially that one must strain to attain the impossibility of
self-recollection, even when the experience moves from an object to its
double. In the real world, where everything is standardized, where
everything is repeated, the whole question is to forget from an object
to its reduplication. If we don't have this power to forget, if today's
art doesn't help us to forget, we will be submerged, drowned in an ava-
lanche of rigorously identical objects.

*Art as you define it then is a discipline of adaptation to the real as it
is. It doesn't propose to change the world but accepts it as it presents
itself. In the name of habit-breaking, it habituates even more firmly!*

I don't think so. There's a term in the problem which you've ignored:
the world. The real. You say: the real, the world as it is. But it isn't,
it becomes! It moves, it changes! It doesn't wait for us in order to
change .... It is more mobile than you imagine. You begin to approach
this mobility when you say: as it presents itself. It "presents itself":

signifying that it's not there, as is an object. The world, the real, this is no object. It's a process.

There can be no custom and no habit in a world becoming... Is that your idea?

Yes, it's an idea of change, as is all my music which could be called a Music of Changes. And I took this designation from the *Book of Changes*, as the *I Ching* is called in English.

I can't help but think that the logos, that logic, has very little hold in this world as you define it.

That's because I am not a Greek philosopher! We used to seek out logical experiences; nothing mattered more than stability. Today, beside stability, we allow for instability. We have come to desire the experience of what is. But this "what is" is neither stable nor unchanging. At any rate, we understand better that we bring the logic with us. It doesn't lie around us, waiting to be discovered. "What is" doesn't depend on us, we depend on it. And it is for us to approach it.

Could you explain your idea of time? How does it cohere with your idea of the future, of a world in flux?

A Zen monk went out with one of his disciples and saw a flock of wild geese, "What's that?" he asked. "It was wild geese," one answered. The master violently tweaked this disciple's nose. "You imagine that they have passed. But they were always here." Thus the disciple was enlightened.

Then you would say that we cannot represent time?

We must not hypnotize ourselves with intellectual categories, such as continuous-discontinuous, stable-unstable, etc. which we imagine will enable us to conceive time.

That could appear as a profession of vitalist faith.

Nothing is further from life than the philosophies of life! No, I am not about to embrace any of those philosophies. An inanimate being has as much life as an animate one. A sound is alive. The philosophers of life don't say that, do they?

And when one of your colleagues, Morton Feldman, affirms that your music is not identical to life in that it re-assembles only a part of life's sonorities…

I would say again that it lets nothing escape. Or better yet that it escapes the idea that it lets anything escape!

Aren't you avoiding the issue?

But everything is possible! My music imposes no restrictions. It just so happens that the life we lead is partial and that many of the sounds are difficult to assemble in the concert-halls we use. I try to avoid this obligation of selecting the appropriate sounds for a concert, an audience, a place, etc. I expand to the maximum the conditions of execution of my music. I go to the circuses, to the clearings, to the galleries, to the rooftops… my music is assuredly partial, but I do not pursue this partiality. If I pursue anything, it is the absence of a goal.

Therein is what must be the difficulty of being a student of John Cage! How could you have students, and teach them without goals?

It turns out that many people have come to study with me. But for each one, I tried to discover who he was and what he could do. Result: more often than not, I became the student.

At the university as well? I have the impression that certain of your students learned quite a bit from you…

In any case, they taught me – at least those of The New School of Social

Research – that I'd rather not teach.

And yet you haven't really renounced all pedagogic activities?

I've tried, as much as possible, to avoid the universities.

Why?

They're too intimate with governments, be it in France where nothing occurs without an official's stamp on it, or in America, where the authority is private; but it comes to the same thing, doesn't it?

But wouldn't that change if someone like you accepted more often to intervene?

Recently, at the University of California at Davis, I offered a class, with, in the guise of an opening condition, the hypothesis that we would not know what we were about to study and that we would not divide ourselves into students and non-students; but that all of us, myself included, would be students.

What happened?

We subjected the library to chance operations, and in this group of about a hundred, each one performed two chance operations to determine the works he would read. Then, by drawing lots, we formed flexible groups: each group was to meet and exchange information on what everyone had read. This technique was supposed to respond to the wishes of McLuhan who feels that our work must consist of freshening information by means of information.

But the "assemblages, environments and happenings," to borrow the title of a well-known book by Allan Kaprow, one of your disciples, aren't they all contrary to your ideal openness to all that is? For he's working with controlled activities, isn't he? The absence of purpose, even with you, can become the purpose: it risks becoming as constraining as the earlier situation in which everything was submitted to a single purpose. Haven't you indicated as much, on the occasion of these happenings where you were told what to do: to go from one room to another, for example?

We are not free. We live in a sub-divided society. We must remain aware of those sub-divisions. But why repeat them? Why must the happenings reproduce the most constrictive aspects of daily life? We always think that, in art, we must erect order everywhere. And if art were to incite disorder?

To want disorder is still to want.

The question is not one of wanting, but of being free in relation to one's own will. In the university, in my music, in my day-to-day activities, I make constant use of chance operations. But I don't perform chance operations exclusively or uniquely. To recognize the importance of chance does not mean to sacrifice all to it.

Then your teaching – if you'll allow that word – could be defined as a pedagogy of non-volition? A detachment in relation to the will?

A progressive detachment, yes, that will not fall back into attachment. A detachment that will repeat nothing.

Which places us dead-square in the Orient...

Before my encounter with Oriental thought, which I situate somewhere around 1945, I already saw no need to bring God into this idea of the life of each thing. But I like to think that each thing has not only its own life but its own center and that that center is, each time, the exact center of the Universe. That is one of the principal themes I've retained from my studies in Zen.

Must we dissociate the idea of life and the idea of the center?

That they interpenetrate signifies that between them there is nothing. Thus nothing separates them...

You speak of nothing, of "rien." I'd like to raise a point of translation here. Would you prefer the English nothing to be translated as "rien" or as "le rien," as "nothing" or as "the nothing"? Can we see the "nothing" of your thoughts as "the Nothing," the Nothingness, the Silence? In the inverse hypothesis, Lecture on Nothing would have to be translated as Discours sur rien. Which should be chosen?

And what did my French translator do?

He hesitates, sometimes opting for the capital N, at other times using the small n. Sometimes for the West, others for the East!

I wonder which one should choose. But it's hard because we still remain mired within the intellectual categories. Of course, to say "the Nothing" is not to go all the way, for it says: the Nothing is still some-thing. It's not very satisfying.

Must we therefore reject the very solution you just finished suggesting as necessary?

As long as you oppose Some-thing to Nothing, you remain in the game of intellectual categories. What I wanted to say, when speaking of the "nothing in between," is that the Nothing is...neither Being nor Nothing.

It is outside the relationship between Being and Nothing.

Right. Each time we establish a relation, each time we connect two terms, we forget that we have to return to zero before moving to the next term. The same goes for Being and Nothing! We speak, we try to think about these notions – like musical sounds – and we forget what's really going on. We forget that each time, to pass from one word to the next, we must return to zero.

Language compels you to return to "absolute" Nothing?

Yes, and thus I can stick to the first choice: the "Nothing." On the condition that we don't let the words take over, we can let it happen.

Your ideas come from Suzuki?

Yes, and also from a fascinating book, entitled *Neti, Neti*, that taught me that in the world of created things, there is some-thing that is, so to speak, no-thing; and moreover: a nothing which has no-thing within it. That is the *nothing in between!* More recently, I re-encountered this idea in Buckminster Fuller: he describes the world as a movement of spheres among which there is a void, a necessary space. It is this space we tend to forget. We over-leap it in order to establish our relations and connections. We think we can slide, in continuity, from one sound to the next, from one thought to the next. In reality, we fall and don't even know it! We live, but to live means to cross the world of relations or representations. After all, we never see ourselves crossing this world! And yet that's all we ever do!

It's all very simple, then?

I would say, inversely, that while our way of thinking is so simple, our experience is always, and in each instant, extreme and complex. When we think, we continually return to the paired opposites, sound and silence, Being and Nothing. This is precisely in order to simplify experience, which is beyond simplification and never reducible to the number two.

Aren't we in danger of returning to the number one? To a sort of monism?

Buckminster Fuller insists on the number three and feels there is hardly a useful idea that can proceed without taking at least three things into account simultaneously. As for me, the best way to escape the two is to perform a chance operation. Because then we allow an infinity of things to enter into a single, complex event. And by that, we avoid that simplification peculiar to our way of thinking.

Nevertheless I wonder how you can not be shocked by the mechanistic, automatic nature of the chance operations. To draw the sounds by lot, isn't that a facile solution? Wherever the role of chance in daily life may be, doesn't chance frequently oversimplify things?

But how will we explain the fact that we are all present here, that we are in the present but not in the same present as the fir-trees in the forest? We owe this complexity to chance .... Our life is an intense complexity on which new layers of chance are constantly imposed. Chance allows this and excludes that.

Does it therefore oblige us to consider presence and absence as complements?

It obliges us to reject the exclusions, the radical alternatives between opposites.

Translated by Daniel Moshenberg

The Dance of Signs
Sylvère Lotringer

"Even when immobile we are in motion."
—Merce Cunningham

"What counts is to put the individual in flux. One must destroy the wall of the ego; weaken opinions, memory and emotions; tear down all the ramparts."
—John Cage

"That which is, cannot contain motion."
—Friedrich Nietzsche

Interpretive power: Freud analyzing Jensen's *Gradiva*. Not a mere "conceptual translation," not a neutral, indifferent explication. An interpretation. But how powerful?

Structuralism obviously blurs the issue. It studies more *possible* than actual literature. At bottom, an exploitation of the categorical capacities of discourse. Conceptual translation: power without interpretation, or interpretation without power?

Language in itself is relational; it equalizes everything. A "science" of literature codifies these relations in terms of a particular system itself part of a more general mechanism. This in turn functions as a repertory of possible forms. The original text returns as a measurable "difference." Was it worth the trouble?

Objectivity is actually a pure fiction, an interpretation in its own right. But disavowed. The choice of elements, their grouping, the logic at work, etc., are anything but neutral. Structuralists insist on hiding behind a self-imposed logical organization; Freud defines a goal and arranges the facts accordingly. The man of pure knowledge boastfully practices self-effacement: he preaches liberation from all effects. Freud also promises access to truth, but he does not renounce the will. His goal is to demonstrate the existence of repression. He does not merely explain. He interprets.

There is a violence of interpretation and Freud assumes it unabashedly. He clearly enjoys it.

My own inquiry begins at this point. If interpretation *is* appropriation and appropriation the inevitable outcome of the will to power, are all interpretations on the same level? How is one to choose among them? What happens if I reject them all?

But is it possible *not* to interpret?

Perspective Valuations

"How much of a piece of music has been understood when that in it which is calculable has been reckoned up?"
The Will to Power

The world has no value in itself; it waits for my evaluation. I never find it, though, in a pristine state: it is always already shaped by interpretations. Evaluation substitutes a new interpretation for another that has become narrow or weak. But what makes a "superior" interpretation in the world of *no truth*?

Reading a text raises similar problems. However much I try to disregard previous evaluations, I have to confront textual configurations whose economy I can never totally upset but merely modify. All interpretation activates, or *reactivates*, the forces at work in the text. *Gradiva*, the final hermeneutic novel, is no exception.

A literary text is not a psychic "object" waiting for the sage to coax it with the tip of his quill in order to shatter cataplexy into light. A text has as many meanings as it has forces capable of dominating it. *Gradiva*, obviously, was waiting for Freud to force it open.

Freud is not blind to this: "The producer which the author makes his Zoe adopt for curing her childhood friend's delusion shows a far reaching similarity – no, a complete agreement in its essence – with the analytical method which consists, as applied to patients suffering from disorders analogous to Hanold's delusion, in bringing to their consciousness, to some extent forcibly, the unconscious whose repression led to their falling ill" (Standard Edition, IX, 88). Such is the powerful thrust of similitude. Freud has no more qualms to reduce "poetic creations" to real persons or the "Pompeian fancy" to a simple "psychiatric study." Beneath the trappings of truth, on the razor's edge of demonstration, forces are confronting each other in order to turn the process – the text – into a product.

If *Gradiva* adheres so perfectly to the analytical mold, the analysis of the novel must serve as an *absolute proof*, in Freud's words, of the theory of the unconscious. Absolute proof – or absolute counter-proof... Even thought "absolute" is clearly too strong a word for such a circumscribed operation, to counter Freud's interpretation and thus unsettle the theory of the unconscious is indeed the substance of the present attempt.

Not to replace Freud's elaborate construct with another, more powerful, mode of evaluation would certainly prove the *wisdom* in the face of the illusion of truth. Although "nihilistic" at heart, such a perspective is not bound to be simply *negative*. It can attest to a growing force. I realize that I can overcome the temptation of total interpretations, whose values are universal (they are actually symptoms of fear and apathy). To destroy the belief in the law, to dissipate the fiction of predictability, to reject the sage recurrence of the "same," this is not just a "critical" stand. It is an act of force. But destruction must not open onto an absence of values, worthless or meaninglessness. It must lead to a new evaluation.

Nietzsche sees in the wisdom of the East a principle of decadence, a weakening of the power of appropriation. Force of intention matters more than will to truth. To reject truth without intensifying the force of invention still participates in the ascetic ideal, thus in *ressentiment*. "To read off a text without interposing an interpretation" therefore is "hardly possible" (*The Will to Power*, 479). I must use my creative forces *to create values* without falling into the inertia of truth or an anemia of will. I must render the text, and the world, to their "disturbing and enigmatic character"; will them incomprehensible, elusive, "in flux," only indebted to perspective valuations: "The greater the impulse toward unity, the more firmly may one conclude that weakness is present; the greater the impulse toward variety, differentiation, inner decay, the more force is present" (WP, 655). Inner decay: to dance away over oneself. Motion, not emotions.

Freud's interpretation resists the false neutrality of science. It only shows a sign of decline when it aims for the truth, when it succumbs to the temptation of unity, the sick security of monism, the illusion of a reconciliation. A *reactive* interpretation, it assumes powerful, but fabricated, weapons: the difference between objects and subjects, cause and effect, means and ends, etc.

That *Gradiva* presents a certain order of succession in no way proves that individual moments are related to one another as cause and effect, that they obey a "law" and a calculus but rather that different factions abruptly confront each other in their attempt to draw their ultimate consequence at every moment. "As long as there is a structure, as long as there is a method, or better yet as long as structure and method exist through the mental, through intelligence, time is trapped – or else we imagine we have trapped it" (John Cage, *Pour les Oiseaux*. Belfond, 1976, 34).

Structural analysis properly discerned that a narrative establishes a confusion between time (succession) and logic (cause and effect). However, instead of "delogifying" time, it forced narrative time to submit to narrative logic. Far from being dispelled, the confusion became the very springboard of analysis! It is high time to take advantage of this latency of the narrative, of the divorce between consequence and construction, in order to "rechronocize" succession.

I will, here and now, stop wanting the story to go somewhere. I will forget what I know feebly, in advance, in order to gather the whole complexity of forces at play in a text. I will learn to resist the melody of casual relations and the torpor of narrative accumulations in order to reinvent the intensity of risks, ceaselessly menacing and forever being reborn.

Repression Now

"Subject, object, a doer added to the doing, the doing separated from that which it does; let us not forget that this is mere semeiotics and nothing real."
The Will to Power

Reading *Gradiva* without any preconceived notion of its destination, the opening scene assumes all the characteristics of semiotic rupture.

The sculpture representing Gradiva holds Norbert, a young archaeologist, in the grip of a powerful fascination. A roman relic, it should invite a decipherment and maintain the archaeologist within the sacred vault of his science. And yet, as Jensen points out, "from the viewpoint of the science he taught, the bas-relief has nothing remarkable." The bas-relief is by no means an inert object. It is at the juncture of unequal forces in a relation of tension with one another. Tapping upon the realm of knowledge, the energy that emanates from the cast is so powerful that it overturns all the young man's sedentary habits, his manic erudition, and thrusts him into an unprecedented nomadism.

For Freud, armed with novelistic retrospection, the outcome leaves no room for doubt: "When Norbert Harold saw the relief, he did not remember that he had already seen a similar posture of the foot in his childhood friend; *he remembered nothing at all, but all the effects brought about by the relief originated from this link* that was made with the impression of childhood. Thus the childhood impression was stirred up, it became active, so that it began to produce effects, but it did not come into consciousness – it remained 'unconscious'" (S.E., IX, 47. My italics). Forgetting, like interpretation, is a force, but an *active* force that struggles to separate cause from effect and exorcise the harsh tamping of the present onto the past (which is still to come) by means of which the present falls into incompletion. Only through the insufficiency of the present can the machinery of repression, the cornerstone of the psychoanalytic edifice, be sustained.

Repression, actually, is an on-going creation. Freud recognizes it, but in a somewhat restrictive way, when he defines the *mobility* of repression in terms of the constant pressure it exercises in the direction

of the conscious: "The process of repression is not to be regarded as an
event which takes place once, the results of which are permanent, as
when some living thing has been killed and from that time onward is
dead; repression demands a persistent expenditure of force, and if this
were to cease the success of the repression would be jeopardized, so
that the fresh act of repression would be necessary." (S.E., XIV, 151).
The mobility of repression is a process by which the repressed is kept
at a distance from the conscious. And yet a unique event is always to
be determined from its mnemic traces, through its deformations, and
even in the blank spaces where it allegedly attempts to annihilate itself.
The eternal search for an origin, a cause, an anterior point of emission
to explain the present psychic reality. A theory of seduction, a seduction
of theory...

The continuity of repression does not arise from that energy clamped
down like a lid over the past; it is *in the present* that the libido unfail-
ingly produces or reactivates its own impasses. At this point, forgetting
does not lack anything. It even becomes assertive, or *affirmative*. It
literally places Norbert beside himself. It liberates him from his spatio-
temporal attachments and projects him into an intensive present by
essence foreign to the consequential logic of repression.

Whatever the causes, *not* to remember is to erase the past in favor
of the new. No wonder that it allows Norbert to feel deeply moved at
the sight of a gait foreign to all intent or signification.

The bas-relief represents a woman in motion, but the archaeologist
is affected not by her formal beauty nor even by her indifferent face, but
rather by the vertical movement of her right foot. The name with which
he dubs her: Gradiva, "she who walks in splendor," who dances and
bounces, like the Antic Graces or the leaping priests of Mars Gradivus,
emphasizes the primacy of the gait over the person, the strength of a
process which refuses to dissociate doing into doer, becoming into
being, effect into cause, in short to produce any subjective affectation.

Gradiva is a pure force, a movement that carries in its wake, a
motion that mobilizes, an emotion that moves everything into trance,
into dance. The dance of signs: Gradiva crossing with her singular
indifference the stiff, cold frame of repression to engage Norbert to
follow her in her flight.

It was imperative to staunch this disturbing motion with a sex, a site, a subject, to freeze it with temporality and fate. Such is the function of Norbert's dream with which Freud now brilliantly joins forces.

The Dreams of Interpretation

"There is no essential difference between dreams and wakefulness."
The Dawn

"Soon after his pedestrian investigations had yielded him this knowledge, he had, one night, a dream which caused him great anguish of mind. In it he was in old Pompeii, and on the twenty-fourth of august of the year 79 A.D., which witnessed the eruption of Vesuvius. The heavens held the doomed city wrapped in a black mantel of smoke; only then and there the flaring masses of flame from the crater made distinguishable, through the rift, something steeped in blood-red light; all the inhabitants, either individually or in confused crowds, stunned out of their senses by the unusual horror, sought safety in flight. The pebbles and the rain of ashes fell down on Norbert also, but, after the strange manner of dreams, they did not hurt him; and, in the same way, he smelled the deadly sulphur fumes or the air without having his breathing impeded by them. As he stood thus at the edge of the Forum near the Temple of Jupiter, he suddenly saw Gradiva a short distance in front of him. Until then no thought of her presence there had moved him, but now suddenly it seemed natural to him, as she was of course, a Pompeian girl, that she was living in her native city and, without his having any suspicion of it, was his contemporary. He recognized her at first glance; the stone model of her was splendidly striking in every detail, even in her gait; involuntarily he designated this as *lente festinans*. So with buoyant composure and the calm unmindfulness of her surroundings peculiar to her, she walked across the flagstones of the Forum to the Temple of Apollo. She seemed not to notice the impending fate of the city, but to be given up to her thoughts; on that account he also forgot the frightful occurrence, for at least a few moments, and because of a feeling that the living reality would quickly disappear from him again, he tried to impress it accurately on his mind. Then, however, he became suddenly aware that if she did not quickly save herself, she must perish in the general destruction, and violent fear forced from him a cry of warning. She heard it, too, for her head turned toward him so that her face now appeared for a moment in full view, yet with an utterly uncomprehending expression; and without paying any more attention to him, she continued in the same direction as before. At the same time, her face became paler as if it were changing to white marble; she stepped up to the portico of the Temple, and then, between the pillars, she sat down on a step and slowly laid her head upon it. Now the pebbles were falling in such masses that they condensed into a completely opaque curtain; hastening quickly after, however, he found his way to the place where she had disappeared from his view, and there she lay, protected by the projecting roof, stretched out on the broad step, as if for sleep, but no longer breathing, apparently stiffed by the sulfur fumes. From Vesuvius the red glow flared over her countenance, which, with closed eyes, was exactly like that of a beautiful statue. No fear nor distortion was apparent, but a strange equanimity, calmly submitting to the inevitable, was manifest in her features. Yet they quickly became more indistinct as the wind drove to the place the rain of ashes, which spread over them, first like a gray gauze veil, then extinguished the last glimpse of her face, and soon, like a northern winter snowfall, buried the whole figure under a smooth cover. Outside, the pillars of the Temple of Apollo rose – now, however, only half of them, for the gray fall of ashes heaped itself likewise against them." ("Gradiva: A

Pompeian Fancy," in *Delusion and Dreams* [D&D]. Boston: Beacon Press, 1958.)

The oneiric images, like the stone images, *"have to be regarded as something distorted, behind which something else must be looked for"*: the repressed. (S.E., IX. 59. My italics.). The repressed, Freud asserts, stems from a "faulty translation." Let's translate then, let's "interpretate," by all sorts of devices, the manifest content into latent thoughts. That Gradiva is specifically designated in the dream as being a Pompeian (she lives "in her native city, and, without his having any suspicion of it, was his contemporary") constitutes the first figure of the unconscious: actually, Norbert has not, like her, become an inhabitant of Pompeii. It is Gradiva rather who, like Norbert, is German. Figure, or better yet, disfiguration: a *distortion by means of a displacement*. Another oneiric transformation, which Freud decodes with as much gusto and elegance, turns the walking Gradiva into a stone-image: actually, Hanold transferred his interest from the living woman he knew as a child to a bas-relief. The dream presents in disguise the very genesis of the archaeologist's delusion, "an ingenious and poetical representation of the real event." (S.E., IX, 60). The dream thus comes to the rescue of the delusion. The third displacement: Norbert's anxiety. Referring to his *Interpretation of Dreams*, Freud suggests that it has nothing to do with the dream-content (the eruption of Vesuvius), but springs instead from a repressed sexual excitement. Fear of love transpires as fear of death.

The dream is the *via regia* to the Freudian unconscious. An intensive constellation, sensory chaos with no direct attachment to the socius, it is indeed the dream-prize of analysis. Freud's intuition led him at the core of this essentially psychotic dream-experience – *in order to better neuroticize it*. He produced within the dream another scene and other signs configuring a new, mental universe equally dependent upon the laws of representation.

The dream simultaneously anticipated and encouraged his pulling in of the reins. First, no dream participates directly in the innocence of becoming. It already incorporates in its narrative form a logic essentially alien to its own elaboration: "Our entire dream life is the interpretation of complex feelings *with a view to possible causes* – and in such a way that we are conscious of a condition only when the supposed casual chain associated with it has entered consciousness" (WP, 479. My italics.). Then isn't non-sense itself an irresistible invitation to the most daring, and costly, translations? Once properly told, folded into language and ironed out, i.e., organized and linearized, a dream is ready for all the total interpretations, not to mention "literary" dreams! We can still try to locate, the best way we can, the blockage-points. Intensify the lines of resistance, emphasize any possible rupture within the stuff of dream.

The Freudian screen channels energies onto figures and gathers figures within a single framework. I will rather distinguish, evaluate and affirm the forces struggling (either openly or covertly) to appropriate this tight and yet exploding sphere, this starburst: the dream.

Since I refuse to plumb this allegedly hidden face of the dream, I have to be especially sensitive to its strategic orientation, to its specific mode of insertion into a system whose main function is to check the initial semiotic break overflow. The *Gradiva-effect* (motion) being alien to all goals and intents can only repeat itself. The power of forgetfulness, though, each time turns the repetition into a new experience of liberation. If, on the other hand – Freud's hand – the dream as a whole contributes to the development of Norbert's "delusion," then the nature of that supplement must be carefully evaluated.

There is no doubt that Norbert's dream, viewed as a whole, *from a holistic perspective*, confirms the "delusion." The dream, to start with, occurs at the time the archaeologist has concluded his pedestrian investigation among the living women and arrived at the conclusion that none of them had Gravida's gait. The dream testifies to the contrary – the woman does exist, and she lives in Pompeii. This is the dream's *function*, to deliver an arresting blow to the intensive motion. Norbert recognizes it immediately in his dream: "Until then no thought of her presence there had moved him, but now suddenly it seemed natural to him (…) that she was living in her native city" (D&D, 153). The dream thus entrusts Norbert with a prospective, or retrospective, awareness: what awaits him at Pompeii arises from the dark regions of his own past. The dream forces upon Norbert a last recognition: the cause and effect relationship between the bas-relief and the dream-vision of Gradiva.

The unpredictable event becomes a prey to all the calculi and succession to consequence. Freud's interpretation does not impose from without logic's quantum power. He merely reinforces the actual degree of resistance of the forces of causality to the forces of becoming.

Norbert's first vision of Gradiva gives us an indication of the tremendous switch of perspective produced by the dream: "He recognized her at first glance; the stone model of her was splendidly striking in every detail, *even to her gait...*" (My italics). No longer is the posture an element racked from the body. It now appears in a position which had been "organically" assigned, after the *global* grasp of a particular corporeality. Once the mobilizing force invested from within, turned against itself and divested of most of its power, it is *represented* in another sphere. It is made to testify for a logic of whole and parts open to all the fetishist interpretations. From an infinitive of movement, the motion has become a codifiable and supplementary feature that qualifies a "substantiality" and corroborates an identity. The rest of the dream will never return to the dancing gait now properly reintegrated into the whole of the person. Once awake, Norbert will recognize with amazement that he hadn't particularly noticed in the dream "whether the living Gradiva had really walked as the piece of sculpture represented her, and as the women of today, at any rate, did not walk. That was remarkable because it was the basis for his scientific interest in the relief..." His realization, though, comes when he is well past the dream's interpretative power."

What did actually happen in the dream? How is it that the movement of becoming, the mobilizing motion ever turned into a mere individual reflexivity? The archaeologist immediately provides us with an answer: "...on the other hand, it would be explained by his excitement over the danger to her life." To invoke here, as Freud does, Norbert's reversed nostalgia toward Zoe is only meant to justify an interpretation of anxiety in terms of repressed sexual excitement. There is, actually, no need to call upon the *meaning* of Norbert's emotion. I will rather consider the *power* it exerts upon him. My question already supplies its answer: the emotion mobilizes forces that reduce the fleeting trait to a subjective indication. The pression of death is no more mysterious nor does it require any more clarification: its role, in the struggle staged by the dream, is to produce a similar effect.

Everything is wed, and everything is said, for the moment Gradiva is seen as a person in her own right. Once deemed alive, she lends herself to the utter simplification, and the brutal imposition of binary order: the life-death dichotomy thus comes to reinforce, and even generate, the eruption of Vesuvius and the terror of internment. Inasmuch as becoming is represented as being, and the impersonal motion's caught into a human, all too human emotion, it is immediately threatened by annihilation: "Then however he became suddenly aware that if she did not quickly save herself, she must perish in the general destruction, and violent fear forced him a cry of warning." Norbert's anguish does not prove in any way the existence of a repression. It does not substantiate Freud's claim that an event, a feeling from the past, are attempting to resurface. Anguish is a product of *the present*. It arises by virtue of the *"living reality"* conferred upon Gradiva.

As soon as the archaeologist sees her in danger of being buried he tries to imprint "her image onto his memory." The becoming unlimited of Gradiva, once objectified, falls back instantaneously upon the *past* (memory) already directed toward the *future* (he will have seen her). Oppositions form anew. Memory arises from Norbert's focalization on a representation, an icon, an *image*. Memory liberates the possibility of repression which does not come *from* the past, but results from the fantasmatic projection of the present *onto* the past. Memory helps to quench the intensity of the present. It limits the power of forgetfulness by means of a specular detachment, i.e., a *speculation* that veneers the motion with depth, difference and temporality.

The oneiric present can always be bounced back onto alleged infantile sources. All Freudian dreams must fulfill this condition: "A normal dream stands, so to speak, on two legs. One rests on essential recent factors and the other on an important childhood event. Between these two events, the dream establishes a communication, it strives to mold the present upon the past" (*Dora*). I would rather say that it shapes the past on the present! Freud recognized this at first, but in terms of *fantasies*. He saw them as delayed products that "starting in the present are thrown backwards, towards earliest infancy." Freud offers an explanation for such a retrogression: "I have found how this happens: it is, once more, through verbal association." (*Letters to Wilhelm Fliess*, 101). Does this come as a surprise? Psychoanalysis exudes a conviction all the more irresistible that it is inextricably bound with the fantasmatic coil it claims to explain. No wonder if repetition prevails...But to simply reverse Freud's proposition still maintains us within a casual-temporal opposition. We already put a limitation to the pure becoming by end-lessly dividing the present between the past and the future.

Freud's reading emphasizes the living present of the dream. The unlimited present, as a result, is weighted down by an anxiety whose matrix is thus internalized and thrust back so as to furnish an unim-peachable causation. Since it is assumed "dreams and delusions arise from the same source – from what is repressed" (S.E., IX, 62), Norbert's wandering will testify to repression.

Norbert's delusion in no way was morbid, but with the dream's help it comes very close to becoming so! Always more meanings, interpreta-tions and images. For fear of losing or of wanting. And one wants because one signifies, interprets, imagines, remembers! A classic *double bind*.

The metonymization of the gait onto the complete body of Gradiva gives rise to another detachment which aims at obliterating the energetic element. Such is the face whose omnipresence in the dream is so force-ful that it ends up replacing the motion.

I could view the substitution in a linear way and oppose, as though it were its dark, negative side, the impersonal, deterritorializing trance of the process to the subjugation generated by the face. This ego effect parallels Norbert's quest to find an equivalence to the posture. While examining the sculpture's "indifferent" face, the archaeologist could not help individualizing the *person* of Gradiva. He invented a rank, a race, a temperament. His interests now seemed to circle around a single point: "From daily contemplation of her head, another new conjecture had gradually arisen. The cut of her features seemed to him, more and more, not Roman or Latin, but Greek... Upon closer consideration he found this also confirmed by the expression of the face" (D&D, 150-1).

Norbert's terror at the sight of a living person as such exposed to death depends heavily on the imposition of the face. It should increase the dream's pressure towards individualization. But a reactive force is not tied down to an intangible object defined independently of the specific situations in which it appears. The archaeologist's neurotic interpretation actually runs up against the same "object" (but is it really *the same*?) which first strived to freeze the motion. In response to his cry of warning, "her head turned toward him so that her face now appeared for a moment in full view, *yet with an utterly uncomprehending expression*: and, without paying anymore attention to him, she continued in the same direction as before." Gradiva's face, far from eliciting Norbert's subjective understanding, resolutely resists any such appropriation. The *face-in-motion* thus opposes its radical indifference to Norbert's differentiating anxiety.

The strategic position of the dream is to initiate a reappropriation of the Gradiva-effect. Within the oneiric scene, however, the active forces continue to elude the sway of expressive signs, the reign of representation.

Gradiva's face-in-motion turns to stone: "her face became paler as if it were changing to white marble." Freud immediately wants to identify the idea that, in his words, is *represented and enacted* by the dream. His interpretation is final: "Hanold had in fact transferred his interests from the living girl to the sculpture: the girl he had loved had been transformed for him into a marble relief. The latent dream-thoughts, which were bound to remain unconscious, sought to change the sculpture back into the living girl; what they were saying to him accordingly was something like: 'After all, you're interested in the statue of Gradiva only because it reminds you of Zoe, who is living here and now.' But if this discovery could have become conscious, it would have meant the end of the delusion" (S.E., IX, 60). It would indeed have ended the delusion as an access to the becoming-nomad of Norbert. But not to the symptom-delusion, to the delusion of the becoming-conscious of repression which only *begins* with the all too intelligent interpretation of Freud.

Another intelligence offers at this point to push the Freudian interpretation to its ultimate consequence. The analyst reverses Zoe's petrification into Gradiva. The science of dreams stages far more elaborate permutations. Sarah Kofman feels therefore entitled to conclude that Zoe's becoming-stone, or Gradiva's becoming-alive actually refer to Norbert's being *medusa'd* by Zoe-Athena as a child: "Stone, symbol (...) of castration and of resistance to castration." (*Quatre romans analy-*

tiques. Galilée, 1973, 124). Who would doubt that the petrification of Zoe was not the sign of Norbert's castration-complex? The becoming-stone is thus properly reintegrated into a subjective representation. Every "subject" is, in essence, the subject of castration...

Norbert cannot become a subject in his own right unless Gradiva assumes the role of an object of desire. Her presence has to be felt as a deprivation, her possession as a loss. The face-in-motion, however, eludes such a reactive role. The archaeologist's expressive interpretation of Gradiva's impassive face is consequently revealed to what it is. Anxiety had pinned down the movement of becoming to a recognizable, sub-jective feature. The becoming-mineral, on the other hand, takes Gradiva away from the powerful machine of logic: "her face became pale as if it were changing to white marble; *she continued to walk...*" Discoloration in no way indicates a *loss* of color, it rather gives access to a non-substantial, non-differential, and even transmortal state. To breathe no more – to become marble – puts to rest all the reductive oppositions: it produces a "supernatural calm" alien to all danger, to all terror. Although Freudian interpretation saturates and dramatizes the oneiric scene through Norbert's own projections, it can at best juxtapose from the out-side its commentary to a set-up that fiercely resists it: "There she lay... as if for sleep, but no longer breathing, apparently stifled by the sulfur fumes. From Vesuvius the red glow flared over her countenance, which, with closed eyes, was exactly like that of a beautiful statue. *No fear nor distortion* was apparent, but a *strange equanimity, calmly* submitting to the inevitable..." The non-representative and non-expressive power of the face is still haunted by the subjective economy (*stifled, submission, inevitable*). An extra twist of the signs and sleep becomes the metaphor of death, indifference a submission to destroy. Gradiva's features, stay-ing clear of such a neurotic reading, quickly become indistinct...

Another phenomenon has become visible through this confrontation. I will now try to define it from another angle.

From a bird's eye view, Norbert's dream appears as a well-defined narrative unity, with a rigorous internal logic and a dialectical progres-sion. Freud did not hesitate to break the surface connections of the dream in order to explain the intricate elaboration of each of the heterogeneous elements he retains for his analysis. He brought to light, along the same lines, the specific distortions and the forceful masks they had to assume under the pressure of censorship before they reached a semblance of verisimilitude.

Dissociation within the dream, however, preludes to a new construction whose outcome is the *thought of the dream*. Freud's prodigious inventiveness in regard to the intensive polyphony of the dream ends up in a weak mental construct. As a matter of fact, does it *end up*, or did it *start* in such a fashion? Totalization is actually at work in the genesis of individual terms through the imposition of language and the powerful assimilations it allows. Such is the *via regia* to psychoanalysis: one adheres closely to the primary processes, one swiftly embraces the libidinal flux only to channel them into the all too willing structures and the implacable logic of language.

Following Freud's example, one must know how to change scales freely in the presence of a dream, so as to avoid petrifying its energetic process and analyzing the decomposed components in relation to a presumptive origin. The elements of a dream refer to nothing, they are raw forces, distant yet proximate, almost combined, to paraphrase John Cage, within the same frame.

I purposely turn to modern music here, primarily, I admit, because of Freud's enduring hostility to music in general. In his introduction to "The Moses of Michelangelo," he says he is interested only in works that allow him to *understand* how they produce their effects: "Whenever I cannot do this, as for instance with music, I am almost incapable of obtaining any pleasure. Some rationalistic, or perhaps analytic, turn of mind in me rebels against being moved by a thing without knowing why I am thus affected and what it is that affects me." (S.E., XIII, 211). "Intellectual orgasm," as they say in brothels.

Everything vibrant and audacious modern art has to offer – from William Burrough's *cut-ups* to Merce Cunningham's ballets, from Bob Wilson's operas to Rauschenberg's constructions – is a million light-years away from the crummy rationalizations of psychoanalysis. The question of meaning has long been forgotten and what matters is how one can gather and mobilize disparate elements without giving in to the demands of resemblance, without resorting to relations, logical causality, the burdensome clogs of finality, in order to restore the flow of events, the overwhelming process of the world, beyond the cloggish need to censure, to abstract, to foresee, to possess: "I wanted to avoid the melodic aspect," says Cage, "because melody entails will and the desire to bend the sounds to the will. Nevertheless, I do not reject melody. I reject it even less since it is self-endangered. But it must not begin by being imposed: I don't want to force sounds to follow me." (John Cage, *Pour Les Oiseaux*, 81).

Why then should one insist on forcing dreams, texts, words, and actions to signify? Keep the dream-bursts apart; let them resound together without filling the intervals that allow them to coexist in all their richness within dissonance.

At this point, no more need to be said of the dream or the text. Merely let them act upon you, for as soon as you try to tie all the scattered ends, as soon as you trade the fluid process for the moral order of relations and the mental order of the object, as soon as you submit to the rule of signs, ambivalence and ambiguity, repression and the uncanny – all the mirages of the subject and of knowledge – are bound to reappear. If you cannot break away from the traps of metonymized desire and relinquish your grasp, what else is there to do but to call in the police of meaning and psychoanalyse, and psychoanalyse, and psychoanalyse…

The archaeologist safeguards his delirium by forgetting the Pompeian dream. Hysterical amnesia, whispers Freud, before relevantly concluding: "the journey is the result not of the direct instigation of the dream, but a revolt against it, as an emanation of a mental power that refused to know anything of the secret meaning of the dream." (S.E., IX, 68). Must repression be invoked once again? The dream is not to be envisioned in terms of secrecy and knowledge, but in terms of power. *Interpretative* power. They send you off in search of something lying beneath the allegedly deformed production of oneiric images, while in reality catching you in the symbol-trap, in the rigged play of meaning.

Forget meaning and with it the subject. Repression cannot resist the folly of winds.

Beauty will be amnesiac or will not be at all.

Translated by Daniel Moshenberg

January – from The Pain Journal

Bob Flanagan

January, 1995

12/27/94 We are in NY. Gramercy Park Hotel. Bed. Forget what time it is – I mean who cares? Sheree's sleeping. Scott's sleeping. It's been an awful Christmas and an even worse birthday. My parents cramped, depressing apartment. No John. No kids. Me, my whiny, wheezy, grumbling self, scaring everyone out of their minds, acting like I'm going to die any moment. Still depressed now. I just want to die – I meant to write "cry" and I wrote "die." Tomorrow's the museum's B'day party. I'm anxious about it. Just want to be left alone, but I don't want to be alone. I don't want to be nice to anybody. Can't stand anyone. Hate myself. Just want to be home.

12/28/94 Birthday party over – Thank God. Success, from the look of it. People. Nice presents. But me? Where the hell was I? People were impressed by me on the nails – but I wasn't really on the nails – not all of me – too chicken shit to let go. "Couldn't breathe," my idiot's lament. Terrified at the sight of Sheree slicing the big marzipan penis on my stomach – afraid she'll go too far – accidents, afraid of accidents, so I can't get into anything. I'm always on the periphery. I'm always terrified, exhausted, annoyed, pissed, anxious, nervous, impatient, just out of it –period, out of the loop, out of my mind, running out of time.

12/29/94 Everybody's out. I'm in. Everybody is Scott, Sheree and her friend, Jake (female). Not so depressed today, but getting around is tough. Chest hurts. Can't breathe. Blah blah blah. Interview by two Spanish guys and *USA Today*. Who am I that they should value my opinion on anything? What am I? I'm so afraid of being stupid.

12/30/94   Long day breathing badly and being scared about it. Thoughts
of going home early. Thoughts of getting chest x-ray (is it a collapsed
lung?) I increased my prednisone and that seemed to boost me a bit.
Last day of VH tomorrow. New Year's Eve. Don't want to go out anywhere tomorrow night.

12/31/94   Happy New Year. *Visiting Hours* are over. Blab. Mitch
Corber – pest from the past. Sheree – yes I love her – but in her normal
state, not when she's stoned, and she's been stoned a lot this week,
thanks to Scott. I don't relate. I wish I could, and I wish she would stop
and just be herself, the one I get along with, the real one I love. But no
such luck. She's out now, with Julia and Shelly, desperately searching
for a good time, never giving up, never giving in, after a nice dinner
(what the fuck is nice?). It was tense for me – too much talk about Bob
Bob Bob Sheree Sheree Sheree art art art. Scott Kirby and Laura were
there also, but mostly Sheree. "Do you want to hear my idea about
Germany?" No! Please not now, but she's off, and she's drunk, and etc.
But I do love her. Am I just saying that to wrap this thing up nicely?
Bob – Mr. Nice Guy.

1/1/95   Of course the blow up. Slow, sleepy day. Wake up from a nap
in the afternoon. Sheree, Scott, Kirby in the living room, stoned. Sheree
bitching about her life, as usual. I toss her a Paxil. Join them. Laughs.
Joking about tv and stuff and Shelly who turned out to be a shit last
night. Suddenly Sheree gets Shelly's manuscript and says she's going to
burn it, or goes to burn it and I say no, the sprinklers, too dangerous.
Kirby and Scott agree. Kirby videotaping. Suddenly Sheree gets up and
comes back with the big candle (the one I got for my b'day) and a bowl –
I guess for the ashes – and I flipped, grabbed the candle and threw it
across the room, where it broke. "So what, it's my candle," I say. But
that's it. Of course I'm the monster, I'm wrong. It's been cool from her
ever since.

1/2/95   Bad stomach most of the day. Sheree out with Scott. Kirby out.
Interviewed by Kathe Burkhardt for Kirby. Sheree, Scott, Kirby, Kathe
stoned, drunk, loud, obnoxious (Sheree, anyway). Dinner at City Crab.

The Piss Twins show up. Come back and they do a little show in the bedroom. But it's all too loud (Sheree) and everyone's too out of it for me. "$80 for a bottle of wine! Are you nuts?" "Oh, $18. That's different." Kathe asks us on tape when was the last time we fucked? We couldn't remember.

1/3/95   Took down the alphabet block wall with Scott, but even though he did the work I still couldn't breathe. Saw myself on the computer internet. "Pussy" letter on my e-mail. Dinner with Scott, Kirby, Laura, and Sheree. Calmer today. Nasty finger fuck, cunt lick, ass lick last night cause she begged me after those piss lesbians got her all hot. I didn't want to give her the time of day. I was just so pissed at her because I was tired of seeing her pissed/wasted/drunk/loud. Felt like George Saunders. Cold. Sadistic. Superior. Mean. But I gave in cause I knew there would be hell to pay if I didn't. I knew how bad I'd feel afterwards. I knew how wrong I was.

1/4/95   Another dinner another night of people. If Sheree says "the internet" one more time I'm going to wish her into a corn field. Everything taken down at the museum it's a great feeling I'm ready to go home tomorrow will I be as out of breath there? Will Sheree get morose and miserable being back with nothing to do? Well, I have lots to do – My life, whatever it is.

1/5/95   Home home home. I know Sheree's not so thrilled. She's in bed sleeping now because she's got to be up for work tomorrow – but I'm glad to be home, even though it's a big mess and there's no food or milk and I don't really know what to do with myself other than sit here on the couch and doze off as I stare at the tv. Not ready for bed, but exhausted just the same. Flight was fine. Anti-anxiety pills. Kirby picked us up, camera in hand. When we get home I get a frantic call from Mom and Dad – TWA in Kansas called them wondering where I was. They said they had my oxygen waiting and I never got on the plane in New York. So of course they panicked and tried to reach us, called the hotel, called the car service – when all the time I was asleep on the plane. Nutty. But here I am. Nothing to say. Lots to do. Am I really in as bad of shape as I felt much of the time away? I can't tell. Too relaxed.

1/6/95 Wake up early morning yelling at Sheree before she leaves for work because I get tired of her moaning and groaning about how bad she has it and how I wasn't able to do very much in New York. She's insatiable. Yelling seemed to help. She's been real good to me ever since, although I physically just don't have it. Made Debbie cry telling her how worried I am about getting worse and slipping away. Exaggeration? Problem is I don't know. Just don't know.

1/7/95 I'm a boring person who's dying. Feel dead. Wish I was but don't want to be. Want to be doing work. New work. It's time. All Sheree can think about is going going going. As far removed from work as you can get. But I was mad this morning because we're involved in some goofy show at Cal Arts and we have to supply the equipment and we have to deliver it. Life's too hard already to have to add more bullshit for little money and no prestige. And while I'm dwelling on death – Preston, 23 year old from cystic fibrosis camp, died a couple of days ago. Funeral tomorrow but I'm not going to go. Should have called him, but what would I have done, wished him luck?

1/8/95 Horrible stomach aches and nausea. Heavy little shits. Should I start taking Wellbutrin? Don't know. Am I sick or crazy? Short of breath everywhere I go. Making like I'm dying. Am I exaggerating? Why would I? Who would I be trying to impress? Drove Sheree out to Cal Arts with the fucking video projector today. Heavy rain. I like driving. It's the only time I can go from here to there and not feel completely wasted.

1/9/95 Cold in here. "Here" is the hospital again. Again I got tired and scared about not being able to breathe. What's the deal? I feel OK now, but – here's the guy to fix the cooler. A few minutes, he says. I keep thinking I'm dying, I'm dying, but I'm not, I'm not – not yet.

1/10/95 Don't write much in the hospital cause nothing happens and there's certainly nothing in my head. Tv tv tv. Low SATS when I walk. At least I know I'm not crazy. But what's wrong with me? Cf, you jerk.

1/11/95 Almost forgot. It's real late. Slept and woke up. Watching *The Conversation* on tv. Never saw it before. Should go back to sleep. Gotta watch my health, you know. By the way – still in the hospital (where else?) Kind of depressed. All this time thinking I'm going to die – am I just talking myself into a frenzy of phlegm and fatigue? Maybe I'm getting better. Maybe I'm not. Now they say I should exercise. Exercise/ Wheelchair. Exercise/Wheelchair. Hard to know what to do or who I am in it all.

1/12/95 Almost slipped off without writing. Have to do a little. Zone out when I'm in the hospital. All day working up a sweat just trying to breathe. Started physical therapy but the little bit of stretching she had me doing was tough. But everyone says I look good. Just feel like shit. Here's the nurse for drugs. Sheree called. *Autopsy* opening at Cal Arts group show. Everybody loves it and us and me, although it's getting harder to understand why.

1/13/95 Don't want to give it up to write anything. Don't have anything. Depressed. Taking big red Wellbutrin pills but still depressed. My shrink, Dr. Obler gone for two weeks. Can't get myself together. Stuck here in the hospital bed again. Too much. Now Boston U wants to exhibit our piece *Visiting Hours*. But it won't include me, just the stuff. "You know, and stuff." That's what Mom says: "You know, and stuff." No stuff here. And I don't know.

1/14/95 Mom and Dad's 45th anniversary – I made the call – no I didn't – they called me cause I'm the sick one in the hospital. Their sick child. Their dying boy. I keep having these flashes of anxiety where I feel I'm under some sort of weight or under water and I want to run but I can't get out. Sweating like crazy too. Sheree's out with Jake tonight. Marnie's party. I'm actually having sexual thoughts – some stirrings. Even masturbated in broad daylight, sitting right here in my hospital bed with a hard-on under my gown while the nurse brought me my dinner tray. "You got everything?" she asks. "Yes," I say. And I don't even lose my hard – on. Coming is always a let down, but at least I can do it – still alive.

1/15/95 The old *Perry Mason* show used to be so depressing when it came on, but now it's almost comforting. You get your comforts where you can these days here in the hospital. Life goes on and so does this depression. When my mother calls and tells me I sound like I'm getting better I tell her no, not really, not yet. I'm almost rude to her about it. No I'm not. I'm not better. I'm not ready to be better, so stop making me better already. And of course I spend the whole day feeling guilty about it, how I almost cut her off because she was feeling good that I might be feeling better. I'll make it up to her – tomorrow I will be better, even though I just now spit up a big wad of blood – I'll still be better, just you wait and see.

1/16/95   I ask for Vicodin and then I put an alligator clip on my left nipple. It's all drugs. Thanks to the Wellbutrin (the lack of Paxil) I'm getting hard-ons again, and renewed fantasies of self torture. Want to be beaten by Sheree – someday I'll tell her. See what happens at home – Wednesday probably.

1/17/95   Tim's birthday. Anniversary of last year's quake. Day of new major quake in Japan. 2,000 killed. Thousands trapped. Scaring the hell out of myself watching this shit. Sheree wants to keep me locked in the cage at night when I get home, but I'm claustrophobic already, imagining myself trapped in the cage in a major quake, unable to find the key, Sheree lost, me screaming for help, out of oxygen. Short of breath already. But then, even without the cage, what's the difference – house, apartment – big cages without bars or sex appeal. I still can't breathe. Going home tomorrow. Home to lots of beatings – I hope.

1/18/95   Home. Buttplug up my ass. IV running through my chest. Sheree asleep downstairs. And I can sleep with her when I'm done, not in the cage like she said. I'm glad – sleeping in the cage would be hard after more than a week in bed without her, and it's so cold here. Yes, I get incredibly excited at the thought of her being cruel to me – endless hard-ons – but I love the reality of her being nice to me. It's all good, but more cruelty, PLEASE!

1/19/95   Late night infusion. Sleeping here on the couch, not in the cage, not yet. Too much to do with these drugs and this nervousness I feel. Career is steamrollering ahead – exciting but crushing. *Visiting Hours Revisited* in Boston, February 9. Berlin, February 12. Otis, also in February. Now add Exit Art to the stew, the performance/body art retrospective. Interviews. Phone calls. Budgets. And I in such a hot mood for sex and submission, but instead I have to work. And what about breathing? Oh, I forgot, I'm sick, yeah. I'm dying, remember? New pieces I want to make. Sue Spaid Gallery. Stuff and stuff and stuff.

1/20/95   Like a camp out here on the couch. Sheree asleep. Me with ear plugs to block that whisper of a snore she has that unnerves me like so many things unnerve me. Watching *Mirage* on tv. Had dinner with Kirby and Rita and watched *Don't Look Back* and *The Wiz Kids* (my term for Maria Beatty and her piss queen mistress). Itchy asshole. Want to be a slave but I'm always uncomfortable, annoyed, distracted, and Sheree's asleep. Me too.

1/21/95   Locked in the cage for two and a half hours bound in strait jacket. Scared at first that I would panic, but it was good. I counted the seconds, I rocked back and forth, and I dwelled on the pain in my lower back and in my right foot against the metal floor. Took deep breaths. Felt calm. Peaceful. Rigged up the video camera so someone could monitor me – baby-sit me – upstairs while Sheree went out, leaving me only slightly unattended. Thought Kirby was going to be the baby-sitter – then I realized Sheree didn't go out like she said she was going to. Kirby was here for a while, too, videotaping. Now it's late. I'm tired. Turned on. Doing antibiotics. Scribbling.

1/23/95   Fell asleep on the couch and I forgot to write last night and almost forgot tonight. Wiped out yesterday after the rigors of breathing while trying to supervise Andy cleaning the garage and setting up my office, and Ed accompanying me to the storage space to take inventory for the Boston show. The *"Sick Superman"* print rattled when I picked it up: broken glass. Panic. Out of breath. But it's OK. But how am I? Bad pain in my chest all day. Felt like collapsed lung or pleurisy. Called

Dr. Riker. Supposed to see him tomorrow morning, but after sleeping on the couch awhile I don't feel so bad. Might just be a cracked rib or pulled muscle. I get so fucking worried because I feel so fucking bad. I have so much to do and I feel so lousy – but I don't want to get worse.

1/25/95   Fell asleep on the couch last night and I didn't write. Fell asleep again tonight and I almost forgot, but here I am, nervous wreck all night. Preparing shit for Boston. Truck comes tomorrow. Went to Debbie's tonight, but forgot to refill my oxygen, so I had to drive home huffing and puffing. Everything's a hassle. Shitty shitty mood. But Sheree's completely understanding, no matter how much I rant and rave. She made me dinner. Don't know why I'm so crazy. Can't relax. Can't sleep. Can't stay anywhere. Too much drugs – prescription. Took a Halcyon and I'm going to sleep, even though Halcyon sleep is weird sleep – not restful – but it's the only kind I can get right now.

1/27/95   Dozed on the couch last night doing drugs. Tonight too, but I'm playing through with the scribbling, even at this late hour, and even though I'm zonked. SM panel at Fullerton tonight with Sheree, Bill S., Ira and his girl toy, Sarah. Bored to tears doing that stuff but this one pays money, so I did it. Ran out of oxygen and Sheree had to run to the car for the spare tank. My lousy breathing is always the main concern. Life is very hard and sometimes it completely panics me.

1/28/95   Took a Halcyon because last night I didn't take a Halcyon and last night I didn't sleep. Aches and pains and complaints. Pain in my right chest, bad all day and night, but now, not so bad. What gives? Depressed as hell. I don't know who I am anymore. I get these nostalgic flashes on the person I used to be – not years ago, weeks ago! But I've got my orgasms back. That's something – used to be everything.

1/29/95   By the light of the bedroom tv. Pain in my shoulder. SOB (short of breath) from the long, grueling trip downstairs. Seeing Riker on Tuesday. Sometimes I feel so bad I worry I might go back in the hospital. So today I went to Otis with Sheree and Ed and set up the casket for next Saturday's show, just in case I'm indisposed during the week.

Still have more to do, so I'm not indisposed. Don't think I'll be in the hospital. Nothing they can do. I just feel like shit. Shitty lungs filled with shit and I feel like shit. Anything else to talk about? No.

1/30/95 What do I have to do tomorrow that makes me so nervous tonight? Too much: Doctor's appointment; draft oxygen letter for Dr. Riker; measure rods for alphabet wall; get gang box for video casket; what thickness are those rods? Fax Pollas; call Exit Art; call Peter; Fedex package to Exit Art –photographs; draft letter of instructions for Boston people; what else needs to be shipped to Boston? Tell Boston about Norm's date for *"Why"* text; find video for NGBK; ship NGBK video; finish coffin at Otis; find AIG forms for Riker; pick up Rx at Long Beach; double check *Visible Man*; tell Boston about *Visible Man* goop; find coffin video tapes; write checks and mail bills; type up this list. Back to today: Saw Obler. "You have money now," he said when I told him about the cost of Wellbutrin, right after I said we were finally getting some money from our art. Is he feeling taken advantage of by me? Could barely move, I was so short of breath. But I picked up photos on Sunset anyway. Picked up Sheree from work. Had dinner with Jack Skelley. He left. Donna arrived. Troubles in married land, i.e. reality. That does tend to rear its ugly head, doesn't it?

1/31/95 Last day of the first month ends with gloom and doom on the horizon for me. The horrible health (bad breathing and pain) comes off and on, mostly on, and the pulmonary tests at the doctor's echoed what I've been feeling: low and getting lower. I'm dying. It sounds like melodrama, but the damn thing is that it's true – and everyone has to face it: Sheree, my parents, me. I'm so sick of the art crap. Sick of *Visiting Hours*. Every day is a pile of work and expectations. Pile of crap. What else do I want to be doing? I don't know – relaxing. Numbness.

Dynasty Reruns

Lynne Tillman

The banner for the show stretched across the width of the National Gallery's East Building. TREASURE HOUSES OF GREAT BRITAIN, FIVE HUNDRED YEARS OF PRIVATE PATRONAGE AND ART COLLECTING. The letters were gold on a royal blue background, edged with a majestic red. Madame Realism hoped the show would have rooms with dioramas like those at the Museum of Natural History – with stuffed lords and ladies at tea or in conversation or at dinner, all behind glass, all perfectly appointed. Because "houses" was in the title, she was looking for rooms as they might have been lived in. When she thought about the past she always wanted to know, But how did they live and what did they talk about?

Madame Realism entered the slide show that introduced the exhibition. A taped English voice narrated the images of beautiful countryside and enormous houses. Why aren't these called palaces or even mansions, she wondered. The Englishman's voice explained: "British Houses are as much a part of the landscape as the oaks and acorns"; the people in these houses, "vessels of civilization," developed a "civilized outlook, which helped to produce parliamentary democracy, as well as the ideals that helped shape Western civilization." The term "civilized outlook" set Madame Realism's teeth on edge. Houses natural like the scenery? The divine right of houses? She doubted that something could be both natural and civilized at the same time.

Accompanied by the disembodied voice of J. Carter Brown, the director of the National Gallery, on the audioguide, Madame Realism entered the first rooms, which were called "From the Castle to the Country House." Carter Brown told her that the country houses began in 1485, with the accession of the first Tudor to the throne. With relative calm in England and Wales, the castle becomes house because it no longer needs defense – high walls and moats. Madame Realism thought there was always some need for defense, and moats and high walls were perfect metaphors for human ones. Listening to Carter Brown's narration, she felt she was back in grade school. His voice, friendly and authoritative, recited dates and facts that jerked classroom memories. Back then she'd absorbed things wholesale, the way kids do, but now she was able to remind herself that there isn't one history, there are at least two. The official version and the unofficial, whose dates were not taught in grade school – the history of those without access to power. There was no doubt which version this would be, inaugurated as it was by Charles and Di, and funded in part by the British government and the Ford Motor Co.

Madame Realism stared hard at the portrait attributed to Rowland Lockey of Elizabeth Hardwick, Countess of Shrewsbury (ca. 1600). Bess of Hardwick had four husbands, outlived them all and inherited everything, making her the richest woman in England, next to Elizabeth the Queen. Bess's almost heart-shaped hair frames a resolute face that is cut off from its body by a high white collar. That old devil issue, the mind/body split, popped into her mind but did it apply to Bess? This portrait was not meant to imply personality or psychology, but, like the other portraits in these rooms, to be emblematic of position and power. Everyone was holding scepters, wearing important jewels, or being represented in allegories that assure their right of succession and that of their dynasties. Even so, Madame Realism wondered if Old Bess was bawdy like the Wife of Bath, what with four husbands – more husbands even than Alexis on TV's *Dynasty* – and were she and the Queen friends? In *Elizabeth I: The Rainbow Portrait* (ca. 1600), attributed to Marcus Gheeraerts the younger, the Queen wears a cloak and dress that have eyes and ears embroidered all over them. J. Carter Brown informs Madame Realism, and others standing with her in front of the painting, that this means Elizabeth had many informers in her employ, maintaining power through a spy system in which she also used her servants. Again Madame Realism thought about *Dynasty*, and imagined that Elizabeth I might have been like paranoid Alexis and Bess of Hardwick like trusting Krystle. Guiltily she looked around her and wondered if anyone else was making such plebeian comparisons.

"There are many symbols everywhere," Madame Realism heard one woman say to another. "Everything means something else." They were standing in the Jacobean Long Gallery, modeled after the picture gallery in the background of Daniel Mytens's portrait of the Countess of Arundel, Alatheia Talbot. Madame Realism and others are directed by the audioguide to pretend they are in the Countess's house, to stroll down the hall and gaze at the paintings. On cue she and several others move in unison. Madame Realism halted in front of the painting of *Barbara, Lady Sydney, with Six Children*, again by Gheeraerts the younger (1596). How had Lady Sydney survived six childbirths? Mother and children look identical, as if stamped rather than painted. Clearly dynasty isn't concerned with individuals, only continuity. So it's faceless. Maybe that was what was so funny about *Dynasty*. Sons and daughters disappear, are thought dead, then reappear with entirely different faces that should be unrecognizable but aren't. Of course the series has to continue, even when principal actors leave for other jobs. The series must continue, she thought, looking around her. And then she heard a man say to his companion, "They don't have beauty. It's the one thing the British don't have." What about, she wanted to argue, Vivien Leigh, Vanessa Redgrave, Annie Lennox, Bob Hoskins. She suspected that the man, awed by how much these people did have, may have been comforting himself with the idea that no one has it all.

Madame Realism would never have been invited, in that time, to stroll down the Countess's picture gallery. The British don't fool themselves about all being one happy classless family. She appreciated *The Tichborne Dole* by Gillis van Tillborch (1670), one of the few paintings on view that depicts workers or the poor, and which explained to her the origin of the term "dole." The painting shows Sir Henry Tichborne and his family about to distribute bread to the poor of the village. It's a tradition, she reads in the catalogue, that exists in Tichborne to this day, even though the dole itself is under attack from Thatcher. This painting may have been made to demonstrate the worthiness of that wealthy family, but at least the poor are shown to exist, she thought to herself, which is more than can be said for Reagan's picture of America.

J. Carter Brown was talking to her over the audioguide, his voice reassuring and almost familiar. The reign of the Tudors passed to the

Stuarts in 1603, and everyone kept collecting and patronizing. Upheavals in other countries, such as French Huguenot craftsmen getting kicked out of France, added to British treasure troves. The British made a killing on social upheavals, and, Madame Realism learned, they became rich tourists, taking what came to be known as the Grand Tour, the title of the exhibition's next rooms. "The Grand Tour" is dated as beginning in 1714, when Richard Boyle, 3rd Earl of Burlington, made his first jaunt abroad, returning to Chiswick and building a villa there after designs by Palladio. What the British brought back – according to Carter Brown, "the fruits of these tours" – were "souvenirs." A villa in Chiswick, paintings by Canalletto, all these Roman sculptures and busts – souvenirs? Two Venetian Lattimo Plates (1741) did look like contemporary tourist views of Venice on dinner plates. Horace Walpole carried back twenty-four of them in his luggage; she wondered whether he and his family had ever eaten off them.

There were paintings of English gents posing among Roman ruins – Narcissistic Neoclassicism. *William Gordon* by Pompeo Batoni (1766) is wearing a kilt, with a view of the Coliseum in the background and a statue of Roma on a pedestal sharing the foreground – the spotlight – with him. Colonel Gordon's kilt was draped like a toga, reminding her of a letter to the *Times* she'd read when she was in London one summer. A man wrote the editor suggesting that, because it was so beastly hot, men wear togas rather than suits, ties and bowlers. To maintain class distinctions, different kinds and colors of stripes could be sewn on the hems of the togas, and, of course, men could still carry umbrellas. Lots of Englishmen walking around the City in togas carrying umbrellas would turn the English summer into a Monty Python skit. Madame Realism laughed out loud, attracting some attention.

A china serving dish shaped like a boar's head made her chortle quietly; porcelain figurines of prominent 18th-century actors were objects any fan could relate to. In gift shops across the U.S. today there'd be something similar – a little figurine of John Forsythe, maybe. Embarrassed to find *Dynasty* so much on her mind – she might explain to scoffers and non-viewers that she watched only the reruns, as if that made her less adolescent than the rest of the nation who were watching it on prime time – she heard a man say to his young daughter, "That's where we got off our gondola to go to our hotel." They were in front of a view of commerce in the Campo Santa Maria Formosa in Venice by Canaletto, one of the souvenirs J. Carter Brown had mentioned earlier. As accurate as any tourist snapshot.

Madame Realism entered the room called "Chinoiserie and Porcelain" and walked immediately to the state bed. It had elaborately embroidered Chinese silk curtains and looked pretty narrow for a bed of state, but then how many heads of state were expected to lie in it at one time anyway? State bed or sex and politics. Musing about 18th-century sex lives of the rich and famous, she wished that Carter Brown would get even more familiar. But instead he directed her to the tiaras and crowns, which rested on shelves in a glass cabinet, so gaudy they looked fake. One woman nudged another and said conspiratorially, "That's why the people rebelled." Madame Realism wanted to tell this woman and her friend, if they didn't already know, about Guy Fawkes Day, when the English celebrate an abortive attempt to overthrow King James I. Were they the only people in the world to celebrate a failed revolution?

The exhibition's brochure claimed that the love of landscape was "essentially English," but to Madame Realism the way the English took the piss out of each other was even more essential. But wait, she said to herself, what did they mean by essential? Natural? By now she was in a room called "The Sporting Life," surrounded by paintings of animals, primarily horses, like those done by George Stubbs. There were gentlemen in red hunting jackets, men on horseback in black jackets, and men surrounded by live dogs and dead game. Britain's contemporary Animal Liberation Front might have something to say about the English love of landscape, populated as it is by dead prey hung next to portraits of dogs who were much loved by their owners.

Sentiment was very definitely in the air, what with these sweet animal portraits and the works in the last, "Pre-Raphaelite and Romantic" room. *Love Among the Ruins* by Burne-Jones (1894) was just the kind of painting she might have had a print of on her wall, when she was a teenager, as consolation for yet another broken heart. Now Madame Realism wished she could steal the title, just as Burne-Jones had stolen it from Browning. She liked the title much better than the picture; it

was tougher than the wistful backward-looking image. But was that
really true? she asked herself, wondering why this kind of adolescent
sentiment didn't appeal to her anymore and *Dynasty*'s did.

Parody, she told herself, and walked into the last room, called
"Epilogue," which was devoted to family photo albums of some late
19th- and early 20th-century collectors and patrons. By comparison
with the rest of the exhibition, "Epilogue" was homey and dimly lit,
small in scale in both size of room and in what was on display. Madame
Realism thought it odd that an exhibition devoted to the display of
wealth and power should end on so mundane a note, though it did allow
the spectator a moment to reorient, as in a decompression chamber, for
reentry into ordinary life.

Spotlights shone on the albums and photographic portraits. The
differences between the paintings and these photographs were overwhelming. Family photo albums compared with paintings meant to last
forever. Casual pictures in black and white and posed portraits in magnificent color. The lords and ladies "captured" at unguarded moments,
letting us know that, in the end, we're all "just folks." Especially in these
dimly lit rooms.

A small plain book caught Madame Realism's eye. It was, the cap-
tion read, a scrapbook of photographs of the servants of a particular
household, taken by the lady of the house. Madame Realism wanted to
see these photographs, but she couldn't because the book was barely
open. These were the invisible people, part of unofficial history, who
built the country houses and packed up the souvenirs so that they
wouldn't get broken on the trip home. Carter Brown directed everyone's attention to the doll's house replica of an English country house,
attributed to Thomas Chippendale (ca. 1745). It was behind glass at the
end of the room, but this wasn't the diorama she had hoped for. There
was a very long line, and Madame Realism stood on it for a while, only
to leave the crowd and return to the small, plain book with its glimpse
into ....The repressed, she said to herself. It's like the return of the
repressed. She wondered what Carter Brown looked like ...Vincent
Price?

When Madame Realism got outside, it was snowing. The White
House was surprisingly and deceptively invisible. The young black

taxidriver, wearing a Coptic cross earring, explained that D.C. had been designed by mystics and visionaries, and that through their writings he knew that the end of the world was at hand. "God makes no accidents," he warned.

Back home, Madame Realism lay in bed, thinking about the exhibition and reading Virginia Woolf's *Orlando*, to satisfy her desire to know how people lived and what they talked about in the treasure houses of Britain. There's a wonderful scene in which Elizabethan poet Nick Greene has dinner at Orlando's country house, and though the poet mocks his host and his efforts at poetry, still Orlando "paid the pension quarterly" to Greene. Woolf is taking the piss out of patrons, while the exhibition had pumped them up. Nothing is sacred in *Orlando*. Madame Realism reached the page where Orlando changes from a man into a woman. She put the book on her lap. Was she expected to be grateful to or respectful of the aristocracy for having first created and then preserved Western civilization? The show's banner could have read: WESTERN CIVILIZATION BROUGHT TO YOU BY.... It was too tall an order, and besides, respect was something Madame Realism didn't like to be asked to give. Just too much to swallow, she said to her cat, who had sat himself down on the sex-change page. Closing her eyes, she had a hypnogogic vision: If Steven, the son on Dynasty who goes from gay to straight to gay, were to come back as a woman, would he be a gay or a straight woman? Madame Realism fell asleep smiling.

May '68 Did Not Take Place
Deleuze and Guattari

In historical phenomena such as the revolution of 1789, the Commune, the revolution of 1917, there is always one part of the *event* that is irreducible to any social determinism, or to causal chains. Historians are not very fond of this point: they restore causality after the fact. Yet the event is itself a splitting off from, a breaking with causality; it is a bifurcation, a lawless deviation, an unstable condition that opens up a new field of the possible. In physics, Ilya Prigogine spoke of states in which the slightest differences persist rather than cancel themselves out, and where independent phenomena inter-resonate. An event can be turned around, repressed, co-opted, betrayed, but still something survives that cannot be outdated. Only traitors could say it's outdated. Even ancient, an event can never be outdated. It is an opening onto the possible. It enters as much into the interior of individuals as into the depths of a society.

The historical phenomena we are invoking were indeed accompanied by determinisms or causalities, but these were of a peculiar nature. May '68 is of the order of pure event, free from all normal, or normative causalities. Its history is a "series of amplified instabilities and fluctuations." There were many agitations, gesticulations, slogans, idiocies, illusions in '68, but this is not what counts. What counts amounted to a visionary phenomenon, as if a society suddenly perceived what was intolerable in itself and also saw the possibility of change. It is a collective phenomenon in the form of: "Give me the possible, or else I'll suffocate." The possible does not pre-exist, it is created by the event. It is a matter of life. The event creates a new existence, it produces a new subjectivity (new relations with the body, with time, sexuality, the immediate surroundings, with culture, work).

When a social mutation appears, it is not enough to draw the consequences or effects according to lines of economic or political causality. Society must be capable of forming collective agencies of enunciation that match the new subjectivity, in such a way that it desires its own mutation. It's a veritable redeployment. The American *New Deal* and the Japanese boom corresponded to two very different examples of subjective redeployment, into all sorts of ambiguities and even reactionary structures. But they produced enough initiative and creativity to conceive new social states capable of responding to the demands of the event. Following '68 in France, on the contrary, the authorities never stopped living with the idea that "things will settle down." And indeed, things did settle down, but under catastrophic conditions. May '68 was neither the result of, nor a reaction to a crisis. It is rather the opposite. It is the current crisis in France, the impasse that stems directly from the inability of French society to assimilate May '68. French society has shown a radical incapacity to create a subjective redeployment on the collective level, which is what '68 demands. In this light, how could it now trigger an economic redeployment that would ever satisfy the expectations of the "left"? French society never came up with anything for the people: nothing at school, nothing at work. Everything that was new was marginalized or reduced into caricature. Today we see the population of Longwy cling to their steel, the dairy farmers to their cows, etc. What else can they do? Every collective enunciation by a new existence, by a new collective subjectivity, was crushed in advance by the reaction against '68, on the left almost as much as on the right. Even by the "free radio stations." Each time it appeared, the possible was closed off.

The children of May '68, you can run into them all over the place, even if they are not aware of who they are. Each country produces them in its own way. Their situation isn't so great. These are not young executives. These are strangely indifferent, and for this very reason are in the right frame of mind. They have stopped being demanding and narcissistic, but they know perfectly well that nothing today corresponds to their subjectivity, to their potential of energy. They even know that all current reforms are rather directed against them. They are determined to mind to their own business as much as they can. They hold it open, hang on to something possible. It is Coppola who created their poetized portrait in *Rusty James*. The actor Mickey Rourke explained: "The character is at the end of his rope, on the edge. He's not the Hell's Angel type. He's got brains and he's got good sense. But he hasn't got any university degree. And it is this combination that makes him go crazy. He knows that there's no job for him because he is smarter than any guy willing to hire him" (*Libération*, February 15, 1984).

This is true of the entire world. What we institutionalize for the unemployed, the retired, or in school, are controlled "situations of abandonment." For these, the handicapped is the model. The only subjective redeployments actually occurring collectively are those of an unbridled American-style capitalism, of a Muslim fundamentalism like in Iran, or of Afro-American religion like in Brazil: the reversed figures of a new orthodoxy (one should add European neo-Papism to the list). Europe has nothing to suggest, and France seems no longer to have any other ambition than to assume the leadership of an Americanized and over-armed Europe that would impose the necessary economic redeployment from above. But the field of the possible lives elsewhere. *Along the East-West axis*, in pacifism, insofar as it intends to break up not only relations of conflict and over-armament, but also of complicity and distribution between the United States and the Soviet Union. *Along the North-South axis*, in a new internationalism that no longer relies solely on an alliance with the third-world, but on the phenomena of third-worldification in the rich countries themselves (the evolution of metropolises, the decline of the inner-cities, the rise of a European third-world, as Paul Virilio has theorized them). There can only be creative solutions. These are the creative redeployments that can contribute to a resolution of the current crisis and that can take over where a generalized May '68, amplified bifurcation or fluctuation, left off.

Translated by Robert Hardwick Weston

GETTING AND SPENDING

Capitalism: A Very Special Delirium
Deleuze and Guattari

Gilles Deleuze: Underneath all reason lies delirium, drift. Everything is rational in capitalism, except capital or capitalism itself. The stock market is certainly rational; one can understand it, study it, the capitalists know how to use it, and yet it is completely delirious; it's mad. In this sense we say: the rational is always the rationality of an irrational. Something that hasn't been adequately discussed about Marx's Capital is the extent to which Marx is fascinated by capitalism's mechanisms, precisely because the system is demented, yet works very well at the same time. What is rational in a society is – the interests being defined in the framework of this society – the way people pursue those interests, their realization. But down below are desires, investments of desire that cannot be confused with the investments of interest, and on which interests depend in their determination and distribution: an enormous flux. All kinds of libidinal-unconscious flows make up the delirium of this society. The true history is the history of desire. A capitalist, or today's technocrat, does not desire in the same way as a slave merchant or official of the ancient Chinese empire. That people in a society desire repression, both for others and for themselves, that there are always some people who want to spy on others and who have the opportunity to do so, the "right" to do so, reveals the problem of a deep link between libidinal desire and the social domain. A "disinterested" love for the oppressive machine: Nietzsche said some beautiful things about this permanent triumph of slaves, on how the embittered, the depressed and the weak impose their mode of life upon us all.

Are delirium and interest, or rather desire and reason, distributed in a completely new, particularly "abnormal" way in capitalism? We believe so. Capital, or money, is at such a level of insanity that psychiatry has but one clinical equivalent: the terminal stage. In other societies there is exploitation, there are also scandals and secrets, but these are part of the "code," there are even explicitly secret codes. With capitalism, nothing is secret, at least according to the code (this is why capitalism is "democratic" and can "publicize" itself, even in a juridical sense). And yet nothing is admissible. Legality itself is inadmissible. In contrast to other societies, it is a regime both of the public and the inadmissible. A very special delirium inherent to the regime of money. Take what are called scandals today: newspapers talk a lot about them, some people pretend to defend themselves, others go on the attack, yet it would be hard to find anything illegal in terms of the capitalist regime. The prime minister's tax returns, real estate deals, invested interests, and the more general economical and financial mechanisms of capital – in sum, everything is legal, except for little blunders. Everything is public, yet nothing is admissible. If the left was "reasonable," it would content itself with vulgarizing economic and financial mechanisms. There is no need to publicize what is private, only to make sure that what is already public is being admitted publicly. One would find oneself in a state of dementia without equivalent in the asylums. Instead one talks of "ideology." But ideology has no importance whatsoever: what matters is not ideology, not even the "economico-ideological" distinction or oppositions, but the organization of power. Because organization of power – that is, the manner in which libido invests the economic, haunts the economic, and nourishes political forms of repression.

To say "ideology is a *trompe l'oeil*," is still the traditional thesis. One puts the infrastructure on one side – the economic, the serious – and on the other, the superstructure, of which ideology is a part, thus rejecting the phenomena of desire in ideology. It's a perfect way to ignore how desire works within infrastructure, how it invests it, how it takes part in it, how, in this respect, it organizes power and the repressive system. We do not say: ideology is a *trompe l'oeil* (or a concept that refers to certain illusions). We say: there is no ideology, it is an illusion. That's why it suits orthodox Marxism and the Communist Party so well. Marxism put so much emphasis on the theme of ideology to conceal what was happening in the USSR: a new organization of repressive power. Once it is admitted that the organization of power is the unity of desire and the economic infrastructure, there is no ideology, there are only organizations of power. Take two examples. Education: in May 1968 the leftists lost a lot of time insisting that professors engage in public self-criticism as agents of bourgeois ideology. This was stupid, and simply fueled the masochistic impulses of academics. The struggle against the competitive examination was abandoned for the benefit of controversy, of the great anti-ideological public confession. In the meantime, the more conservative professors had no difficulty reorganizing their power. The problem of education is not ideological, but a problem of the organization of power. The specificity of educational power makes it appear an ideology, but it's pure illusion. Second example: Christianity. The church is perfectly pleased to be treated as an ideology. This can be argued; it feeds ecumenicism. But Christianity has never been an ideology; it is a very original, very specific organization of power that has assumed diverse forms since the Roman Empire. It was able to invent the idea of international power. It's far more important than ideology.

Félix Guattari: It's the same thing in traditional political structures. One finds the old trick played again and again: a big ideological debate in the general assembly and questions of organization reserved for special commissions. These questions appear secondary, determined by political options. But on the contrary, the real problems are those of organization, never specified or rationalized, but projected afterwards in ideological terms. There the real divisions show up: an organization of desire and power, of investments, of group Oedipus, of group "superegos," of perverse phenomena, etc. And then political oppositions are built up: the individual takes such a position against another one, because in the scheme of organization of power, he has already chosen and hates his adversary.

It's a whole axiomatics, down to the phonological level – the way of articulating certain words, the gestures that accompany them – and then the structures of organization, the conception of what sort of relationships to maintain with the allies, the centrists, the adversaries.... This may correspond to a certain figure of Oedipalization, the reassuring, intangible universe of the obsessive who loses his sense of security if one shifts the position of a single, familiar object.

One must explain the role of party machines – the groupuscules and their work of stacking and shifting – in crushing desire. It's a dilemma: to be broken by the social system or to be integrated in the pre-established structure of these little churches. In a way, May 1968 was an astonishing revelation. The desiring power became so accelerated that it broke up the groupuscules. These later pulled themselves together; they participated in the reordering business with the other repressive forces, the CGT [Communist worker's union], the PC, the CRS [riot police]. I don't say this to be provocative. Of course, the militants courageously fought the police. But if one leaves the sphere of struggle to consider the function of desire, one must recognize that certain groupuscules approached the youth in spirit of repression: to contain liberated desire in order to re-channel it.

Take desire in one of its most critical, most acute stages: that of the schizophrenic – the schizo who can produce something within or beyond the scope of the confined schizo, battered down by drugs and social repression. It appears to us that certain schizophrenics directly express a free deciphering of desire. But how does one conceive a collective form of the economy of desire? Certainly not at the local level. I would have a lot of difficulty imagining a small, liberated community maintaining itself against the flows of a repressive society, an addition of individuals emancipated one by one. But if desire constitutes the very texture of society in its entirety, including its mechanisms of reproduction, a movement of liberation can "crystallize" within the whole of society. In May 1968, from the first sparks of local clashes, the shake-up was brutally transmitted to the whole of society, even to groups that had nothing remotely to do with the revolutionary movement – doctors, lawyers, grocers. Vested interests carried the day, but only after a month of burning. We are moving toward explosions of this type, but more profound.

There are militant revolutionaries who feel a sense of responsibility and say: Yes, excess "at the first stage of revolution." But there is a second stage, of organization, functioning, serious things…. For desire is not liberated in simple moments of celebration. See the discussions between Victor and Foucault in the issue of *Les Temps Modernes* on the Maoists. Victor consents to excess, but only at the "first stage." Victor calls for a new apparatus of state, new norms, a popular justice with a tribunal, a legal process external to the masses, a third party capable of resolving contradictions among masses. One always finds the old schema: the detachment of pseudo-avant-garde capable of bringing about synthesis, of forming a party as an embryo of state apparatus, drawing out of well-raised, well-educated working class; and the rest is a residue, a lumpen-proletariat one should always mistrust (the same old condemnation of desire). But these distinctions themselves are another way of trapping desire for the advantage of a bureaucratic caste. Foucault reacts by denouncing the third party, saying that if there is popular justice, it does not issue from a tribunal. He shows very well that the "avant-garde-lumpen-proletariat" is a distinction introduced by the bourgeoisie to the masses in order to crush the phenomena of desire, to *marginalize* desire. It would be strange to rely on a party or state apparatus for the liberation of desire. And then we are told: how would you unify isolated struggles without a party? How would you make the machine work without the state apparatus. It also requires an instance of analysis, an analysis of the desire of the masses, but not by an apparatus external to syntheses. Liberated desire escapes the impasse of private fantasy: it is not a question of adapting it, socializing it, disciplining it, but of plugging it in in such a way that its process not be interrupted in the social body, and that its expression is collective. What counts is not the authoritarian unification, but rather a sort of infinite spreading: desire in the schools, the factories, the neighborhoods, the nursery schools, the prisons, etc. It is not a question of directing, of totalizing, but of plugging into the same plan of oscillation. As long as one alternates between the impotent spontaneity of anarchy and the bureaucratic and hierarchic coding of party organization, there is no liberation of desire.

Capitalism remains a formidable desiring machine. The monetary flux, the means of production, of manpower, of new markets, are all the flow of desire. It's enough to consider the sum of contingencies at the origin of capitalism to see to what degree it has been a crossroads of desire, and that its infrastructure, even its economy, has been inseparable from the phenomenon of desire. And fascism too – one must say that is has "assumed the social desires," including the desire of repression and death. People get hard-ons for Hitler, for the beautiful fascist machine. But was capitalism revolutionary in its beginnings, has the industrial revolution ever coincided with social revolution? No, I don't think so. Capitalism has been tied from birth to a savage repressiveness; it had its organization of power and its state apparatus from the start. Did capitalism imply dissolution of the previous social codes and powers? Certainly. But it had already established its wheels of power, including its power of class in the fissures of previous regimes. It is always the same: things are not so progressive; even before a social formation is established, its instruments of exploitation and repression are already there, still turning in a vacuum, ready to work full capacity. The first capitalists are like waiting birds of prey. They wait for their meeting with the worker, with the one who drops through the cracks of the preceding system. In every sense this is what one calls primitive accumulation.

Leash
Jane Delynn

14

In the morning the sky was distant, the sun cold. I was cold too, though
it could have been the Restoril, making me foggy and slow. My throat
was dry, as if I had drunk too much, and my muscles were stiff, perhaps
from the cold. Worst was a peculiar smell on me, almost of urine, which
I was suddenly afraid would not wash off. I had been near people who
had such odors, which seemed strangely resistant to water and soap.
What if I were to be marked hereafter by some such smell, as old
people and mothers are?

I was getting out of the shower when the Current (the one with
whom I exchanged rings, the one whom, to be honest, I cannot swear
I like) called, as she had warned me she would. It was, after all, my
birthday.

As she chattered I stared at my drawings and paintings, most of
which she co-owned, along with the 2300 square foot loft with the 11
foot high ceilings and six 4' x 7' windows, the red leather chair with
its matching leather couch, the Thonet chairs and Philippe Starck
cabinet, the art by Bill Sullivan, Perry Bard, Martha Diamond, Helene
Aylon, Zoe Leonard, Peter Noble, Liz Rosenblum, Donna Dennis, Judy
Somerville, etc., the kilim rugs and marble table, the 54" projection TV
with digital picture-in-a-picture and its SurroundSound sound system,
the laserdisc and 3 VCRs, the two CDRom changers and palmsize
Camcorder, the 600 watt speakers and infrared cordless earphones
and universal remote control, 4 computers (two portable), one black
and white and one color printer, a flatbed scanner and a Visioneer
Paperport, 3 phone lines, 6 phones (including the one on the plain
paper fax, two of which are portable), two digital T.A.D.s (telephone

answering devices), a hundred or so CDs, endless tapes, homemade and otherwise, and a huge collection of records we couldn't bring ourselves to throw out not to mention piles of cameras, radios, Walkpeople, binoculars, too numerous to count.

Did these bring me happiness? Not at all. Yet I was sure I could not survive without them.

After the obligatory congratulations and an apology for not getting my present to me in time, she launched into a critique of my half of our email correspondence, which she considered deficient in terms of frequency, duration, and the platitudes of affection.

Lying on my back on the bed, I dangled the phone a little above me in the air, so I would have to strain to hear the words. It was more interesting that way.

"Do you miss me?" she asked. The voice was far away. I brought it to my ear. "I asked if you missed me," she repeated.

"Of course," I sighed. "I've been a bit distracted, that's all."

"Are you getting your work done?"

Long sigh. "No."

"So come join me."

"I'm not in the mood."

"You used to love to travel," she said plaintively.

"Not to Sweden."

"I thought you thought it was the greatest country in the world."

"Conceptually. To be honest, I'd probably rather live in South Africa." A longer silence. "Are you ill?" she finally asked.

Although I'm sure she'd rather I be ill than prefer living in South Africa to Sweden, I said no.

After a long silence, she asked about Esmeralda. More than once we had reverted to "pet" discussion in preference to argument.

"She's fine." I got Esmeralda and held her ear up the phone. "Say 'hi.'"

Esmeralda squirmed and I put her down. I listened for awhile as the current mouthed inanities about "being a good girl ...not knocking over the water bowl ....not scratching the couch," etc.

"People sound so stupid when they talk to their pets," I said.

"Fuck you." She hung up.

This little show of independence made me like her better, though not enough to call her back. But, lying on the bed, I thought about it, with the same kind of enjoyment I got on hot summer evenings when I lay in bed thinking about whether it was worth it to get out of bed, stumble over to the air-conditioner, and fiddle with the controls.

I decided it was a bad idea, as it would only reinforce her hanging up on me when she was angry, an action which, although I rather admired it at the moment, would over time become melodramatic and tedious.

I burrowed through drawers until I found an old baggie with bits of dried twigs and leaves in it. My tampons now came encased in plastic, and it had been years since I had rolling papers, so I took a pencil and wrapped aluminum foil around it, leaving some extra at the end which I fastened into a little bowl. I stabbed the bowl several times with the point of a knife, then, having placed some twigs and leaves into the concavity, and discarding the pencil, held the hollow tube to my mouth and lit a match. After which I inhaled the only illegal substance the government had ever managed to get even somewhat under its control as demonstrated by the extraordinary sum I was forced to pay for my quarter ounce.

It felt pleasant, as if I were a criminal especially because I was not in some East Village dump, but in an expensive loft most people I knew would kill to be in.

But although they would kill to be in it, if they were here they wouldn't have smoked dope with me, as most of them were in programs to help keep themselves free from various addictions (but not from the addiction of the programs themselves).

Nonetheless, because they still lived in the East Village, because in years or decades past they had staggered down the street, because they had woken up swathed in vomit in the apartments of strangers they did not remember meeting, they still thought of themselves as criminals and me as bourgeois, though in truth probably the only criminal thing they had done in years was underpay their income taxes.

But what poor person can underpay their income taxes as much as I can?

I realized I was humming "Mr. Soul" under my breath. I searched for it among the records we hid in the closet for just such moments. I had not played it (or perhaps any record) in years. It was scratchy and full of hisses. I reminded myself there had been a time, not so long ago, that I could listen to entire stacks of records filled with scratches, through a 25 watt amplifier hooked to speakers that cost perhaps a tenth of what mine (ours) did, and enjoy it utterly.

Such philosophizing helped me to enjoy it (if not utterly), but I made a mental note to buy the compilation CD the next time I went to Tower Records.

Thus it is that Capitalism encases us in its chains. Does not every phone call the TAD records, every program one buys for one's computer, every hunk of frozen meat one feeds to one's microwave, serve to enslave us further?

But if I were not enslaved, could I want anything?

I realized I was hungry, and made some tuna fish.

15

Before leaving the apartment, I put the various notes I had received, along with the *Village Voice* ad and receipt for the P.O. box and the East Village address to which I was shortly going, in a 10" x 13" manila envelope which I sealed and left by the front door. On the front I wrote in a thick black permanent marker "In case something happens to me." I wore khaki twill shorts, a new shortsleeved offwhite shirt of an astonishing weave and price, and expensive sandals with molded rubber buttons. With great trepidation (lest I have a heart attack, be hit by a car, be chopped in pieces, etc.) I left my health insurance card at home, though I carried (both for a good luck token and to help in case of amnesia) a matchbook of a restaurant one block north of where I lived.

Having debated (and rejected) bringing flowers, out of fear it would signal (relative to the East Village) either wealth or sentimentality, I bought a sixpack of Rolling Rock – a deliberately anonymous beer, for I wanted to confine whatever quirkiness I possessed to a single sphere. But near her building I abandoned it, partly because it might give a faulty impression of nervousness and/or alcoholism, and partly because she might be in AA, like everybody else in the East Village.

Two Spanish men eyed my abandonment of the sixpack with suspicion. Halfway down the block I turned; they still had not retrieved it. Though they were looking at me looking at them, I went back and got it.

16

Not just the outer but the inner door was unlocked, as they often are in crummy tenements.

I walked up the stone stairs, indented from decades of footsteps, walls bumpy from ancient attempts to make "the texture" interesting, paint chipped, graffitied, peeling, names of old lovers (Mike & Cathy forever, Julio loves Sandy) etched by key or knife into its surface. Garlic, marijuana, fried chicken, rotting food – Spanish music and kids screaming and TV in various languages mingling in a way that was pleasantly familiar. In the past I had known buildings like this so well, with their geographically-labeled (NE, SE, NW, SW) apartments, the chains through which old ladies peeked before opening the door, tied-up bags of garbage (brown bags inside plastic) waiting outside doors to be carried downstairs – all the joys of downward mobility, whether involuntary or chosen.

I went up the stairs as far as I could until I faced a metal door to the roof. I assumed this was where I was supposed to wait, and I put the sixpack down. On the floor was a little brown paper bag, on top of which was a printed note that read: 'Put this on.'

Inside the bag was a kind of large blindfold, almost a partial hood, of black leather, with an arched area to go over one's nose and what seemed like real fur behind the eye-patches. The back was a thick band of elastic, but there were also velcro straps to make it even tighter.

Feeling stupid, but also intrigued, I placed the blindfold over my face. In my life, of course, I have had occasion to make use of blindfolds, but none this elaborate or so intelligently designed. Once on, there was no way to dislodge it to catch a glimpse of anything; in any case, the tickling of the fur on the eyeball made it impossible to open your eyes more than a second.

As I waited, I leaned against the wall, stiffening and relaxing various muscles of my back so that the pressure of the wall worked against them

almost like a massage. Then somehow, despite my curiosity and nervousness, I grew sleepy, as has happened more than once in a dentist's
chair. Ignoring my concern re my twill shorts, I sat down on the floor.

"Is the blindfold on?" a voice startled me.

"Yes," I said truthfully, though my heart pounded as if I had been
caught lying.

"How much can you see?"

"Nothing."

"Good. Stand up, but keep your back toward me." A bit awkwardly,
for I was still startled by the intrusion of her voice inside my unconscious,
I pushed myself to my feet.

"Now reach out with your left hand, until you feel the bannister."

I fumbled around, my palm against the wall, until, reaching backward, I felt the metal railing, cool and knobby from decades of paint.

"Good. Now move over…more…more…a little backward…Stop.
The stairs are right behind you." I shuffled my feet very slowly until I
could feel my heel sliding off the edge of the step. "Good. Now lift your
right foot and place it behind you. Hold on tight so you don't fall, and
walk slowly down the stairs."

"Backwards!"

"Yes."

"I can't." I was petrified, afraid I'd fall into the void, or that she'd
push me (even though her voice was below me).

"Of course you can. You just feel with your foot until there's no step,
then lower yourself carefully."

"What if I fall?"

"You won't."

"But what if I do?"

"I'll help you. Don't worry."

Still I waited. "What about the beer?"

"We don't need it."

'I don't need any of this,' I told myself, but nonetheless I let my left
hand slide slightly down the bannister, which was now becoming wet
from my sweat and, gripping it hard as I could, reached behind me with
my right leg until I found the lower step.

Carefully shifting my weight onto this leg, I fumbled in the air with my left leg. Thus, proceeding cautiously, but slightly faster, like a precocious child learning to walk, I made my way down the stairs.

"One more step," she said. I lowered my foot, then a jarring went through my body, as my foot landed unexpectedly on the floor.

She turned me around, so her voice was in front of me. "What do I look like?"

"I don't know."

She laughed, then placed one hand on my right shoulder, and one on my left arm, and pulling with one arm and pushing with the other, began to spin me around. Then she removed her hands and told me to do this myself until I got dizzy. When I stopped she took me by the hand and told me to follow her.

"Where are we going?" I resisted.

"You'll...see."

"Will I?"

"Don't you trust me?"

"I don't know."

I tried to figure out which way I was facing, but the spinning had confused me. I liked the feeling of my hand in hers, though, and the quality of her voice, which was musical but slightly husky, as if she were thirsty, or getting a cold, or had talked all day on the phone.

She stopped. I heard a slight creak (a door being pushed open), then, after warning me to lift my foot a little, my foot landed on a somewhat softer and more absorbent surface, which I realized was wood, and then I realized that what I had been standing on before was tile.

I felt wind, I heard a kind of aching sigh, I heard the click as she turned the lock on the door.

Energumen Capitalism
Jean-François Lyotard

In spite of its title, *Anti-Oedipus* is not a critical book. Rather, like the *Anti-Christ*, it is a positive, assertive book, an energetic *position* inscribed in discourse, the negation of the adversary not by *Aughebung*, but by forgetting. Just as atheism is religion extended into its negative form – is even the modern *form* of religion, the only form in which modernity could continue to be religious – so the critique makes itself the object of its object and settles down into the field of the other, accepting the latter's dimensions, directions and space at the very moment it contests them. In Deleuze and Guattari's book you will see everywhere their utter contempt for the category of transgression (implicitly then for the whole of Bataille). Either you *leave immediately* without wasting time in critique, simply because you find yourself to be outside the adversary's domain, or else you critique, keeping one foot in and one out, in the positivity of the negative, perhaps, but also in the nothingness of the positivity. And this is the critical impotence one finds in Feuerbach and Adorno. Marx said in 1844 that socialism doesn't need atheism because the *question* of atheism is *positionally* that of religion. What is important in the question is not its negativity, but its position (the position of the problem).

From atheism (which Marx considered to be utopian communism) to socialism, there is no critique, no barrier crossed, no transcrescence; there is a displacement. Desire has wandered into another space, another mechanism has begun to operate, it works differently, and what allows it to work is not the fact that the other, older machine has been criticized. For the same reason, all things being equal, the lines that follow will not be a critique.

Contrary to all expectations, or in fact *because* the shattering title works an illusory effect, what the book subverts most profoundly is what it doesn't *criticize*: Marxism. This is not to say that, symmetrically, it does not subvert psychoanalysis, which it attacks. On the contrary, beneath the different speeds at which the book/machine runs, whether with Freud or Marx, there remains an evident identity of *position*. What is silently borrowed from Marx is no less serious or important than what from Freud is rendered up to the crackling blaze of the *Anti-Oedipus* counterfire. On one hand, the machine/book unplugs itself from the psychoanalytical network and *exposes* it, forces it to expose itself, just like the man with the tape recorder does, reducing and projecting all the libidinal energy which should have flowed away into the transferential relationship, onto the paranoiac configuration of the Arch-State which, according to Deleuze and Guattari, underlies the network of psychoanalytical practice, theoretical and practical flows, cutting them off here and there, dropping without a word whole parts of the Marxist apparatus. Nonetheless, the two Elders are in fact put under the same banner: in their works the libidinal economy always communicates with the political economy as a transforming force and thus a potential departure. For Deleuze and Guattari, on the contrary, that by which the libidinal conceals the political in Freud or the libidinal in Marx must be leapt out of and danced upon. Thus, as the visible axis of the book, everything that is *unconsciously* political in psychoanalysis will be profoundly subverted. *Anti-Oedipus* being Anti-State, the despotic configuration unconsciously libidinal in Marxism will be detached, a libido imprisoned in the religious scaffolding of dialectical politics of economic catastrophism, a libido repressed in the interrupted analyses of commodity fetishism or of the naturality of work.

It is of no importance that what we do ends up being melodic.
—C. Wolff to Stockhausen

Marxism says: there is a frontier, a limit past which the organization of flows called capital (capitalist relations of production) comes apart, and the group of correspondences between money and commodities, capital and labor, and between other parameters, go haywire. And it is the very growth of production capacities in the most modern capitalism which, reaching this limit, will cause the whole system of production and circulation to wobble. This growth will not fail to allow the passage of new energy flows, and to unleash and disperse their "regulation" systems within capital, that is, within the relations of production.

All Marxist politics is built on seeking in this frontier, this limit, or this chain, a cornerstone ready to crumble, the strongest weak link – or one considered so pertinent as to bring down the whole structure. This is all a politics of limits and of negativity. It requires an exteriority beyond the reach of capital. Capital extends the law of value to new objects, or rather it remodels all the old objects formerly "coded" according to the intricate rules of the production of "trades," according to religious rituals, and according to the customs of older, more "savage" cultures, so that they may be decoded into modern "objects" stripped of all constraints other than that of exchangeability. Here, capital itself approaches a limit it cannot exceed.

What is this limit? The disproportion between flows of credit and flows of production? Between quantities of commodities and quantities of available currency? Between invested capital and the expected profit rate? The disequilibrium between projected production capacity and effective production? The disproportion between fixed capital and salaries of variable capital? Between surplus value created by the exploitation of the labor force and its realization or reconversion in production? Or is the limit the lowering of the profit rate? Or the rising up of revolutionary criticism within the ranks of a growing proletariat? Or should it on the contrary be bitterly but symmetrically (by remaining within the given theoretical and practical field) recorded that the impetus to invest, discouraged by the lowering of the profit rate, is enforced by the State; that workers are less and less open to a revolutionary upheaval in spite of their growing numbers (to the extent that Communist parties are obliged *practically* to exclude such a perspective and to present themselves as capable managers of a nearly identical system where there are simply a few less owners of capital and a few more high-level functionaries)?

These are not speculative hesitations, but practical and political. They are the legacy of a century of the Communist movement, and from a good half-century of socialist revolution: as if around 1860, one had examined the dynamics of the French society, the contradictions within the society of the *Ancien Régime*; the direction imposed by Robespierre during the French Revolution, the historical function of Bonaparte, and finally, the fundamental difference between French society under the last kings and under the last emperor, realizing that the movement is found not in the Age of Enlightenment, where bourgeois ideology places it, but to the side, in the Industrial Revolution. The same goes, all things displaced, for the Russian "socialist" state. It diverges from bourgeois society not where its discourse claims; not in the power of the Soviets, that is, not in the greater, theoretically maximum proximity of the workers to economic and social decision-making; thus in freer flows of production, words, thoughts and objects. On the contrary its difference lies in restraining these currents just as strongly as under czarism, just as rationally (that is to say, irrationally, and in just as unconscious a fashion (in the Freudian sense) by a sociovorous state that absorbs civil, economic and intellectual society, that infiltrates all through circulatory canals, pouring into them the cement of its bureaucratic suspicion. Thus no more fluctuating, less representative, just as centralized, totalizing and paranoiac. Here, again divergence: the socialist revolution engenders a new kind of despotic state, where the police-like, paternalistic contempt for the masses and for the libido seeks to work with the technical efficiency and initiative of (American) capitalism, and fails. When Lenin stated that socialism was the Soviets' power plus electrification, Cronstadt replied: it is the Party's power plus execution. Neither is capitalism the reign of freedom, for it too is the mapping back of the flows of production onto the *socius*. Capital *is* this mapping back-onto; but it must occur *only as profit*, and not at all in the form of some gain in sacred power (*numen*), in what Deleuze and Guattari call code surplus value, a gain in prestige presupposing an emotional attachment. Capitalism offers nothing to believe in, cynicism is its morality. The Party, on the contrary, as a despotic configuration, requires a mapping-back-onto that is territorialized, coded and hierarchized, in the religious sense of the terms. Russia, Mother Russia, the people, folklore, dances, customs, and costumes, baba and little father, all that comes from "savage" Slavic communities is kept up, preserved and transferred to the figure of the Secretary General, to the despot who appropriates all production.

If one wonders what can effectively destroy bourgeois society, it is clear that the answer can be found neither in socialist revolution nor in Marxism. The "dialectics" of history not only belies speculative dialectics, but it must be admitted that there is no dialectics at all. Configurations and vast networks dispute energies; the way to tap, transform and circulate them varies completely, depending on whether the configuration is capitalistic or despotic. They may combine, producing no contradictions, no totalization of history leading to other configurations, only effects of compromise on the social surface, unexpected monsters: the Stakhanovist worker, the proletarian company head, the Red Marshall, the leftist nuclear bomb, the unionized policeman, the communist labor camp, Socialist Realism... In this economic-libidinal mixing, it is surely the despotic configuration that dominates. But in any case, if the outcome were different, it cannot be seen how and why this machinery would be a result of dialectics, even less why and how the libidinal configuration of capitalism might "lead to" this kind of arrangement as a "result of its intrinsic organic development." In fact, capitalism leads only to itself: there is no transcresence to expect, no limit in its field that it does not cross. On one hand, capitalism leaps over all the pre-capitalist limitations; on the other, it draws along and displaces its own limit in its movement.

What if this idea of an impassable economic, social, "moral," political, technical, or whatever, limit were a hollow idea? – this is where Deleuze and Guattari begin. What if instead of a wall to breach or transgress, it were capitalism's own wall that always passed increasingly farther inside itself (this kind of set-up was already established in the old idea of the expansion of the "internal" market)? Not that it would thus suppress itself by simple extension; but neither would the question of its overthrow be found to be obsolete and necessitate joining the ranks of revisionists and reformers promoting development, growth and a little more "democracy," or nothing more than a 3% increase in the GNP and better distribution. But there is no exteriority, no Other of Kapital – no Nature, Socialism, Festival, whatever – only in the very interior of the system there are the regions of contact and war ceaselessly multiplying between what is both the fluidity and near indifference of capital, and what is "axiomatic," repression, plugging up of flows, "reterritorialization," and mapping back of energy onto a body supposed to be its origin but only drawing energy from it, whatever the name it assumes; Nation, Civilization, Freedom, Future, and New Society have only one Identity: Kapital.

There is no dialectics in the sense that one or several of these conflicts should one day result in the breaching of the wall, that one day the energy should find itself freed, dispersed, fluid, on the "other side." Rather there is a kind of *overflowing* of force within the same system that liberated it from its savage and barbaric origins. Any object of exchange can enter Kapital. From the moment it is exchangeable (according to the law of value), what can be metamorphosed from money into machines, from merchandise into merchandise, from work-force into labor, from labor into salary, from salary into work-force, is an object for Kapital. And thus nothing is left but these enormous movings around. Objects appear and disappear like fins of dolphins on the surface of the sea, and objectness gives way to sheer obsolescence. What is important is no longer the object, a concretion inherited from the codes, but metamorphosis, fluidity. Not a dolphin, but a trail, an energetic trace inscribed on the surface. It is perhaps in this liquidity, in these lukewarm waters, that the capitalist production relationships will sink, in the simple rule of equality of exchangeable values, in the whole set of "axioms" that Kapital keeps on creating to make this rule compulsory and respectable at the same time it unceasingly derides it.

ENERGUMEN CAPITALISM

At once very deep and superficial, a Marxist subversion never stated.... This configuration of Kapital, the circulation of flows, is imposed by the predominance of the point of view of circulation over that of production in political economics. (Production, for Deleuze and Guattari, is the branching on and breaking off of flows, a gush of milk sucked from the breast and cut off by the lips, energy extracted and converted, a flow of electrons burned in the rotation of a milling machine, spurts of semen sucked in by the uterus.) This predominance of the point of view of circulation will inevitably be attacked. When Deleuze and Guattari write that capitalism must be conceived of in the category of the bank rather than in that of production, it will be denounced as Keynesian ideology, techno-bureaucratic representation of the system by intellectuals cut off from practice, and that in abandoning the point of view of production, labor, worker, struggle, and class are all ignored. There is not a word, in fact, on work-value theory; and only an enigmatic word on a hypothesis of machine surplus value. In truth, the great river of the book washes up several major cadavers: proletariat, class struggle, human surplus value.... It spreads the image of a decoded capitalism full of contemporary circulations, of such intense potential circulations that only a series of dikes ("re-territorializations") can restrain and keep them within the banks, only a whole battery of expressions led by the fundamental State, the Arch-State and its Oedipus.

Capitalism as metamorphosis without an extrinsic code, having its limit only within itself, a relative, deferred limit (which is the law of value): there is in fact an "economics" already present in *German Ideology* and again in manuscripts of 1857–58 (*Grundrisse*, introduction to the *Critique of Political Economics*), and in *Capital* itself. And the traces of this economics' concern with the libido can be seen at one end in the *Reading Notes* of 1843, and at the other in the chapter on fetishism in *Capital*, as Baudrillard has shown. The critical universality of capitalism is outlined as well, the hypothesis that with indifference, with the effect of the principle of equivalence – of decoding – the empty space, the void in which the great categories of work and value are constituted, arises in labor or in the capitalist practice of capitalism. The assumption is made that it will be possible to apply these categories retroactively to systems ("precapitalist" forms) in which the modalities have been covered over by codes, by markings and representations that do not permit a generalized political economics, that is, maintain political and libidinal economics exterior to one another, the latter diverted into religion, customs, rituals of inscription (tattooing, scarification), cruelty and terror. With capitalism, all becomes equalized, the modalities of production and inscription are simplified within the law of value, and thus anything can be produced-inscribed from the moment when the inscription-production energy, put into a trace or an object, is reconvertible into energy, into another object or another trace. A portrait of a nearly schizophrenic capital. If it's occasionally called perverse, it is a *normal* perversion, the perversion of a libido operating its flows over an organless body on which it can cling everywhere and nowhere, just as the flows of material and economic energy can, in the form of production – that is, of conversion – invest themselves on (to) any region whatsoever of the surface of the social body, of the smooth and indifferent *socius*. Transient cathexes causing all territories confined and marked by codes to disappear in their wake – not only on the side of *objects* (prohibitions of production and circulation all collapse, one after another), but as well on the side of "subjects," whether individual or social, which can only appear in this transit as indifferent concretions themselves exchangeable and anonymous, whose illusion of existence can only be maintained at the price of special expenditures of energy.

What fascinates Marx is quite recognizable in the configuration of Kapital proposed by Deleuze and Guattari: the capitalist *perversion*, the subversion of codes, religions, decency, trades, education, cookery, speech, the leveling of all "established" differences into the one and only difference: being worth…, exchangeable for …. Indifferent difference. *Mors immortalis*, in his words.

Deleuze and Guattari have brought this fascination to light, freed it from bad conscience. They help us dislodge it all the way into today's politics. It was bad conscience for Marx himself, and is increasingly so for Marxists. Thus in proportion, their piety is meant to conceal and expiate this appetite for capitalist liquefaction: this piety – dialectics – amounts to maintaining the positive perversion of capitalism inside a network of negativity, contradiction and neurosis which will permit a detection and denunciation of the *forgetting of the creditor (the proletariat) and of the debt (surplus value)*, in a freedom declared to be factitious and guilty, in a positivity judged to be a façade. Marxism will then be the repairing and remonstrating enterprise in which one will demonstrate the system to be a faithless debtor and direct all political energy on the project of repairing the wrong – not just any wrong, said Marx in 1843, but a wrong in itself, this living wrong that *is* the proletariat, the wrong of alienation. A not unfamiliar device, inherited from Christianity, that took on paranoiac dimensions under Stalin and Trotsky before it fell into the routine of wilted belief of today's "communism."

It is from this system of negativity and guilt that *Anti-Oedipus* frees Marxism. Cendrars said that "artists are, above all, men who struggle to become inhuman." The book's silence on class struggle, the worker's epic and the function of his party, as they encumber political language, leads one to believe that for the authors, today's true politicians are in fact those who struggle to become inhuman. Its muteness on surplus value springs from the same source: looking for the creditor is wasted effort when the *subject* of the credit must always be *made to exist*, the proletariat be incarnated on the surface of the *socius*, that is, represented in the representative box on the political stage. In nucleus, this is the reappearance of the Arch-State. It is Lenin and Stalin, and can also be a nameless subject, the Party, a Void, the Signifier – and it is never anything more, since a creditor is simply the name of something missing. So forget bad politics, the politics of bad conscience, the processions of bedecked and bannered wisdom of a simulated piety: capitalism will never croak from bad conscience, it will not die of lack or of a failure to render unto the exploited what is owed them. If it disappears, it will be by excess, because its energetics unceasingly displace its limits. "Restitution" comes not as a paranoiac, but a passion to render justice, to give everyone his due, as if it were not self-evident that in addition to the market value of his energy expenditure, a worker's "salary" in any of the ten wealthiest nations did not contain a redistributed share of surplus value.

NEITHER STRUCTURES, BE THEY INFRA- NOR EXCHANGE, BE IT SYMBOLIC

What are the prohibitions capitalism opposes to the incessant wandering of flows? "Reterritorializations" necessary for the maintenance of the system in place, say Deleuze and Guattari. Such localizations are neoarchaisms circumscribed on the surface of the socius, disconnecting whole regions and sheltering them from schizo-flows, they say: Indian reservations, Fascism, exchange, Third World bureaucracies, private property – and, assuredly, Oedipus and *Urstaat*.

How superficial it seems to ascribe the same function to reservations and capital, Stalin and Hitler, Hitler and private property! What do they do with super- and infra-structures? Not a word, of course, on this subject. There are only desiring-machines and the organless body, their stormy relationships already in molecular order, relationships between the anus making shit, the mouth making words or the eyes making eyes, and a surface of the hypothetical body where they are to posit, inscribe and compose themselves – and then in the order of the conjectural, great social body, of the *socius*, now in the molar order. The violent disjunction between on one hand, the blind, mechanic repetition of the production-inscription of small organs and social segments, and on the other, the mapping back and monopolization of these segmentary productions on (to) the surface of the socius, thanks to the Arch-State in particular. No structure in the linguistic or semiotic sense; only dispositions of energy transformations. And among these dispositions, no reason to privilege (in the name of infrastructure) what regulates the production and circulation of *goods*, the so-called "economic" apparatus…. For there is no less an *economy*, an energetics in that which will regulate lineages and alliances and thus distribute the flows of intensity in concretions of roles, persons and goals on the surface of the socius, finally producing the so-called organization of savage society (an organism that is in fact never unified, always divided between the thousand poles of small, multiple organs, partial objects, libidinal segments, and the vacuum-unifying pole created, at the summit, at and in the head, by the signifier) – no less an economy in the laws of kinship, no less an economy even in the distribution of the libido on the surface of the organless body, in the hooking-up of small, desiring, energy transforming, and pleasure-seeking organs, than in the economics and distribution of capital, no less of a producing-inscribing apparatus there than here. Conversely, the Oedipal formation is no less political-economic than Kapital's, and finally, no less eco-libidinal and deviant than the primary process it taps. Thus in considering these dispositions, the problem is not in discerning which is subordinating and which subordinated: it is a reciprocal subordination. But the infra/super hypothesis would require that the organic totality of the social field be presupposed, that a social whole be presupposed and perpetuated, that structures be mapped out in a macro-structure, that the whole be the point of departure, that it be assumed that the whole is given or at least discernible and analyzable.

But the whole problem is that the *whole is not given*, that society *is not* a unified totality; it is, rather, displacements and metamorphoses of energy that never stop decomposing and recomposing sub-units and that pull these units along, now towards the organs' perverse-schizo functioning, now towards the neurotic-paranoia of the great absent signifier. If you speak in terms of super- and infra- you order dispositives according to high and low and you have already adopted the point of the signifier, of the whole, and *it will not let you go*. When you want to conduct a revolutionary politics or to imagine a subversive process, if you don't attack this edifice, you will have at best a dialectics, at best "after" the negative moment, "after" the revolution, that is, *already before* (a party, for example, or a need for effectiveness or for organization, or the fear of failure), and the same hierarchized arrangement will be reproduced: the same worker-militant on the bottom and the same chief-boss on the top, the same confiscation of flows and partial production for the common good, that is to say, for the good of the despot.

What allows us to say this – once again, it is no fantasy – is capitalism itself. By sweeping through the most forbidden regions with its influxes of work and money – through art, science, trades and festivals, politics and sports, words and images, air, water, snow and sun, Bolshevik, Maoist and Castroist revolutions – capitalism makes the coded dispositions that govern the economy appear as libidinal configurations at the very moment that it casts them into disuse. It thus reveals that infra/superstructural oppositions, or economic/ideological structures and relationships, of production versus social relationships, are themselves paired concepts that cannot show us what happens in savage, feudal or Oriental societies, or even in capitalist society itself. For they are either too much or too little: too much because it is unquestionable that in the former, kinship, ritual and practical relationships decisively determine the production and circulation of goods, that is, the configuration of the "economy," and they cannot be reduced to an illusory ideological function; too little because in the latter the term economics covers much more than political economy, much more than production and the exchange of goods. Economy is also the exchange of labor force, images, words, knowledge, power, travel and sex.

If political economics is a discourse that establishes the phenomena of production and circulation by anchoring them in a nature (the Physiocratic Nature, the interests and needs of *Homo Oeconomicus*, the creative power of the workers' expenditure of energy), it is never applicable past the level of survival given by hypothesis. Archaic societies are no less arbitrary than capitalism, and capitalism fits no better than they into categories of interest, need or work. Nowhere is there a primary economic order (of interest, need or work) followed by effects, be they ideological, cultural, juridical, religious, familial, etc. Everywhere these are set-up aimed at tapping or discharging, but in archaic or Oriental societies, energy and its concretions in "objects" (sexual partners, children, tools and weapons, food) must be *marked* – a seal, an incision, an abstraction. The marking of archaic arts are "representation" in the sense of the Quattrocento, but rather code what is libidinally invested or investable, authorize what may circulate and produce pleasure; these codes are thus sorters, selectors, brakes-accelerators, dams and canals, mitral valves regulating the inputs and outputs of energy in all its forms (words, dances, children, delicacies…) in relation to the socius, to the non-existent, postulated Great Social Body. In capitalism, however, all is swept away – these codified functionings, these specific adjustments in their concrete abstractions, this or that inscription on a certain region of the skin to denote puberty, the distinctive distortion in the neck, the ear, the nostrils, or the confection of a hat of chicken or pig entrails (Leiris in Gondar) to denote a particular function in a religious or magic ritual, this tattoo for the right to bear arms, that ornament on the chief's face, those words and chants and drum beats inscribed in the ritual scenario of sacrifice, the mourning of excision: all of this is surpassed and dissipated. Capitalism deculturalizes peoples, dehistoricizes their inscriptions, repeats them anywhere at all as long as they are marketable, recognizes no code marked by the libido but only exchange value: you can produce and consume everything, exchange, work or inscribe anything anyway you want if it comes through, if it flows, if it is metamorphosizable. The *only* untouchable axiom bears on the condition of metamorphosis and transfer: exchange value. Axiom, not code: energy and its objects are no longer marked with a sign; properly speaking, *there are no more signs* since there is no more code, no reference to an origin, to a norm, to a "practice," to a supposed nature, to surreality or reality, to a paradigm or to a Great Other – there is nothing left but a little price tag, the index of exchangeability: it is nothing, it is enormous, it is something else.

Neither the territorial mechanism of savagery nor even the great barbaric despotic machine (as Nietzsche sometimes envisioned it) gives a good perspective for viewing the machinery of capitalism. After Marx, Deleuze and Guattari say that capitalism is *the* proper perspective for seeing it all. If you look at capitalism through castration, you think you see it from the despotic Orient or from savage Africa, but in fact you perpetuate the nihilism of Western religion; your position is still inspired by bad conscience and piety for Nature and Exteriority and Transcendence. Capitalism, much more positively than atheism, the indication of a profound liquidity of economic flows on the surface of the socius, retroactively makes us see the precapitalistic codes and lets us comprehend what in it and related only to itself, *index sui*, blocks up and channels this liquidity in the law of value. The only axiom of this system entirely made up of indifference and equivalence (*Gleichgultigkeit*, says Marx again and again, young and old), the law of value, is as well the only *limit*, the impassable limit if you wish, always displaceable and displaced, keeping capitalism from being carried off by the meandering flood of molecular energetics.

Translated by James Leigh

Uncle Fishhook and the Sacred Baby Poo Poo of Art
Jack Smith

Sylvère Lotringer: How did you get the idea to make Flaming Creatures?

Jack Smith: I started making a comedy about everything that I thought was funny. And it *was* funny. The first audiences were laughing from the beginning all the way through. But then *that writing* started – and it became a sex thing. It turned the movie into a magazine sex issue. It was fed to the magazines. Lesbian writers were finding purple titillations. Then it fertilized Hollywood. Wonderful. When they got through licking their chops over the movie there was no more laughter. There was dead silence in the auditorium. The film was practically used to destroy me.

There wasn't a trial?

There was a trial and I lost. Uncle Jonas's [Jonas Mekas] lawyers were doing the trial, and at some point it was dropped. And if a case is dropped, it can't be appealed. Now the movie is permanently illegal in New York.

Can't it be shown in some places, under certain conditions?

Uncle Fishhook [Jonas Mekas] was showing it at his mausoleum [The Anthology Film Archives], but that's because no one has complained.... It would be inconvenient to have anybody complain. But when he need-ed a complaint, there was a complaint. At one time it was fashionable to have a work of art in the courts. All the mileage gotten out of Henry Miller's books.... And Uncle Fishhook wanted to have something in court at the time, it being so fashionable. The publicity. It was another way by which he could be made to look like a saint, to be in the position of defending something when he was really kicking it to death. So he would give screenings of *Creatures* and make speeches, defying the police to bust the film. Which they did. And then there was the trial... I don't know what the lawyers were doing. I wasn't even permitted to be in the court. I walked into the courtroom and my lawyer said, "Go out of the courtroom," and I said, "Why?" – "because the judge is upset by too many men with beards." I was ordered to leave by the marsh-mallow lawyer that Uncle Mekas had. So I couldn't even see the trial. You know: it goes on and on.

I must say that when I saw the film at the Cinemathèque, people were laughing their heads off.

Mumble, mumble. It inflated Uncle Fishhook; it made his career; I ended up supporting him. He's been doing my traveling for 15 years. He's been conducting a campaign to dehumanize me in his column. There's just a list of monstrosities. I don't want to start that.... So from supporting Uncle Fishhook, now we're left years later with nothing. There's nothing anybody can do with their films. *He's* got the original.

You don't have any copy?

I have a miserable beat up inter-negative that's shot. He must have sucked 1,000 copies out of it. It needs to be restored or something.

Why don't you make another film?

I don't want to let somebody go running off with... I am. I've already made new films; I have a roomful of films that I've made since then.... But there's nothing in the world that I can do with them, because Uncle Fishhook has established this pattern of the way film is thought about, and seen, and everything else...

Did you actually mean anything through your film?

No, I didn't then. But the meaning has to come out in what is done with the art – is what gives it meaning. The way my movie was used – that was the meaning of the movie.

You mean that meaning comes afterwards?

What you do with it economically is what the meaning is. If it goes to support Uncle Fishhook, that's what it means. Movies are always made for an audience. But I didn't make it that way. I was just making it completely for myself. At the time, that seemed like an intellectual experiment. But that point got lost.

But that happens every time someone wants to make art.

If they weren't making this deliberately pointless art, then it wouldn't happen…. And it wouldn't have happened to me if I had been perfect. It wouldn't have been taken up and used by somebody else.

I read recently what Susan Sontag wrote about Flaming Creatures…

It showed that she was just as hypnotized by him as I was… but by that time I was no longer hypnotized by him and she…

She said it didn't mean anything, and that was the strength of the film. I liked that. It's not just that it was comical, but that it makes fun of all sorts of ideas we have, and definitions…

Was it being exploited like Hollywood? Uncle Fishhook's use of the word co-op just drifted past Miss Sontag…. And nobody seems to expect anything from that idea. They don't seem to know what a co-op is.

What is it about?

It's a thing that controls all the activities of a certain activity. And then everyone engaged in this is sharing the money.

Is that the way your film was done?

A film co-op sounded like something I wanted to do, to support. I turned over my film to this film co-op. And then it became a grotesque parody of Hollywood. Uncle Fishhook seemed heroic in her review. What was heroic? Taking someone's film away from him.... Uncle Roachcrust perpetuated the monstrosity of discrediting co-ops. That's why he is a symbol, an Uncle Pawnshop, a symbol of fishhook co-ops. The only reason for the pattern of the 2 night screenings he has established is so somebody's film will spend one night in the safe – if you get my meaning.

Didn't you want to destroy your work?

Uncle Fishhook says all kinds of fantastic things about me. If anybody that can only comprehend capitalism would look at my behavior and the only conclusion that they could come to was that I was trying to destroy myself –

When capitalism is in fact trying to destroy you?

And he's printed things like that in his column. Once he printed that Jack Smith's art is so precious that it cannot be exported. You know: seeming to be saying something complimentary when actually killing the chance of the economic possibility of my going to Europe. Everything on earth like that he's been doing. My life has been a nightmare because of that damn film. That sucked up ten years of my life. For a while I was being betrayed on an average of about twice a week to Uncle Fishhook. It was like being boiled alive. People would turn me in because Uncle Fishhook wanted to get me and everybody knew that...
(Sounds of the radio)

Is that WBAI? Have you ever done anything for them?

I tried; I tried. I went there a number of times. There are some dummies there. And I just had the bad luck of running into all the dummies, I guess. I get these incredible over-reactions because I'm a very strange looking person.

What happened there?

Once I was thrown out by the receptionist. I was asked not to wait inside the building. I was listening to their begging for money and it really gripped my heart. I went there. Four or five times. Every time I ran into some dummy at the place, so I just gave up. I wanted so much to help. It is the only source of information in the city. I think you have to be Jewish, number one. And normal, number two. The very first sign of the trouble *they* had was when they attacked the homo who had a program called *The Importance of Being Earnest,* a gay program. And he was forbidden to put on one of his programs. People with their snot impacted voices that they paid for in college: their rumbling snot. They wanted normalcy. Later the whole station was turned off by the same management.

In Italy, little independent radios like Radio-Alice have a more direct political impact on the population. It's starting in France too. They do it with very limited means.

There's always been political art in Europe. There's never been any political art in this country.

Do you consider your art political?

I wouldn't put any program out now unless it had an overtly political title.

How about your slide-show, do you consider that political?

If you can put an explicit title on something implicit, that's almost enough – because you're giving the indication of how to see it. Not everything has to be cerebral at every moment.... But the title does have to be explicit. The title is 50 percent of the work. That's why I shudder with the title of your magazine. You have that chance to say something.

A title is language, and I'm not sure language can be that effective.

But thought can. The world is starving for thoughts. I worry about the thoughts. A new thought must come out in new language.

So it didn't really matter if you actually had a slide show or not because you've advertised the title: the title is sufficient.

Almost. You don't have to see the slide show as far as I'm concerned. The slide is entertainment, the icing. I mean there's a thought, there's a socialist thought in it, but the information and all the intellectual content is being conveyed by the title. You can become so explicit that you can state something the world didn't know and to know and this you can state very clearly in the title. The images could be made to mean anything, but the title's got to be explicit because it's your only chance. You have to struggle to make more of it more and more explicit, but, still glamorous. If it is not done glamorously, it's no good because it wouldn't have been dramatized.

What title would you choose now for Flaming Creatures *if you had a choice?*

Let me think, a new title... I have to think about it... What's its content... there never was any content. "Connecting Sugar with Hollywood," maybe...

You mean your film was some sort of parody of Hollywood?

Of course. My mind was filled with it... Everybody is filled with Hollywood.

Did you watch television?

Not until later. Then I became addicted to it... No longer though.

What sort of thing did you read?

My favorite book was *The Count of Monte Cristo.* Sinclair Lewis is my

favorite writer. They think they're through with Sinclair Lewis. I just
finished a book of his called *King's Blood Royal*, in which the most typical WASP in the world finds out that he has one percent Negro blood;
and then the book ends with everybody in the neighborhood marching
on his house with rifles. But it could be about any minority group.

What do you think of the gay movement?

They've become a ghetto, already: they just want to talk about gay
things. They're trying to cut it off from being in any context.

Don't you think it's becoming something of an industry too?

Oh sure, of course. It's just one of the unexpected bad side developments of it that's making it possible to be so happily ghetto-ized. But
that's where the people in the theater are supposed to be coming in and
helping the atmosphere. And, you see, they're not. I took my program
to a gay theater, and he couldn't understand how it was gay, because he
was unable to see it in a context. If it wasn't discussing exactly how
many inches was my first lollipop, well then it wouldn't be anything
they'd be interested in. And so I couldn't get this gay theater. It was one
of the places I tried. Getting theaters is one of the 7 labors of Uranus.

What was that: "I Was a Mekas Collaborator!"

I put the ad in the paper and then I didn't go to the theater. The ad was
as far as I could get with a lobotomized, zombified...

What do you mean by that?

That if a program has any intellectual interest at all then it can only be
given one or two nights – but you can be entertained to death in this
country.

Is that the slide show you want to present?

That slide show is just the same mass of slides: I've been showing it for years. Every once in a while I have a new shooting session and add a new scene to it. Nobody has ever complained. It's always, you know, completely interesting. The Penguin Epic is all new, though.

That's why Burroughs uses cut-ups: to try to prevent the words from being twisted around.

Oh, that's one way.

It's an extreme way.

That's the wrong extreme. What I mean is the extreme in the other direction – by being more and more specific about what you're thinking. The title is supposed to serve the idea. If I am lucky enough to get a socialistic idea...

What do you mean by a socialistic idea?

To me, socialism is to try to find social ways of sharing. That's all. And to replace the dependence upon authority with the principle of sharing. Because it's very likely that there would be much more for everybody, thousands and more times for everybody if things were shared. We're living like dogs from all the competing.

Were you ever competitive? Did you ever believe in that?

Yes, of course, when you're young. It's drilled into you, and you have to slowly find your way out of it, because you find it doesn't work. Capitalism is terribly inefficient. The insane duplication, the insane waste, and the young only know what's put in front of them... But then, by experience, things are happening to you and you find out that this doesn't work. I mean this is *not* productive.

It produces waste.

I looked through your magazine and I was repelled by the title. It's so dry, you just want to throw it in the wastebasket, which I did. Then I picked it out... Listen: *Hatred of Capitalism* is a good name for that magazine. It's stunning. I'll never admit that I thought of it.

I doubt that by saying that directly you'll change anything. Language is corrupt.

Listen, you are a creature, artistic I can tell, that somehow got hung up on the issue of language. Forget it. It's *thinking*. If you can think of a thought in a most pathetic language... Look at what I have to do in order to think of thoughts. I have to forget language. All I can do with no education, nothing, no advice, no common sense in my life, an insane mother I mean, no background, nothing, nothing, and I have to make art, but I know that under these conditions the one thing I had to find out was if I could think of a thought that has never been thought of before, then it could be in language that was never read before. If you can think of something, the language will fall into place in the most fantastic way, but the thought is what's going to do it. The language is shit, I mean it's only there to support a thought. Look at Susan Sontag, that's a phenomenon that will never occur, only in every hundred years. Anybody like that. She says things that you would never have thought of. And the language is automatically unique. Whatever new thoughts you can think of that the world needs will be automatically clothed in the most radiant language imaginable.

Have you ever thought of another type of society...

I can think of billions of ways for the world to be completely different. I wish they would invent a scalpbrush. Do you realize that there is nothing on earth that you can brush your scalp with?... I can think of other types of societies... Like in the middle of the city should be a repository of objects that people don't want anymore, which they would take to this giant junkyard. That would form an organization, a way that the city would be organized... the city organized around that. I think this center of unused objects and unwanted objects would become a center of intellectual activity. Things would grow up around it.

You mean some sort of center of exchange?

Yes, there could be exchange, that would start to develop. You take anything that you don't want and don't want to throw out and just take it to this giant place, and just leaving it and looking for something that you need...

And there wouldn't be any money?

Then things would form the way they always do around that.

Will people still own anything?

Yeah, I don't mind... Buying and selling is the most natural human institution: there's nothing wrong with that... Buying and selling is the most interesting thing in the world. It should be aesthetic and everything else. But capitalism is a perversion of this. Nothing is more wonderful than a marketplace. It gives people something to do... and it can be creative. Wonderful things come from commerce... but not from capitalism...

What do you mean exactly by landlordism?

Fear ritual of lucky landlord paradise. That's what supports the government.

You mean property?

The whole fantasy of how money is squeezed out of real estate. It supports the government; it supports everything. And it isn't even rational. When is a building ever paid for? The person that built the building is dead long since, and yet it can never be paid for, it has to be paid for all over again, every month. That's as irrational as buying a pair of shoes and paying for them again. It supports the whole system that we have to struggle against. We have to spend the rest of our time struggling against the uses they make of our money against us.

They call it "rent control." That's exactly what it is about: control through rent.

But if the whole population has no conception of how irrational that is, that's how far they are from doing anything about it, or any of the other things that oppress them. All the money that runs the government comes from the fantasy of paying rent.

As if we owned something.

Alright. So we don't own it. But do they own it? People that live in a place and maintain it and build it, why do they own it less than the government? Then you're saying that the government owns it more than you do. And that's also silly.

The difference is that in a capitalist country you owe money to an individual and in a communist country you owe money to the state. It still holds...

Well, you don't own your own property... but even if you could understand that, why would you understand that, why would you understand that somebody else has some claim, or owns, your property.

You mean then that everyone should own what they use?

You want to start making more laws and more rules. But that's how a lot of strange things began... from the expectation that you need all the laws and rules...

But if no one had to own anything... if you use something, you don't have to pay for it, but it doesn't belong to you.

What's so incredible about that? There is a new movement called

Housing in the Public Domain – maybe the first idea on the subject since feudal times. I never had sunlight. I was always so naíve I just kept taking places that had no sunlight. But the next time I move there will be some sunlight involved, somehow, coming through a window, or anything. But I can't build it; I can't be permitted to build my own house. You can build exotic architecture or strange houses if it's outside the city if there are not other people around that would complain. All the complaining!

You want to build an exotic house?

I'd like to invent a building that wouldn't be a rectangle, that would utilize the pouring qualities of cement.

It would be closed?

I don't know what in the world it would be. It would be open in the middle: sunlight could come in the middle. They cling to rectangles because it's the preferred shape of capitalism; it's easy to manufacture a rectangle, to manufacture the components of a rectangle. But why should I live in a house for the convenience of the manufacturers? I think the normal idea of the house is more circular, whatever it is, and it would have an opening for sunlight to come in. The house would be arranged in that way. It would also have all the ugly non-design of manufacturers banished from it. Everything to do with water would be in one place and it would be in the form of a waterfall; and it would be enclosed, and plants would be happy there; washing the dishes would become a Polynesian thing, it would not be an ugly thing washing the dishes; and washing clothes, taking a bath would also be done in this place; the dishes would wash themselves. It would use much less water; all the water would be utilized; there wouldn't be any wasted water; the waterfall would be turned on and off, of course. It would be in the central part where the sunlight is… the water would be mixed with the sunlight, a steamroom would then be created, steam is very healthful, it cleans your lungs. And I can imagine anything on earth like this. But if I try to build it there would be a million laws saying that I can't build it.

It sounds like a building you could build in Miami.

I heard of someone building their own building in Miami, and the city
officials made him tear it apart ten times until he got every little thing
just to comply with the city regulations. So you wouldn't do it in the
city. You might do it outside the city. As long as there aren't people
complaining. And then this would dispense with the ugly rectangular
monstrosity of the kitchen sink; bathtubs wouldn't exist. All this duplication wouldn't exist; it would save space. It's got to be built to be a
model to do away with the ugly designs that now surround us completely.

*I think it is like art; as soon as there is a model it's going to be dupli-
cated and then it becomes an industry. It's very difficult to avoid that.*

That's what I want: I would want them to duplicate my ideas. But all
that's happened to me so far is that my idea that I never had doesn't
register – and they duplicate my icing. I know how just a thing like the
ugly design of kitchen sinks destroyed my childhood… 'cause I had to
fight with my sister all the time over who had to do the dishes. It was
the ugliness, the ugliness of capitalism, making it impossible for anybody
to live a life that isn't made ugly.

Where did you grow up?

In the Midwest. My father's family were hillbillies in West Virginia. They
went to the hills because they wanted to be more independent in the
first place, and then they became more independent because they were
living in the hills. Hillbillies, nomads, gypsies are natural anarchists.

Do you like that?

Yes, basically I'm an anarchist, that's not to say that I think there will
ever be any state of anarchy, but I don't think that you should stamp
out anarchy… You need it to flavor other ideas, because anarchy is the
giving part of politics. In this country they have stamped it out, and

made it a dirty word, made it synonymous with chaos... They want to tell you that it's the same as chaos. It isn't. All it means is without a ruler. And if people don't try to make a start of getting along without authorities, they will never be in a position where they are not being worked over by these authorities. And so naturally they don't like anarchy. We have never had anarchy, but we do have chaos. There's always going to be government agents that are going to be throwing bombs, saying that the anarchists did it, to set up a reaction.

There are so many rulers now. Authority is everywhere.

They're dreaming of more authority.

I could do with a little more chaos myself.

All it is is an idea of gradually working toward doing things without authorities. Under an anarchist system you would phase authorities out slowly, as much as could be. That seems a fantasy, just because it's been so stamped out and ridiculed. Until the twenties you could go anywhere in the world without a passport. But they want to put you in the frame of mind where you accept more and more authority. You just are required to go through this ritual in which you give them the right to tell you where I can go. And if you don't, you'll be clapped in prison.

It is not easy to live in the way you want and not suffer from it.

I don't mind a certain amount of trouble. I can't take these exaggerated doses of pasty cheerfulness of capitalism in which you have to be happy all the time. That can only produce a crust like Warhol. I don't want to be too happy. I don't want extremes, I mean getting pinnacles of happiness. I can't live with it. What goes up must come down. I tried it. I was a pasty celebrity, I was very fashionable ten years ago... is this being recorded?

Yes.

(laughing) Wonderful. I was hoping it was. I was very fashionable but I couldn't live with it. I will never, never go near anything like that again. This was the golden gift of Uncle Fishhook to me. Please let him keep the blessings of publicity. You see, attention is a very basic human need. It's terribly important. If the baby doesn't get attention, it won't be fed.

If society makes you unhappy, then it has won no matter what.

I don't think so. I can be happy from being unhappy, if I know what I'm doing. I mean I have to struggle against Uncle Fishhook, that's my job, and I'm not running away from it. Everybody else that has been worked over by Uncle Fishhook has just faded out, folded up and creeped out of the city. But I won't do that. Usually in life nothing is ever clear cut. How many people are lucky enough to have an archetypal villain for an adversary.

Do you know Nietzsche at all?

It's probably trash because he was jealous of Wagner. I don't like his attitude towards Wagner. It was just the typical, very mediocre attitude expressed in very fancy language, but it was the very typical *Village Voice* attitude toward anybody that is making a success, but a success based upon their need to transform somebody into an object, and then sacrificing him.

Nietzsche defines a nihilist phase which corresponds to what you call "anarchist": to question everything. There is a second phase which is more interesting: once you've realized what everything is and how it works, how it's going to repeat itself, endlessly, you just step out of it, and affirm other, positive values. You don't waste any more energy criticizing and destroying.

Tell me what I am to do with the energy. I'm supposed to rush into the turquoise paradise of the Bahamas? After two days, I would be bored. I've got to have something to hate.

Flaming Creatures *was about fun, not denouncing.*

I made a comedy. Now I want to make a drama. The movie I'm now preparing is going to be an Arabian Nights architecture film and it will be in Super-8. 35 millimeter is insanely wasteful. And it's never cleaned. It gives me the horrors. Uncle Fishhook represents the idea of expectations from authority, which is also perfect for me since I could spend the rest of my life demolishing very happily. I can be happy in this way. You couldn't, but it has just been my lot to have to clean out the toilets. I mean that's the job that's been inherited by me in life and I have run away from it. I spent the last fifteen years running away from it. Nobody wants to open a can of worms, but that's the thing that has been handed for me to do. And maybe that's a part of all bigtime manufacturers and capitalists, that they're Uncle Fishhook. Maybe I've found a key to them in some way from having to deal with the evil that's come into my life.

ECSTASY

In the White Winter Sun
Fanny Howe

1-0

I locked my husband in a closet one fine winter morning. It was not a
large modern closet, but a little stuffy one in a century-old brick building.
Inside that space with him were two pairs of shoes, a warm coat, a
chamber pot, a bottle of water, peanut butter and a box of crackers. The
lock was strong but the keyhole was the kind you can both peek through
and pick. We had already looked simultaneously, our eyes darkening
to the point of blindness as they fastened on each other, separated by
only two inches of wood. Now I would not want to try peeking again.
My eyes meeting his eyes was more disturbing than the naked encounter
of our two whole faces in the light of day. It reminded me that no one
knew what I had done except for the person I had done it with. And
you God.

1-1

A gold and oily sun lay on the city three days later. Remember how
coldly it shone on the faces of the blind children. They stayed on that
stoop where the beam fell the warmest. I wasn't alone. My religious
friend came up behind me and put his arm across my shoulder.
"We have to say goodbye," he murmured.
I meant to say, "Now?" but said, "No."
I had seen *I'm nobody* written on my ceiling only that morning.

Brick extended on either side. The river lay at the end. Its opposite
bank showed a trail of leafless trees. My friend was tall, aristocratic in his
gestures – that is, without greed. He said the holy spirit was everywhere
if you paid attention. Not as a rewarded prayer but as an atmosphere

that threw your body wide open. I said I hoped this was true. He was very intelligent and well-read. He had sacrificed intimacy and replaced it with intuition.

I wanted badly to believe like him that the air is a conscious spirit. But my paranoia was suffusing the atmosphere, and each passing person wore a steely aura. "Please God don't let it snow when I have to fly," he said and slipped away. My womanly body, heavy once productive, and the van for the children, gunning its engine, seemed to be pounded into one object. It was Dublin and it wasn't. That is, the Irish were all around in shops and restaurants, their voices too soft for the raw American air and a haunt to me. "Come on. Let's walk and say goodbye," he insisted. We walked towards St. John the Evangelist.

"I've got to make a confession," I told him. "Can't I just make it to you? I mean, you're almost a monk, for God's sake."

"No," said Tom. "The priest will hear you. Go on." Obediently I went inside. The old priest was not a Catholic. He was as white as a lightbulb and as smooth. His fingers tapered to pointed tips as if he wore a lizard's lacy gloves. It was cold inside his room. Outside – the river brown and slow. A draft came under the door.

I think he knew that a dread of Catholicism was one reason I was there. He kept muttering about Rome, and how it wouldn't tolerate what he would, as an Anglican.

Personally I think pride is a sin. But I said "a failure of charity" was my reason for being there. This was not an honest confession, but close enough. The priest told me to pray for people who bothered me, using their given names when I did. He said a name was assigned to a person before birth, and therefore the human name was sacred. Then he blessed me. Walking out, I felt I was dragging my skeleton like a pack of branches. After all, a skeleton doesn't clack inside the skin, but is more like wood torn from a tree and wrapped in cloth.

Outside Tom was waiting and we walked over the snow. "I missed that flute of flame that burns between Arjuna and Krishna – the golden faces of Buddha, and Yogananda, Ramakrishna, Milarepa, and the dark eyes of Edith Stein and Saint Teresa. Are all Americans Protestant? The church was cold, austere. I'm a bad Catholic."

He nodded vaguely and said: "But you're a good atheist. Catholicism has an enflamed vocabulary, don't worry. You can transform each day into a sacrament by taking the Eucharist. You just don't want to bother."

Even the will to raise and move a collection of bones can seem heroic. Only an object on one side – or a person – can draw it forwards – or on another side an imagined object or person. Maybe the will responds to nearby objects and thoughts the way a clam opens when it's tapped. "Mechanistic…. We really should put more trust in the plain surface of our actions," I said.

"Do we really have to say goodbye? And leave each other in such a state?"

"We do."

"But first, Tom – I have one favor to ask you."

1-2

Exactly ten years before, during a premature blizzard, I left all my children at home and went to meet my best friends in the Hotel Commander. I did so carrying the weight of my husband like a tree on my back. This was a meeting I couldn't miss, no matter how low I stooped.

The walk from the subway to the hotel was bitter, wet and shiny. Traffic lights moved slowly on my right, while the brick walls and cold gray trees sopped up the gathering snow. I kept my eyes fixed on the left where dark areas behind shrubs and gates could conceal a man, and stepped up my pace.

Lewis and Libby were already seated in a booth in a downstairs lounge. I shook off my coat and sat beside Libby and we all ordered stiff drinks, recalling drunker meetings from earlier youth. I leaned back and kept my eyes on the door, in case my husband appeared and caught me off-guard.

"Relax, Henny," Lewis reproved me.

"I've never met him!" Libby cried. "It's unbelievable."

"He's unbelievable," said Lewis.

"He can't be that bad."

"He is. He should be eliminated. He won't let her out of the house, without her lying. She probably said she had a neighborhood meeting tonight. Right?"

"Henny's not a coward."

"She likes to keep the peace though. That's not good."

"I'm going to be back in the spring. I'll meet him then," Libby said. "And if he's all that bad, I will do something to him."

"Henny has a mercenary army of children around her, protecting her against him," Lewis explained. "They aren't even her own."

"Hen, tell me the truth. Do you wish he would die? I'll make him leave you if you want me to," said Libby.

A renunciatory rush went down my spine when I saw, out in the lobby, the back of a man in a pea-jacket and woolen cap. Gathered over, I left the table for the rest room, and Libby followed breathless. She was wringing her hands, smelling of musk rose, and dancing on her pin-thin legs in high heel boots that had rings of wet fur around the tops while I sat in the sink. "Was it him? Was it him?"

We never found out.

That was the same night we climbed out the hotel kitchen window and walked up a slippery hill, one on each side of Lewis, hugging to his arms, while the snow whipped against our cheeks and lips, and we talked about group suicide.

"Phenobarbital, vodka and applesauce, I think."

"No, Kool-aid, anything sweet."

"For some reason."

"Jam a little smear of strawberry on the tongue."

"Or honey."

"Catbirds and the smell of jasmine and we all lie in a line under the stars."

"With great dignity."

"Despite the shitting." "And die." "Die out."

"I can dig it," said Lewis. "I can dig it."

"But we have to do it all together," Libby said.

1-3

There is a kind of story, God, that glides along under everything else that is happening, and this kind of story only jumps out into the light like a silver fish when it wants to see where it lives in relation to everything else.

Snow is a pattern in this story. It was snowing the day of my first visit to the Federal Penitentiary. The ground was strung with pearly bulbs of ice. I had visited many social service offices in my day, but never a prison. I associated prison with sequence and looked around for a way to break out. As a first-time visitor, and in the early moments, I remembered nervously standing with a crowd of strangers waiting for someone familiar to emerge from behind a green door with a big light over it. For each one of us, the familiar person would be a different person, but our experience would be the same. I already know that some conflicts in life have no resolution and have to be treated in a different way from common problems.

But prison seemed to relate to issues of privacy in ways that were unimaginable to those who had never been forcibly hidden. Simplistically I was scared of being in a jail because it was a space that was unsafe from itself, the way a mind is. But I forced myself, as I sometimes do, to go to the place I dreaded the most – to the place that was so repugnant, it could only change me. Maybe the sacred grove of our time is either the prison or the grave site of a massacre. I have always believed I must visit those sacred groves, and not the woodlands, if I want to know the truth. In this case, I only wanted to see someone I loved and to comfort her by my coming. And surely enough, I did undergo a kind of conversion through my encounters with the persons there. When you visit someone in prison, this paranoid question comes up: Do I exist only in fear? The spirit hates cowards. It broods heavily in the presence of fear. I only felt as safe as a baby when I was holding a baby or a child and so, sitting empty-armed, in a roomful of strangers, watching the light over the heavy door, was a test of will.

Then I saw a child – a little boy in the room with me – he was like leaf blowing across an indoor floor. And while waiting for my friend to come out the door, I moved near him.
I asked him what book he had brought with him. He kept his face down and said, "Gnomes."
"Do you read it yourself, honey?"
"No, I can't. Tom reads it to me."
"Do you want me to read some?"
"Sure," he said and lifted his smile. His eyelids were brown and deeply

circled and closed, as long as the eyelids of the dead whose lashes are strangely punctuated by shadows longer than when they were alive and batting. He wore a limpid smile that inscribed a pretty dimple in his right cheek.

"I'm getting obsessed," he said, "with books about gnomes, goblins, elves, hobbits."

"How do you mean obsessed?"

"I want to know everything about them. And sometimes I'm sure they really exist and run around my feet."

"How can you tell?"

"My shoelaces come untied sometimes, and I think I feel them on my shoes."

"I don't know, honey. I've never seen one. Let's go read about gnomes."

When I took his hot little hand in mine, I felt the material charge of will and spirit return to me. I had an instinctual feeling that the room held me fast by my fate. To be here was to be physically "inside" but the way a ghost is inside the world when it returns to haunt someone and still can depart at will. The ghost is confused, paralyzed by its guilt at being present without paying the price for it. Punishment is easily confused with safety.

1-4

There are sequences of sounds that musicians arrange by twelves, repeating the same twelve notes but in alternating and random sequences. They themselves don't know which three or four notes will come out close, in relation to each other.

It is sort of as if someone I loved indicated that he loved me too, but in unexpected moments and ways. And the three words "I love you" only popped into place once, by mistake, and after he had died, as in "too late." There were no witnesses to our relationship, and this created a credibility gap. I didn't trust that the experience that he and I had had had actually taken place because there were no witnesses; the verb tense was queer. No conventions stuck. I was the missing person at the graveside ceremony – an eyeball behind a bush. The person I loved would say "me... too... you," and this would be months after he died. Would anyone believe that I just heard him say it, no?

1-5

It was in that prison that I met a religious man for the second time in my life. Almost every time I visited there the small boy was there too with his beautiful ringed eyes, serious long face, and this man beside him. The child often wore a strange sidelong smile, the way the blind do. I could tell that his guardian was weirdly unlike a blood father. He always brought along a book that the boy ran his hand over. This man was either distracted or brooding when he talked to the boy's mother, a prisoner who was tiny and wild-haired and dressed in a green uniform which was fitted to say "not my own."

They talked about the boy, eyeing him simultaneously. The mother's expression was sad and inverted. Her eyes pulled their surroundings inside, and then didn't let them out again. This was a common expression on many prisoners' faces here. Many of the women were locked up for drug crimes. Either they were users or else they lived with a dealer and took the rap for him. I found out all about this in upcoming visits. My friend, who had been framed, told me the stories of the prisoners around us. Often the guy was free while his girlfriend and/or mother of his child was locked up for her unwillingness to speak his name to the Feds. Already I knew from experience how quickly a woman's children could end up in foster care if there was no functioning family person. I assumed that this was the case with those three. The man might be a foster father, or a friend. Or was he her boyfriend? I was pretty sure maybe the woman was one of those people who were political prisoners left over from the sixties and seventies. In any case, I concluded there should be a whole separate set of laws for women and watched the boy back onto his mother's lap. Her name was Gemma. One day before jail the man told me about Gemma the prisoner and how he knew her. We stood in puddles that looked like mirrors of shadows around our feet.

"I used to work for a small legal aid firm in Boston," he told me. "I hated law already by then. But a friend called me asking me to defend this woman. She had been part of a bank heist with the Weather Underground. I told him I'd never been in court before, but he persuaded me, and I did it. And failed. Lost. She got forty years. Life, basically."

"And her child?" I asked him. "She was pregnant with him when she went in. It was before they had any maternity programs in prison. She and the kid never really bonded. I have watched out for him ever since. You know. Made sure he had a home."

"What about the father?" was the natural question I asked.

"Never mind, nothing. He couldn't."

"Why? Was he in hiding too?"

"Right, but they are friends. Sort of."

I pressed him: "Why is the child blind? How?"

"She tried to kill herself. With some poison."

"After the trial?"

"During."

We walked from the parking lot towards the prison. I then had a vision of this man having huge lies inside of him, lies like helium that swelled up his spirit until it almost exploded.

I was sure now that he was the father. "What's your name?" I asked with a squint as if I had only forgotten it.

"Tom," he said pleasantly. "I'm in preparation for entering a monastery. What's yours?" The sun seemed to be setting at two p.m. It shriveled and paled like a coin dropped into still yellow milk.

Inside the checking area I handed over my wallet and keys and found my tongue loosened. I am known for my silence, and liked for it, but with Tom I could talk. "I'm used to seeing the children, not the mothers, when they are lost, separated," I told him.

"I see the beginnings of their lives, not the conclusions, as in this case." "What do you mean?" "I'm a foster mother – or was – I took children home."

"That's interesting. Want to go for a walk later?"

Outside again, Tom and I went for our first walk. It was early spring when the forsythia branches were yellowing up for the arrival of their flowers. The reservoir was scalloped behind a chain-link fence. The air was between black and oyster. He told me he was going back to Canada ultimately. He was going to live as a monastic in a Benedictine community. "Why wait?" I asked.

"To get the boy settled. I can't leave until he has a home."

"That could take awhile, because of his age, and affliction."

"Maybe, maybe not.... but I would love to be somewhere warmer than this!"

"Me too." There was a tolerant if melancholy quality to him that eased me. My breathing slowed, I believed I could express myself well in words, and nothing bad would happen. He seemed desireless, without being cold and ironic. I already dreaded saying goodbye although that word was planted and fated, because of his stated plans. On many of our walks, no words in fact passed between us. As soon as I had no fear of speaking to him, I had nothing much to say. It was in this silence that we grew familiar enough to travel side by side.

Armed Anti-Imperialist Struggle

(and the Defensive Position of the Counterrevolution in its Psychologic Warfare Against the People)
Ulrike Meinhof

Anti-Imperialist Struggle

Anti-imperialist struggle, if not meant to be merely a phrase, aims at destroying the imperialist system of powers – politically, economically and in militaristic terms; the cultural institutions through which imperialism provides homogeneity of the ruling elites and the communications systems for its ideological predomination.

Proletarian Internationalism

Anti-imperialist struggle here is not and cannot be a national liberation struggle. Transnational organizations of capital, world gripping military alliances of U.S. imperialism, cooperation of police and secret services, international organizations of ruling elites within the power range of U.S. imperialism are matched on our side by revolutionary class struggles, by the liberation struggles of third world peoples, by the urban guerrilla in the metropoles of imperialism: by proletarian internationalism.

Since the Paris Commune, it has been obvious that the attempt of one people in an imperialist state to liberate itself on a national level will summon revenge, armed retaliation, and the mortal hatred of the bourgeoisie of all other imperialist states.

"One people suppressing others cannot emancipate itself," Marx said. The urban guerrilla, RAF (Red Army Fraction), Brigade Rosse in Italy, United Peoples Liberation in the U.S. receive their military significance from the fact that they can, aligned with the liberation struggles of third world peoples, attack imperialism from behind, from where it exports its troops, its weapons, its training personnel, its technology, its communications systems, its cultural fascism to suppress and exploit third

world peoples. This is the strategic destiny of the urban guerrilla: to bring forth the guerrilla, the armed anti-imperialist struggle, the people's war, it is a long process from within the backlands of imperialism. World revolution is not a matter of days, weeks, months, nor a matter of a few people's uprisings. There is no short-term process. It is not a matter of altering the state apparatus, as revisionist parties and groups imagine or rather claim, since they really don't imagine anything.

About the Term "National State"

The term "national state" is a fiction. It no longer has any reality within the metropoles. Millions of labor emigrants can be found in the rich states of West Europe. Through internationalization of capital, through the news media, through reciprocal dependencies of economic development, through enlargement of the European community, through crisis, an internationalism of the proletariat in Europe now emanates even on the subjective level. European trade unions have been working for years at its suppression, institutionalization and control.

The fiction of a national state, to which the revisionist groups cling, is matched by their fetishistic legalism, their pacifism, their mass opportunism. Members of these groups come from the petit bourgeoisie – itself always organized complementary to the national bourgeoisie, to the ruling class in the state.

Arguing that "the masses are not yet ready" reminds us not that the RAF and captured revolutionaries in isolation, in special prison sections, in artificial brainwash collectives, and in prison, only of the arguments of the colonial pigs in Africa and Asia for over 70 years. Black people, illiterates, slaves, the colonized, tortured, suppressed, starving, the peoples suffering under colonialism, were not yet ready to take their bureaucracy, their school system, their future as human beings into their own hands. This is the argument of folks who are worried about their own positions of power, aiming at ruling a people, not at emancipation and liberation struggle.

The Urban Guerrilla

Our action of May 14, 1970 (freeing Andreas Baader from prison), is and will remain the exemplary action of the urban guerrilla. It combines all elements of the strategy of armed anti-imperialist struggle. It was the liberation of a prisoner from the grip of the state apparatus. It was a guerrilla action, the action of a group, which, through its decision to undertake the section, became a military – *political* cell. It was the liberation of a revolutionary who was essential to the urban guerrilla organization – not just because revolutionary is essential to the revolution, but because he incorporated all qualities needed to make guerrilla, military-political offensive against the imperialist state possible: decisiveness, the will to act, the ability to define oneself only and exclusively through one's aims, while keeping the collective process of learning going, from the very beginning practicing leadership as collective leadership, passing on to the collective the processes of the learning for every individual.

The action was exemplary because anti-imperialist struggle deals with liberation of prisoners, as such, from the prison, which the system has always signified for all exploited and suppressed groups of the people; from the imprisonment of total alienation and self-alienation, from political and existential martial law, in which the people are forced to live within the grip of imperialism, consumer culture, media, the controlling apparatuses of the ruling class, dependent on the market and the state apparatus.

The guerrilla always emanates from nothing. This is no different in Brazil, in Uruguay, in Cuba or with Che in Bolivia. The first phase of its organization is the most difficult. There is a group of comrades, who have decided to take action, to leave the level of lethargy, verbal radicalism, strategic discussions, which become more and more nonsubstantial, to fight. It only becomes evident at this point what kind of a person one is. The metropole individual is discovered. He or she comes from the process of decay, the false, alienated surroundings of living in the system – factory, office, school, university, revisionist groups, apprenticeship and temporary jobs. The results of this separation between professional and private life, the psychic deformation caused by the consumer society begun to show.

But that is us, that is where we come from: bred by the processes of elimination in metropole society, by the war of all against all, the competition between each and everybody else, the system of fear and pressure for productivity, the game of one at the expense of somebody else, the separation of people into men and women, young and old, healthy and sick, foreigners and natives, the fight for reputation. That is where we come from: from the isolation of the suburban home, the desolate concreted public housing, the cell-prisons, asylums and special prison sections. We come to the guerrilla organization brain-washed through the media, consumerism, physical punishment and the ideology of non-violence; from depression, sickness, declassification, insult and humiliation of the individual, of all exploited people under imperialism. Eventually we perceive the misery of each of us as constituting the necessity of liberation from imperialism, the necessity of anti-imperialist struggle. We understand there is nothing to lose by destroying this system through armed struggle, but everything to win: our collective liberation, life, humanity, identity. The concern of the people, of the masses, the assembly-line workers, the bums, the prisoners, the apprentices, the poorest masses here and of the liberation movements in the third world is our concern. Our concern: armed, anti-imperialist struggle – even if this can and will prove to be real only during the long-term development of the military-political offensive of the guerrilla, through the unleashing of the people's war.

The Guerrilla is the Group

The function of leadership in the guerrilla, the function of Andreas Baader in the RAF is orientation: not just to distinguish the main points from the minor ones in each situation but also to remain with the entire political context in all situations; to never lose sight, among technical and logistic details and problems, of the aim, which is the revolution; when formulating policies of alliances, to never forget the class question: to never to succumb to opportunism. It is *"the art of dialectically combining moral rigidity with smoothness of action, the art of applying the law of development to the leadership of revolution, which turns*

progressive changes into qualitative steps," Duan said. It is also an art
"not to withdraw with fright from the immenseness of one's own pur-
poses," but to pursue them rigidly and unwaveringly: the decisiveness to
learn from mistakes, to learn first and foremost. Every revolutionary
organization, every guerrilla organization knows that. Practice demands
the development of such abilities. Every organization, which aims for
victory in the people's struggle rather than the establishment of a party
bureaucracy, requires them.

   We do not talk about democratic centralism. Urban guerrillas in the
Metropole Federal Republic cannot have a centralistic apparatus. We
are not a party but a political-militaristic organization, developing our
leadership collectively from every single unit, group – with the tendency
to dissolve it within the groups, within collective learning. The emphasis
is always on the independent, tactical orientation of the fighter, the
guerrilla, the cadre. Collectivization is a political process, noticeable
everywhere. We learn from one another in all work and training.
Authoritarian structures of leadership lack material basis in the guerrilla,
because the true, i.e. voluntary development of the productive energy of
every individual contributes to the effectiveness of the revolutionary
guerrilla: to be able to intervene in a revolutionary way, to unleash the
people's war.

Psychological Warfare

Psychological warfare is used by the state to set the masses against the
guerrilla, to isolate the guerrilla from the people, to make the perceiv-
able non-perceivable, the rational seemingly irrational, the humanity
of revolutionaries seem inhuman. The technique is: instigation, lies,
dirt, racism, manipulation, mobilization of people's hidden fears of the
reflexes of existential fears of authorities, which have been burnt into
the flesh through decades and centuries of colonialism and exploitative
control.

   The pigs attempt to destroy revolutionary politics through personification and psychologization. They imagine that the structure of the
RAF is the same as the one through which they rule. The pigs adopt
character masks such as the Ku Klux Klan, the Mafia and the CIA as

their puppets in order to force through their interests by/blackmail, bribery, means of competition, protectionism, brutality, to cut a path across dead bodies.

The pigs count on fear in their psychological warfare against us, fear which the system has burnt into the flesh of everyone forced to sell their working energy just to be able to exist. They count on anti-communism, anti-Semitism, sexual repression, religion, authoritarian school systems, racism, brain-washing through consumer culture which has been directed against the people for decades, centuries.

In its first phase the guerrilla is shocking, in the way that our first action was shocking: by having people act without being determined by the pressure of the system, without seeing themselves with the eyes of the media, without fear. It is shocking to see people acting on true experience, both their own and of others. The guerrilla acts upon facts which people experience every day: exploitation, media terror, insecurity of living conditions despite the great wealth and refined technology in this country – the psychic illnesses, suicides, child abuse, distress within the schools, the housing misery. What shocked the imperialist state about our first action was that the RAF has been perceived in the consciousness of the people as what it really is: the practice, the thing, which results logically and dialectically from present conditions. Action returns dignity to the people and meaning to their struggles, enabling the people to have a consciousness of their history. Because all history is history of class struggle, people who had lost a sense of the dimensions of revolutionary class struggle are forced to live in a state of no history, deprived of self-consciousness, i.e. its dignity.

In reference to the guerrilla, everybody can define for himself where he stands – is able, after all, to see for himself where he is standing, his position in the class society, within imperialism. For many think they are standing on the side of the people – but as the people start to fight, they run off, denounce, step on the brakes, move to the side of the police. This is the problem which Marx cited endless times, that a person is not what he claims but what his real functions, his role in the class society, defines him as. This is what, unless acting consciously against the system, i.e. taking up arms and fighting, he has been practically instrumentalized to be for the aims of the system.

Through their use of psychological warfare, the pigs try to reverse those facts which are revealed through guerrilla action: that the people do not depend upon the state, but the state upon the people; that the police was created not to protect people from criminals but to protect the system of imperialism from the people; that we do not depend on the presence of American troops and institutions here, but U.S. imperialism depends upon us. Through personification and psychologization they project upon us their identity: the pig enjoying its alienation, the existence based upon career, upward mobility, stepping on and living at the expense of others, exploitation, hunger, misery, the misery of some billion people in the third world as well as here.

The ruling class hates us because in spite of a hundred years of repression, the revolution is lifting up its head again. The pig state has dumped on us, and especially on Andreas Baader, all they hate and fear about the people: he is the incarnation of the mob, the street fighter enemy. They recognized in us what is threatening them and will overthrow them: the decisiveness towards revolutionary force, and political military action. In it they see their own helplessness, and the limits of their means, once the people take to arms and start fighting.

The Dialectics of Revolution and Counterrevolution

These are the strategic dialectics of anti-imperialist struggle: through the defensive reactions of the system, the escalation of counterrevolution, the transformation of the political martial law into military martial law, the enemy betrays himself, becomes visible. By his own terror he makes the masses rise against him, allows contradictions to escalate and thus forces the revolutionary struggle.

Marighela: *"the basic principle of revolutionary strategy under the conditions of a permanent political crisis in city as well as countryside is to undertake such a range of revolutionary actions that the enemy feels compelled to change the political situation of the state into a military one. Then dissatisfaction will seize all layers and the military will be the only one responsible for all misconduct."* And A.P. Puyan, a Persian comrade: *"Through the pressure of the worsening, counterrevolutionary force against the resistance fighters, all other controlled groups and classes will inevitably become even more suppressed. Thus the ruling class intensifies the contradictions between itself and the suppressed classes and by creating such an atmosphere, which will come by force of things, it pushes the political consciousness of the masses way ahead."*

And Marx: *"Revolutionary progress determines its direction when it rouses a powerful, self centered, counterrevolution by engendering an adversary that can only cause the insurgent party to evolve, in its battle against the counterrevolutionaries, in to a veritable revolutionary party."*

When the pigs in 1972 created a total mobilization with a staff of 150,000 in their search for the RAF, all material and personnel forces of this state were set into motion because of a small number of revolutionaries. It became evident on a material level that the force – monopoly of the state is limited, its powers can be exhausted. Tactically speaking, imperialism is a man-eating monster, but strategically it is a paper tiger. It became evident on a material level that it is up to us whether suppression continues and it is up to us as well whether it will be smashed.

Translated by Sigrid Huth

Full Stop for an Infernal Planet

or The Schizophrenic Sensorial Epileptic and Foreign Languages
Louis Wolfson

We shall see at the times of the noblest, the most glorious, the most musical ("One Hundred Thousand Love Songs"), the sexiest, the most transcendent, the most altruistic and equally the most selfish, the most excusable, the most intelligent, especially the healthiest, and the holiest, the most divine instant that a humanity can attain anywhere and anytime, while the redemptive flame of one hundred thousand good H-bombs is lit and one hundred thousand new happy little celestial bodies are born, we shall see whether we suffer or lick the flames or if we are too stunned by the shock to understand what's happening or too blessed, or one or the other according to personal, individual fate, chance, Providence... Or perhaps the blessed apocalypse would come immediately after some scientists succeed in producing momentarily four whole ounces of so-called anti-matter, supposedly consisting of anti-particles, which alone would suffice for the sanctification of everyone of us, four ounces of anti-water, for example, somewhat less than one hundred and twenty-five grams (the contents therefore of one fourth of an enema, or little enema [or shouldn't we rather say "anti-enema"]). All dead, all "equal," all good socialists, good communists, good democrats, good republicans, good crusaders, good Zionists, good islamized... all beatified... no more reaction, revolution, counterrevolution, "establishment," consumer society, gadgets, or consumption of any kind... and finally the world-wide revolution consummated... no more need to seduce the voters, to agree with the leader or the *troika* of the party, to pander to presidents of the republic, to erect altars to dead old enemas of politicians, to lick the arses of their corpses... no more need to fart, to piss, to shit... no more need to suffer, to make suffer... to ratiocinate, to philosophize on a frightful, monstrous phenomenon, to pray to God, all of us being triumphantly in His kingdom, with the angels...

a planetary kamikaze or Massada, a perfect Islamic submission...

N****

(date)

Mister President (or Minister, Chancellor, Senator, Ambassador, Representative, Mayor....) Y**Z**

(Dear) Sir,

I have sent a letter similar to what follows to the Secretary-General of the UN:

I cannot understand why people at the UN and elsewhere, who are supposed to be intelligent and who apparently like to think of themselves as "good people" keep talking about the limitation of nuclear arms or even about disarmament!

If you consider that around three thousand years ago our poor planet was infected with only 50 million (perhaps a slightly low estimate) copies (while, certainly, a single specimen would already have been too many) of the unfortunate human species; if you imagine having had at the time a pile of good H-bombs at your disposal and having used them to crumble the crust of this damned planet Earth and possibly to convert it into a second chain of asteroids, a first large ring of such little celestial bodies being located between the orbits or Mars and Jupiter; and if you consider then what a litany of unspeakable horrors which still continue and are synonymous with humanity would not have occurred...!! What philosopher would have even dreamed, thirty-five years ago, of thus attacking the so-sick matter which we all are? What philanthropist? What man of good will?

But now we absolutely must not miss the chance – and to have such a chance is too good to be true – finally to bring to an end at last this infamous litany of abominations that we all are (collectively and individually); and I mean by that, obviously, in a complete atomic-nuclear way! Don't they say that the best medicine is prophylactic medicine? The tragedy, the true catastrophe – despite what the notable liars seem

to want to sell us – is that humanity continues... while the divine bene-
diction would be qualified as thermonuclear or some equivalent thereof.
Not to be of this opinion is to be selfish, criminal, monstrous, if not
stark mad.

Yours faithfully,

L...

P.S.   I suppose that all, or nearly all, religions, if one also wants
to look at things from that angle, conceive of Hell or Hades as a subterranean place. But if the Earth were converted into a large ring of
planetoids around the sun, then no more "under world"....! As go the
words of a certain popular song: "No more problems in the sky." And
as the Pope said during his trip to the Far-East: "God is light," and
without a doubt included there is the resurrectional light at the time of
a planetary disintegration... the disintegration of an infernal star.

....

However, such letters naturally having no perceptible effect, perhaps
even an effect contrary to the one sought, our protagonist would become
a partisan of violence, of arsons and assassinations, and would hope –
all the more naïvely, since a certain ignorance, a certain cowardice, a
certain indifference reign... over all – that men and women of true good
will would suppress as quickly as possible the monsters of cruelty all
over the world who speak of the limitation of armaments... and thus
reveal their "prenuclear," outdated, infantile, unrealistic, backward,
hypocritical, inhuman way of thinking... and likewise a fanatical zeal for
turning their backs on certain marvelous properties of matter which are
known at last and infinitely beneficial....! (It is not then, for example,
visits, be they reciprocal and with a minimum of red-tape, between East
and West Berliners or between East and West Germans, that are needed,
but rather the audacious attempt to enable *all* humanity, in as short a
time as possible, to take intergalactic trips through the skies...! It is
quite understandable that so many made such a big deal over the
famous lunar expeditions ["a giant step...!"], which however took a
week for the round-trip in space although our natural satellite is only
two light-seconds away. So if you consider that, flying at the speed of

light [300,000 kilometers per second], it would still take one hundred thousand years [diameter of the disc] to traverse only our own galaxy [the Milky Way: 100,000 million { = 100 billion} stars among which our sun is only one of average size {less then two-thirds of a million typographic characters in the present work}[and that it would take one hundred sixty thousand more years at the same "giddy" speed to reach the nearest neighboring galaxy, one among hundreds of millions of others and whose numbers seem limited only by the lone power [extending however to a distance of billions of light-years] of man to penetrate his cosmos and these hundreds of millions of galaxies seem to move away from each other at unbelievable speeds [an exploding universe, but alas! not quickly enough for the great salvation of all Earthlings]…!)

Whatever heights science may attain, it may only make more and more patent two facts: 1. Those heights can only be attained by mercilessly crushing and walking over mountains of human beings. 2. And indeed be it for this single reason, all of planet Earth should become as quickly as possible a radioactive desert or disappear through disintegration. Do those who hold power have to wait, before they'll submit to the obvious, until the world population becomes so enormous that more people will die every day than there are in a nation of respectable size today? Until the chaos and the impossibility of finding legitimate meaning are multiplied by the infinite? Until everyone has become raving mad? And the "future generations" down here that we talk about so much, are they anything but mineral salts in the earth, fluid or even solid water, gas, molecules in the air, and such little "tripe", which – in the course of the processes of germination and growth – would become plants which would be guzzled up by pregnant women or gobbled by herbivores, whose flesh in turn, would be ingested by those same pregnant women…?! The true good fortune of the "future generations" would be for them not to materialize at all!!

Translated by George Richard Gardner, Jr.

The Wild Celebration

Frédéric Rossif

Jean-Pierre Barou: First of all, by what single trait would you define love in the animal world?

Frédéric Rossif: By madness. One thing that has always seemed amazing to me is that when they're in heat. Animals lose all their inhibitions; for some of them, you can't even get close enough to film except at that time. Because that's when they're really out of their senses. They're hopelessly distracted. You can even kill them. You really have to have seen animals supremely "in love": they don't move anymore.

The motionless of madness...

To the extent that several small tribes in antiquity, and still today, prohibit hunting during this period, in the course of spring and autumn.

You have filmed many love scenes between animals. That must be much more than just a spectacle.

Sometimes, there's a fear in the face of it. I shall repeat something Michel Foucault told me one day: It's really the feeling of animality, of this animality which drives us crazy, which makes us happy, which makes us sad. The spirit of celebration is so complete. You run after one another, you fall, you fall again. Wild goats coming down from mountain tops by the hundreds, jump, turn and fight. They have become so crazy, so magical, that they leap 20 or 30 meters. Some die in the fall. The flock doesn't stop; it keeps going, dragged along by a strong wind...

Does absolute love exist?

Certainly. Take for instance antigonal cranes. Antigonal cranes whose love dances last for hours. They talk to one another; spread their wings, and walk around each other. They jump up with their feet, like wild dancers. And then, when one dies – the Indians say – the other lets himself die, too. It's a discontinuity of life, maybe due to a kind of symbolic relationship between two beings who help one another.

The lion, too, is faithful...

The lion is faithful because the lioness beats him; he receives terrible beatings. That's completely different.

It's the law of the jungle.

In a way. Take the case of prairie dogs in Africa, licaons. You know, they're terrifying animals that kill everything in their path. Nothing can stop them. They attack collectively, be it a hyena, buffalo, giraffe or a lion. Yet, one of the greatest animal specialists, if not the best, in my eyes, Miss Jane Goodall, followed for a year a band of licaons whose leader was a female. This female had three or four males directly depending on her sexually. One day, one of the males cohabitated with another female who became pregnant. The licaon, the head of the band, first relegated her rival to the very end of the group; then, when the latter gave birth, she took her babies and killed them all, except for one, the puniest, which she gave as she would a toy, or a slave to her own children, only after that did she definitively exclude her rival from the group. You see, one can also find absolutely ferocious jealousy.

At the same time, it's a very ordered world.

It depends on the species, the groups. One of the most beautiful love stories I know is about the orchid and the bee, the huge wasp of New Guinea. The orchid smells like female genitalia (of the wasp). SO the male goes straight at it and makes love to the plant. He rubs his stinger against it. Afterwards, the female smells his odor and comes and rubs herself in it, in her turn. That's how she is impregnated, through the plant. Strange ... why doesn't the couple ever meet, except through the plant? What physiological, biological laws of the world of smells and feelings give rise to this trio?

And, how about possible homosexual or incestual relations?

There's lots of homosexuality, even though it really doesn't make sense to put it in those terms. Lets just say that caresses between females exist as well as do those between males and between children and parents. The young lion, from his first and a half year up, begins to desire his mother; sometimes, his father kills him. And the mother defends her son, who is her lover. You know the love celebration is often preceded by fatal battles. Animals fight each other to death. Males fight to get the female. Death precedes this great love madness, that great leap where everything changes. Afterwards, they become very mournful. They make themselves up, decorating and painting themselves.

Decorate themselves?

In Australia, in New Guinea, birds decorate their nest in red, blue and green.

Yes, but, paint themselves?

That too! Some even change color and appearance.

In order to seduce?

Of course! You also have love songs and cries. It's a characteristic of that period. The wolf makes love cries for hours. The sound, the sonorous welcome, the sonorous relationship are very important. Something really amazing: giraffe are deaf animals who, in that situation, start what one might call long mime routines: each wraps and rubs his neck around the other one's, and – who knows? – thus, compensating for an absence of sound.

For you, this animal world, when you look at it, does it correspond to a salvation?

It is to live in salvation. It's especially to live in something unlearned. For me, animals, as Bachelard said so well, are our oldest companions in dreaming. While filming them, I'm filming a lost dream, a dream which goes back thousands of years, well into prehistoric times. I'm able to hear love, the deep cry, death, the forest, water and rhythms. And all because there was a mask, masks, walls set up, historical circumstances. All of which were a continual turning-away-from our animality.

Are you recommending this animality?

What I mean is that there are lost celebrations deep in our memory. We must endeavor to remember them. If we succeed, we'll be like the poets and prophets. If we rediscover the poetry of our cradle, we'll have the memory of the future. Because, either we disappear, or, assuming there is a future for man, it will once again be poetic.

You have repeatedly reminded us that animals, before dying, fight once again.

A wounded animal is dangerous. A wounded man is wounded; he's good for a stretcher. A wounded lion attacks with all his might. Same with the elephant. Man thinks of God. Animals don't have Gods. They have only the present. An animal doesn't bargain with his death. We do! That indicates a lack of animality.

Translated by Stamos Metzidakis

We All
Can't Die
in Bed

Guy Hocquenghem

Pasolini was killed by a swindler.

We all can't die in bed, like Franco. The Italian extreme left is indignant. M.A. Macciocchi, in *Le Monde*, speaks of a fascist plot. More perceptively, Gavi and Maggiori show how the incident was a microfascist coup: the assassin, Pelosi, wasn't used by fascism, he was the voluntary instrument of racism and the refusal of difference, the day-to-day non-politicized kind of fascism.

Probably, probably. Something all through this explanation does not convince me: the external and political nature of this viewpoint on the murder of a homosexual. Certainly you can't help but agree with the analysis of the Pelosi case, you can't help but to refuse to consider him, too, as a victim. Turning the other cheek is out of the question.

At the same time, Pasolini's death seems to me neither abominable, nor even, perhaps, regrettable. As far as I'm concerned, I find it rather satisfying. So much less stupid than a highway accident. In a way, I would want it for myself and for all of my friends.

Sadian estheticism? I hope not: it is only that a fundamental aspect of this story of the murder of a homosexual, of homosexual murder, necessarily eludes the political analysts and those who mean to protect homosexuals from their potential murderers.

It is the intimate, ancient, and very strong bond between the homosexual and his murderer, a bond as traditional as their delinquent prescription in the big cities of the nineteenth century. We too often forget that dissimulation, the homosexual secret or lies, were never chosen for themselves, through a taste for oppression: they were necessary for projecting a desiring impulse towards the underworld, for a libido attracted by objects outside the laws of common desire. Vautrin, in

Balzac, represents this underside of the civilized world born of the corruption of big cities where homosexuality and delinquency go hand in hand, very well. As an urban perversion, illicit homosexuality has, always been linked with underworld crime. There is a specific "dangerousness" which surrounds homosexuality, homosexual blackmail, homosexual murder.

Gavi and Maggiori quite rightly point out that in the Pelosi trial, the victim is just as guilty as the murderer. Which is certainly scandalous, but it constitutes a distinctive feature of the homosexual condition. In the eyes of the courts and the police, there is, in these cases, no difference between victims and murderers. There is but one suspicious "milieu", united by mysterious bonds, a free-masonry of crime where the homo and the murderer intersect. Homosexuality is first of all, and perhaps for a short while will continue to be, a category of criminality. Personally, I prefer this state of affairs to its probable transformation into a psychiatric category of deviance. The libidinal link between the criminal and the homosexual ignores the rational concepts of law, the division of individual responsibility and the distribution of roles between victims and murderers. A homosexual murder is a whole, complete unto itself. A captain of the Belgian gendarmerie writes in an article devoted to the situation of homosexuals: "An attentive surveillance of this particular milieu makes it possible to compile a very useful dossier for the discovery of future swindlers, murderers, and possibly spies."

"Decriminalizing" Homosexuality?

Some will tell me that this is precisely what we're fighting against. So? Are we going to demand the rational progress of justice in distinguishing victims and the perpetrators? Are we going to require, as do the respectable homosexual associations, that the police and the courts accept complaints from homosexuals who are mistreated or blackmailed? Will we see gays, exactly like women, demand the condemnation of rapists by the courts and request protection under the law?

I think on the contrary that even in a struggle for liberation, homosexuality's hope still lies in the fact that it is perceived as delinquent. Let us not confuse self-defense with "respectabilization." The homosexual has frequent contact with the murderer: not only through masochism, suppressed guiltiness or a taste for transgression, but also because an encounter with such a character is a real possibility. Of course, one can always avoid it. All one needs do is avoid cruising in the criminal world. To stop cruising the streets. Not to cruise at all, or only to pick up serious young men from the same social sphere. Pasolini wouldn't be dead if he had only slept with his actors.

This is what eludes all those who sincerely want to "decriminalize" homosexuality, to defend it against itself by severing its bonds with a hard, violent and marginal world.

These combatants are unaware that they are thus joining the vast movement, in France and America for example, of respectabilization and neutralization of homosexuality. That movement does not progress by increased repression, but relies, on the contrary, on an intimate transformation of the homosexual type, freed from his fears and his marginality and finally integrated into the law.

The traditional queen, likeable or wicked, the lover of young thugs, the specialist of street urinals, all these exotic types inherited from the nineteenth century, give way to the reassuring modern young homosexual (aged 25 to 40) with mustache and brief case, without complexes or affectations, cold and polite, in an advertising job or sales position at a large department store, opposed to outlandishness, respectful of power, and a lover of enlightened liberalism and culture. Gone are the sordid and the grandiose, the amusing and the evil. Sado-masochism itself is no longer anything more than a vestiary fashion for the proper queen.

A "White" Homosexuality

A stereotype of the legal homosexual, integrated into society, molded by the Establishment, close to it in his tastes, and reassured, moreover, by the powerful presence of an undersecretary who himself is a homosexual without any false shame – homosexuality is no longer a secret shared only by a few initiates – progressively replaces the baroque diversity of traditional homosexual styles. Finally the time will come when the homosexual will be nothing more than a tourist of sex, a gracious member of Club Med who has gone a little farther than the others, with a horizon of pleasure slightly broader than that of his average contemporary.

We cannot suspect any of this unless we frequent the homosexual circle, a rather closed whole which forges, even for the most isolated homosexual, the social image of his condition. Normalizing pressures move quickly, even if Paris and the bars of the rue Sainte-Anne are not all of France. While there are still queens seeking Arabs in the suburbs or Pigalle, a movement has undeniably been launched for a truly white homosexuality in every sense of the term. And it is rather curious to note, looking at ads and films or at the exits of the gay bars, the emergence of a unisexual model – common to homosexuals and heterosexuals – offered up to the desires and identification of all. Homosexuals become indistinguishable, not because they hide their secret better, but because they are uniform in body and soul, rid of the saga of their ghetto, reintroduced fully and completely not into their difference but into their similarity.

And everyone will fuck in his own social class, the dynamic junior executives will breathe with rapture the smell of their partners' aftershave, and even the Pope will no longer be able to detect anything wrong with it. A very natural thing, as a recent film said. The new official gay will not go looking for useless and dangerous adventures in the short-circuits between social classes. He will surely go on being a sexual pervert, he'll experiment with fist-fucking or flagellation, but with the cool good sense of sexological magazines, not in social violence, but in sex techniques. Pasolini was old-fashioned, the prodigious remains of an epoch that is now being left behind.

Translated by George Richard Gardner, Jr.

BECOMING

Friendship as a Way of Life
Michel Foucault

Q: You're in your fifties. You're a reader of "Le Gai Pied," which has been in existence now for two years. Those who contribute to it and read it are between 25 and 35. Is the kind of discourse you find in the magazine something positive for you?

Michel Foucault: That it exists at all is the positive and important thing. Yet reading it does force me to ponder the question of my age. Very simply I have no place there. The problem is not that it is written by young people and concerns young people. It makes me wonder what can be done in relation to the quasi-identification that exists between homosexuality and the love among young people. Another thing to distrust is the tendency to relate the question of homosexuality to the problem of "Who am I?" and "What is the secret of my desire?" Perhaps it would be better to ask oneself, "What relations can be established, invented, multiplied and modulated through homosexuality?" The problem is not to discover in oneself the truth of sex but rather to use sexuality to arrive at a multiplicity of relationships. And no doubt this is what accounts for the fact that homosexuality is not a form of desire but something desirable. So we have to work at *becoming* homosexuals and not be obstinate in recognizing that we are. The development towards which the problem of homosexuality tends is the one of friendship.

Did you think so at twenty, or have you discovered it over the years?

As far back as I remember, to want boys was to want relations with boys. That has always been important for me. Not necessarily in the form of a couple, but as a matter of existence: how is it possible for men to be together? To live together, to share their time, their meals, their room, their leisure, their grief, their knowledge, their confidences? What is it, to be "naked" among men, outside of institutional relations, family, profession and obligatory camaraderie? It's a desire, an uneasiness, a desire-in-uneasiness that exists among a lot of people.

Can one say that desire and pleasure, and the relationships one can have, are dependent on one's age?

Yes, very profoundly. Between a man and a younger woman the marriage institution makes it easier: she accepts it and makes it work. But two men of noticeably different ages – what code would allow them to communicate? They face each other without terms or convenient words, with nothing to assure them about the meaning of the movement that carries them towards each other. They have to invent, from A to Z, a relationship that is still formless, which is friendship: that is to say, the sum of everything through which they can give each other pleasure.

One of the concessions one makes to others is not to present homosexuality as a kind of immediate pleasure, of two young men meeting in the street, seducing each other with a look, grabbing each other's asses and getting each other off in a quarter of an hour. There you have a kind of neat image of homosexuality without any possibility of generating unease, and for two reasons; it responds to the reassuring canon of beauty and it cancels everything that can be uncomfortable in affection, tenderness, friendship, fidelity, camaraderie and companionship, things which our rather sanitized society can't allow a place for without fearing the formation of new alliances and the tying together of unforeseen lines of force. I think that's what makes homosexuality "disturbing": the homosexual mode of life much more than the sexual act itself. To imagine a sexual act that doesn't conform to law or nature is not what disturbs people. But that individuals are beginning to love one another – there's the problem. The institution is caught in a contradiction; affective intensities traverse it which at one and the same time keep it going and shake it up. Look at the army, where love between men is ceaselessly provoked and shamed. Institutional codes can't validate these relations with multiple intensities, variable colors, imperceptible movements and changing forms. These relations short-circuit it and introduce love where there's supposed to be only law, rule or habit.

You were saying a little while ago: "Rather than crying about faded pleasures, I'm interested in what we ourselves can do." Could you explain that more precisely?

Asceticism as the renunciation of pleasure has bad connotations. But ascesis is something else: it's the work that one performs on oneself in order to transform oneself or make the self appear that happily one never attains. Can that be our problem today? We've rid ourselves of asceticism. Yet it's up to us to advance into a homosexual ascesis that would make us work on ourselves and invent, I do not say discover, a manner of being that is still improbable.

That means that a young homosexual must be very cautious in regard to homosexual imagery; he must work at something else?

What we must work on, it seems to me, is not so much to liberate our desires but to make ourselves infinitely more susceptible to pleasure. We must escape and help others escape the two ready-made formulas of the pure sexual encounter and the lover's fusion of identities.

Can one see the first fruits of strong constructive relationships in the United States, at least in the cities where the problem of sexual misery seems under control?

To me it seems certain that in the United States, even if the basis for sexual misery still exists, the interest in friendship has become very important: one doesn't enter a relationship simply in order to be able to consummate it sexually, which happens very easily. But towards friendship people are very polarized. How can a relational system be reached through sexual practices? Is it possible to create a homosexual mode of life?

This notion of a mode of life seems important to me. Will it require the introduction of a diversification different from the ones due to social class, differences in profession and culture, a diversification which would also be a form of relationship and which would be a "way of life"? A way of life can be shared among individuals of different age, status and social activity. It can yield intense relations not resembling those that are institutionalized. It seems to me that a way of life can yield a culture and an ethics. To be "gay," I think, is not to identify with the psychological traits and the visible masks of the homosexual, but to try to define and develop a way of life.

Isn't it a myth to say: here we are enjoying the first fruits of a socialization between different classes, ages and countries?

Yes, like the great myth of saying: there will no longer be any difference between homo- and heterosexuality. Moreover, I think that it's one of the reasons that homosexuality presents a problem today. Many sexual liberation movements project this idea of "liberating yourself from the hideous constraints that weigh upon you." Yet the affirmation that to be a homosexual is, for a man, to love another man this search for a way of life runs counter to the ideology of the sexual liberation movements of the '60s. It's in this sense that the mustached "clones" are significant. It's a way of responding: "Don't worry; the more one is liberated, the less one will love women, the less one will founder in this poly-sexuality where there are no longer any differences between the two." It's not at all the idea of a great community fusion.

Homosexuality is an historic occasion to re-open affective and relational virtualities, not so much through the intrinsic qualities of the homosexual, but due to the biases against the position he occupies; in a certain sense diagonal lines that he can trace in the social fabric permit him to make these virtualities visible.

Women might object: what do men together have to win compared to the relations between a man and a woman or between two women?

There is a book that just appeared in the U.S. on friendships between women. The affection and passion between women is well-documented. In the preface the author states that she began with the idea of unearthing homosexual relationships but she perceived that not only were these relationships not always present but it was uninteresting whether relationships could be called homosexual or not. And by letting the relationship manifest itself as it appeared in words and gestures, other very essential things also appeared: dense, bright, marvelous loves and affections or very dark and sad loves. The book shows the extent to which woman's body has played a great role, and the importance of physical contact between women: women do each other's hair, help each other with make-up, dress each other. Women have had access to the bodies of other women: they put their arms around each other, kiss each other. Man's body has been forbidden to other men in a much more drastic way. If it's true that life between women was tolerated, it's only in certain periods and since the 19th century that life between men not only was tolerated but rigorously necessary: very simply during war.

And equally in prison camps. You had soldiers and young officers who spent months and even years together. During WWI men lived together completely, one on top of another, and for them it was nothing at all, insofar as death was present and finally the devotion to one another and the services rendered were sanctioned by the play of life and death. And apart from several remarks on camaraderie, the brotherhood of spirit, and some very partial observations, what do we know about the emotional uproars and storms of feeling that took place in those times? One can wonder how, in these absurd and grotesque wars and infernal massacres, the men managed to hold on in spite of everything. Through some emotional fabric no doubt. I don't mean that it was because they were each other's lovers that they continued to fight. But honor, courage, not losing face, sacrifice, leaving the trench with the captain all that implied a very intense emotional tie. It's not to say: "... Ah, there you have homosexuality!" I detest that kind of reasoning. But no doubt you have there one of the conditions, not the only one, that has permitted this infernal life where for weeks guys floundered in the mud and shit, among corpses, starving for food, and were drunk the morning of the assault.

Finally, I would like to say that something like a publication that is reflected upon voluntarily ought to make possible a homosexual culture, that is to say the instruments for polymorphic, varied, and individually modulated relationships. But the idea of a program of proposals is dangerous. As soon as a program is presented, it becomes a law and there's a prohibition against inventing. There ought to be an inventiveness special to a situation like ours and to these feelings that Americans call "coming out," that is, showing oneself. The program must be open. We have to dig deeply to show how things have been historically contingent, for such and such reason intelligible but not necessary. We must make the intelligible appear against a background of emptiness, and deny its necessity. We must think that what exists is far from filling all possible spaces. To make a truly unavoidable challenge of the question: what can we make work, what new game can we invent?

Translated by John Johnston

Goth-N-Roll High School
Boston, 1987
Michelle Tea

At the back of this nightclub called the Channel was a wooden pier that sat squatly over the Charles river and that's where the guys were taking this woman. They were metalhead guys, really Kenmore Square with their long flyaway hair and fringed everything. All I could see of the woman was her ass, wrapped in a bit of black leather and slung over the shoulder of the tallest guy. She was wearing one of those skirts I wanted so badly but couldn't afford, a leather miniskirt, the sides pinned together with skull buckles. She wasn't wearing any underwear, you could tell when she kicked her legs and she kicked her legs a lot, batted the guy on the chest screaming *put me down* and laughing, a shrill sound that got lost inside the deeper laughter of the guys who carried her around to the back of the nightclub, gone.

I had spent the earlier part of the evening inside my bedroom with the nailpolish graffiti marking up the cracked linoleum, with the tinseled windowshades and mutilated Barbie knick knacks. In front of the long mirror affixed to the aluminum wardrobe that held my clothes, taking my hair in thick black chunks, and raking the comb through it backwards, blasting it with some Extra Super Hold, and watching it slowly fall back onto my head, hopeless. My mother was clucking in the doorway, a cigarette in hand, Vantage, the ones with the gross little tunnel in the filter that you can watch turn yellower and yellower as you smoke, like lungs. She still had her white nurse uniform on, the pin with her name, the soft white shoes. She blew smoke into my room and bit her lip. *You got such nice hair* she clucked, watching my desperate attempts to destroy it.

It was an extra special night, the Lords of the New Church were playing at the club in Boston, the one by the water. I was fifteen and too young to actually go to the show, but I figured I could maybe meet them. I didn't meet them. I met Joez, while the Lords played loud inside, and outside, in the parking lot, gloomy teenagers chain-smoked and glared at each other. I was with my friend Tracey, we were in our shaky beginners makeup. Some boy who had Nina Hagen and a bunch of spaceships on the back of his jacket called us poseurs and smoked sulky cigarettes. There was long haired Laura with the bolero hat, and Joez, who had the most perfect mask of makeup I'd ever seen. Her eyeliner slunk from the corners of eyes, tapering into sharp little points. She wore impressive lipliner, shaping her mouth into two red peaks, and her eyebrows arched thinly. Joez's makeup was sharp and deadly on her soft round face. She wore a perfect coat of white on her skin, like a slipcover over good furniture. In the dark Channel parking lot she held a dusty compact in her palm and patted the powder all over her face, slid red lipstick over her lips.

Joez was beautiful. Her hair was big when I met her and like her melancholy it swelled with time, starting out thick red and clumpy, held back with black lace, and by the time she hated me it was longer and brown, the clumps welded solid by her ritual of Aqua Net and a crimping iron. Soak the long tangles in hairspray and feed it to the hot teeth of the iron, the silver zig-zag sizzling. You could actually hear Joez destroying her hair. Then more hair spray and the skinny teasing comb that looked like an ice pick. Joez had it down. She lived in Salem so she was quite authentic in her black cloth and glinting metal spiderwebs. She was very sarcastic about the Salem pseudo-witch culture that me and my Boston friends loved. There was that woman, Laurie Cabot, the Official Witch of Salem, she had a book and a shop and blessed the Salem High football team in her long black cape. The media loved her each October, she'd be on talk shows and the Boston *Globe* explaining how Halloween was a holy day for her. Laurie Cabot drove a spooky black car and almost ran Joez over in it once, earning her the nickname The Official Bitch of Salem. Joez said Laurie Cabot's little witch shop was for dumb tourists who wanted love potions and voodoo dolls and ugly satin jackets with flashy pentacles silkscreened on the back. Joez knew where the real witches shopped, wooden places with shelves of glass jars and an earthy smell. Joez was smart.

Almost right away she was my best friend, though at first there was that really bad boyfriend she had, Rox. He wanted to be Jim Morrison, and did in fact resemble the lizard king. He needed leather pants. I thought he was a dork and told Joez so. I'd see them shopping together in Harvard Square, all in black with those round pilgrimy hats on their heads. Rox would tense up when anyone talked to Joez, you could tell he didn't want her to have any friends.

One night they came to the library steps where everyone hung out and drank vodka. The library was in Copley Square, and the scene there was a real mishmash. Mostly everyone was some form of death rock or goth, but they were skaters too, and sleek-looking artsy girls. Everyone was young, in high school, and some of the skater boys weren't even that old. Tyler and Kenny had to be about 12. They were adorable, they were our mascots and all the girls would coo maternally at them.

They called me ID Lady because I had found some girl's drivers license at a Siouxsie show and used it to buy everyone liquor. It was really perfect because the girl in the picture had fucked up purple hair and all this makeup, so you really didn't know what she looked like. The guys at the liquor store would just shrug and bag up my order. I collected everyone's money, I'd have to write it all down the orders were so long: vodka, rum, 40 ouncers for the boys, sometimes a six pack, wine coolers and there was that time I turned everyone on to Manischewitz, a Jewish table wine that tasted like Zyrex and was only two dollars an bottle. Usually there would be money left over. As much as 10 or 20 dollars, and I kept it as a tip. It was like a job. Basically, everyone would just stand around and get really drunk, smoke lots of cigarettes, some of the more disturbed gothic girls would start to cry and maybe cut up their arms. It was a phenomenon I didn't understand but it was very popular. Lots of girls had scars going up their forearm and down their shoulder, they wore them like proud tattoos. I thought it was dumb. Sometimes kids would puke or cops would come and tell us to move. We peed inside this incredibly ornate hotel near the library, chandeliers and great persian rugs. We'd be totally wrecked with tangled hair and black lipstick, scaring the wealthy. We stole flowers from the vases in the ladies room, and on the way out swiped a glass bowl of peanuts from the bar.

When Joez first started coming to Copley she always had stupid Rox on her arm, that hat like a big black dinner plate hiding his disappearing hairline. Rox would climb up onto one of the moldy-looking statues at the front of the library, and perch there like a gargoyle, watching Joez, looking down at his skinny nose at all the drunk and hyper kids. Me and Joez stumbled past, our arms looped around each others' waists. *I bet she wouldn't like you if she knew...*he called down at Joez. Knew what? She yelled. About you and Monica he taunted. *I Know About Her And Monica* I shot at him and pulled Joez away. Joez made out with a girl once, her friend Monica who was so goth and quiet and cool you thought she was on drugs. Monica actually slept with Stiv Bators the last time the Lords of the New Church were in town. Joez told me how Monica's mother was banging on the hotel room door while Joez and Monica hid in the bathroom and Stiv searched the floor for his pants. Joez had exciting stories. Not so much things she had done, it was more the wild behavior of others that pulled her along and I thought maybe she thought I was also wild and felt inspired to bring her adventures.

Joez had quit high school, got her GED and enrolled in poetry courses at a community college. She just hit fast forward and skipped over the segment of life I was currently mired in, attending my vocational high school, miserably asleep at my computer. The teachers didn't care if we lived or died. I hung out in the bathroom smoking and explaining my hairdo to other smoking girls with their awful just-out-side-Boston accents. Acted crazy in the hallways so that boys would leave me alone. Tried to write sad poetry in math class and the teacher would hurl dusty erasers at me leaving big chalk marks on my black lace dresses.

Joez's poems were better than mine. Her pen name was Phiend, the second half of her full name Josephine, though her parents called her Jennifer or even worse Jenny. It made her crazy. Joez had exceptionally bad parents. Her mother was a tight fake woman with a shrill voice. She had grown up really poor and had never stopped telling Joez how good she had it, how she had walked through the cold New England winters with barely a jacket to keep the wind off. She seemed determined to make Joez relive her experience. Joez wore pointy death rock boots wrapped in electrical tape because she couldn't ask for a new pair without hearing about how her mom never had new shoes when she was growing up.

Joez would take the commuter rail into Boston each weekend with a twenty-dollar bill in the square snapped pocket of her leather jacket. She would be terrified to break the twenty and do this annoying trick where she would ask you to buy all these little things for her, subway tokens and cans of Jolt, because she didn't want to break her bill. By the time the weekend was up you would've spent six or seven dollars on her. Joez never worked. I always had some crappy job, convenience stores, copy shops, hair salons. Joez worked maybe a week at a supermarket and that was it. It was hard because Salem is a small town and she looked like such a freak with her spider hair and exquisite makeup.

Later when we hated each other I heard she got a job at the witchcraft store she made fun of, but while we were friends she just took her poetry classes and rode the train in each weekend with her twenty-dollar bill and a container of guar gum, this powder she mixed with water so she wouldn't have to eat. Joez spent her twenty on vodka and wine and if there was enough left over, records. Joez's favorite was Sisters of Mercy and mine was Christian Death and we both loved Siouxsie, the Cure, Lords of the New Church, the Mission U.K., Bauhaus.

This is how the weekend worked: I would ride the bus into Boston on Friday night, alone with my book on my lap and all my weird makeup, black hair and black lipstick, and hopefully the bus riders of Chelsea Massachusetts would leave me alone but usually I had to endure some kind of humiliation that only strengthened my idea of myself as a beautiful and noble martyr. I had gone to Catholic School and I understood that the most special and most perfect were always persecuted, I would sit in my collar and black lace dress and gaze out the window as we passed over the choppy harbor. And Joez would be there on the other side of the bridge, holding a plastic Tower Records bag packed with clothes for the weekend, books, a walkman for the train. She'd ditched Rox, that drag, it had taken forever and he had all but stalked her but he was gone now, and Joez was mine.

If it was really terrible weather like snow or rain we would climb down into the Hayward Station and take the green line, but it was best when we walked. Climbing the slowly rising steps at Government Center where boring normal people ate lunch during the week but at night it was big and empty like a swimming pool with all the water drained out. We'd walk downtown where it was busier and more exciting, people darting around beneath the streetlights. We were walking into a great drunken adventure. Past the rat-ridden alley that led to the Orpheum Theatre where bands we liked often played. Joez saw the Cure there which was amazing because now they were so huge they only played enormous alienating places where it was impossible to jump on stage or meet them.

Down the street from the Orpheum was a teeny little liquor store that sold 2 for 1 bottles of wine and I would grab a couple by their slender necks, the dark red sloshing around inside, and we would walk across the street to Boston Common and start our journey through the winding path that always looked different depending on the season. If it was white and icy and the ugly naked trees were hung with lights we would take quick steps, hurried in the cold but careful not to slip. Maybe duck into the underground garage and drink our drinks there, but only if it was really freezing. If it was autumn we would kick through crunchy leaves, and summer was best, the most perfect slow stroll beneath trees that had leaves on, us maybe bare shouldered but probably not because part of the gothic aesthetic was keeping yourself covered. In humid Boston summers it was hard, sweating under black sleeves and tights, makeup melting, hair collapsing damply on your head. But summer nights were perfect when we would cross the street into Public Gardens, nicer than the Common with empty fountains and rows of flowers and the shallow pond where the swan boats sat tethered and sleeping.

We'd go beneath the bridge to the pier where in the daylight lines of tourists twist and sweat, waiting for a ride in a big floating swan. At night it was just me and Joez and bunches of spiders that spun webs all over the wood of the pier, you had to be careful not to lean your head back onto one. Me and Joez liked them, they were the pets of this our little clubhouse where we would pull the corks from our bottles and drink. Don't ask me what we talked about but we never shut up. Lots of laughing. We were death rock but we weren't depressed, though Joez did have her moments and there were more and more as time progressed. I would smoke, Marlboro Lights, and Joez wouldn't. The more I drank the more I smoked the more I talked. The more I drank the more I fell in love. With everything. The scuzzy pond beneath us, the buildings twinkling beyond the trees, cars zooming by somewhere. And all of my life would just swell up inside me and soon I'd have to pee. So we'd leave our little pier, legs cramped and drunker when we stood. Leave the park and be on Newbury Street in front of the Ritz-Carlton. Push through the revolving door and glide across the marble floor like we were supposed to be there, hotel people giving us awful looks. If they kicked us out we'd go back to the park and pee under a tree or in an empty fountain, but normally we would just walk proudly down the carpeted stairs and pee in the tasteful white bathroom of the Ritz-Carlton. No paper anything, they had plush facecloths and fluffy towels and a wicker hamper to toss them in when you were finished primping. Joez would fix her makeup in the long lit mirror. I would tease my hair, give it a spray, maybe put on some of Joez's lipstick. My eyeliner was always thicker than hers, like I used a crayon and she had some sort of elegant paintbrush. We would leave the bathroom a mess and I would always steal something completely useless like a bottle of softsoap or a towel. Things I would inevitably forget on a sidewalk later, when I was drunker. Being in that placid white bathroom just made me want to destroy. I took the plant that sat on the sink and tore the thick green leaves from its vine, threw them all over the floor. Stomped on them till they left smudges of green plant blood on the floor, me and Joez laughing. She thought it was mean but she didn't stop me. She stuffed her Tower Records bag with facecloths and we left.

After ruining the bathroom at the Ritz-Carlton me and Joez would stroll up Newbury Street, a street that starts out old and wealthy with fur shops and Shreves, and grows gradually hipper and wealthier with haute couture shops and millions of hair salons. We'd have our bottles, Joez and I, if not wine then juice and 100 proof blue label Smirnoff, though Joez did like to mix hers with Jolt, a cocktail affectionately called Brown Vodka. So strong it stung the raw windburned skin of my lips. Joez laughed at my cringe and said *mother's milk.*

Me and Joez would hold hands and be so obnoxious because glassy rich Newbury Street was not us, the fawning window shoppers weren't weird like us and it made us yell and sing loud and laugh at how normal and dumb everything was. And we turned onto Boylston Street where the fat gray library sat the feeling of entering something would overwhelm me, like the first chords of your favorite song but we were the song, moving through the street to the place where all the kids were. Skater boys jerking around on their boards, clean girls with dyed hair huddled together over their bottles. Sometimes real punks like the crew of mohawked homeless kids from Orange County, a place we all knew from Suburbia. We all felt fake around them.

And then what would happen. Everyone was drunk, running around. Someone would know about a party and we'd go, someone would have acid and a real adventure would begin. A cop would tell us to move and we'd walk down to the river. Or we'd hang out on the library stairs all night, peeing in the alleys behind the building, helping the ones who got too drunk and puked or started crying. I did that once, after my grandmother died. It was actually a good six months after her death and I realized I hadn't done anything meaningful to say goodbye to her, and I started bawling and burping and carrying on to this boy PJ about how I had to bury an amethyst in the ground beneath my grandmother's headstone because she had been an Aquarius, like me.

PJ and his boyfriend Jimy were the only out queers we called them the Gay Punks. PJ was tall and thin and pockmarked with bright red hair and he did a lot of acid. He and Jimy would drink too much and have fist fights that ended up with PJ crying and Jimy storming off. PJ used my weepy outburst as a channel to express his own misery and we sat hugging and sobbing until I got up and barfed.

I remember a girl named Mercy who I didn't really like took care of me, got me into Peter's car where I sat on someone's lap and puked out the window. They were all going to *Rocky Horror* and I had been so excited to go that I drank too much and ultimately passed out, was deposited at Tracey's house, carried onto the couch and whoever took off my boots must have lost patience with me because the laces were busted. My favorite necklace was somehow broken. I woke in the morning so hungover, with no idea where I was. A scratchy little noise woke me and I found Tracey scrubbing a puddle of bile I'd thrown up in my sleep from the carpet. *That's how Jimi Hendrix died* she told me.

Everyone had the best time at *Rocky Horror* and I was sad. At that time *Rocky Horror* was the big thing to do each weekend, the Friday and the Saturday shows at the little cinema in Harvard Square. We were groupies, we knew all the things you yell at the screen, we were friends with the cast of the floor show. James who did Columbia was my first drag queen friend. He would go down to the Greyhound terminal where all the young boys leaned against the buildings waiting for tricks, but James would mug his. He and his boyfriend would beat the guy up and steal his wallet. James told me if he ever got AIDS he would take as many people with him as possible. *James*, I said. He did an OK Columbia. I was dying to be Columbia, but I wasn't really allowed to go to *Rocky Horror*. I had to lie and say I was at other people's houses. For a little while I had a boyfriend, Percy, who wanted to be Frankenfurter. Percy cultivated an evil persona and everyone said he did black magic so I got a crush on him. I was with him in the empty theatre and he was acting seductive like a vampire. *Are you scared of me* he asked and I wasn't scared but said *Yes* because I wanted to be. Percy wore a black cape, he fingered my dog collar and said *I'll put velvet on this so it won't chafe your neck*. Percy was such a fag. We'd make out and I'd go home with his red lipstick smudged on my face and my mother would be really tense. Once we were together in the trunk of Peter's car and I gave him a hickey and experimented briefly with his dick in my mouth. I heard from friends that he didn't really enjoy it.

Percy got to be Frankenfurter one night when the regular Frank was out of town. He was so excited. I brought him a bouquet of baby blue balloons tied with shiny ribbons. He was magnificent. The outfit, the makeup, the perfect cruel pout, the curl of his mouth when he sneered. I had been thinking about breaking up with him but when I saw him like that, all tough in his corset, I swooned. When on the big screen Frankenfurter dies, plummeting from the radio tower, Percy hurled himself off a chair, hitting the floor with a thud and a scream. It was spectacular. I sat in the front row with Joez, whose big white face made her Magenta, and we clutched each other and cheered at the passionate demise of our painted hero.

Sometimes the skinheads would come around. We knew about the skinheads before the news show on Channel 5 did a piece on them and before the big article in the Boston *Globe* that listed their nazi bootlace code, similar to the fag hanky code but entirely different. We knew that white meant white power, but red meaning beat 'em till they're red and bloody was a new color to scan for. The legend was that the skinheads had come down from Rhode Island, a whole gang of them. The photo in the Boston *Globe* showed them posed menacingly before a huge swastika tapestry in some dingy apartment, probably Allston. I half-recognized them. It was hard because you tried not to look at them when they came by and also because they were so identical in their uniform round white heads and puffy jackets. The hairdos on the girls were baffling, shorn save for a bleach blonde fringe that circled their scalp. Really unattractive. It was so they looked fearsome like the boys but still retained some femininity. Stormy was the scariest. She had a baby, you'd see her pushing the stroller, surrounded by her gang of thugs. The rumor was that the baby had an American flag tattooed on its arm, but no one could get close enough to verify.

You should understand the different neighborhoods of Boston counterculture in the 80s. There was Harvard Square which, while it did have a family of hippies wandering around in their ratty layers, was really for punks. I mean real punks. These kids had safety pins in their faces and really filthy clothing and I think many of them didn't have homes. They were authentic. I was kind of scared of them, particularly the girls, who looked incredibly tough.

I had a job in Harvard Square, handing out coupons on the street. One of the annoying people in red shirts attempting to hand-deliver you some junk mail. The coupon books were called The Square Deal and I would stand on the corner with my arm outstretched barking Square Deal, Square Deal, mortified at how low I had sunk. I would see people I knew on their way to their real jobs at boutiques and record stores.

One day I was assigned the part of Harvard Square known as The Pit. It was a wide depression in the middle of the sidewalk with concrete benches and a slope for skateboarding, and it was there that the punks hung out. I was terrified. What a dorky job, I was sure they would hassle me, maybe even beat me up. A blonde girl, short with a nose ring, came up and asked me how much I got paid. I got paid for the book, so much for each one handed out. Why don't you just throw them out she asked, jerking her head towards the trashcan. But I had been warned about the Square Deal spies that cruised by your post and peeked into trashcans to make sure you weren't cheating. *We can take a bunch and dump them into the river for you* she said. I couldn't believe it. I am always so astounded by niceness. These kids must have been really bored. It was the girl and a couple of equally scruffy punk boys, they hefted up my stack of Square Deals and hauled them down to the Charles River. I gave them some cigarettes. A week or so later I lied to my job and said my aunt died because I'm really wimpy about just quitting a job. The Square Deal people were really sad, they said I was one of their best workers.

The kids that hung out in Kenmore Square were older, out of school, and a lot of them played in bands. They didn't look punk but they were really into the music. They looked like jocks actually, the boys did. They looked like boys who would beat them up for looking weird and some of them did. I have never understood this little subculture of frat boys into hardcore but it does exist. There were always fights in Kenmore Square. The boys from New Kids on the Block hung out there before they got so disgustingly famous.

One night I was hanging out with some of the jocky hardcore boys, I was drunk and we were spare-changing for money. This little terror on a skateboard named Damian was chanting *get the punks drunk, get the punks drunk* to the throngs of normal people leaving the Red Sox game. The boys I was with were starting a band and I was telling them how I was learning to play bass and they thought maybe I could wear a skimpy leather outfit and play with them. One boy lifted me up and started carrying me around, he was drunk too, everyone in Kenmore Square was usually drunk, and all of a sudden one of the boys from New Kids on the Block was there grabbing my ass. It was Danny, the one that looks like an ape. I kicked him in the shoulder. This was before everyone knew who they were. Later, when they were on MTV my boyfriend bumped into him at a club and embarked upon a retroactive defense of my soiled honor. *My girlfriend said you grabbed her ass once*, he said. As if he would remember. I'm sure he grabbed asses all the time, those boys are such pricks. *I don't grab a girl's ass*, said the superstar, *I FEEL a girl's ass. But tell her I'm sorry.* Thanks, Danny.

The death rockers of Copley were hated by all the other Boston sub-cultures. The punks thought we were silly and pretentious and came from rich families, and the hardcore boys thought all of our boys were fags and they were probably right. The martyrs this made of us was a good fashion accessory, but it sucked to have no allies when the skin-heads started coming around. First they were just kind of intimidating, they'd huddle in a group a few feet away and mock us, whisper and laugh and yell things like *what the fuck are you looking at* when the truth was we avoided eye contact with the skinheads like we avoided sunlight.

Once Stormy was there and the baby was out of the stroller, crawling around on the library stairs. Stormy was drinking beer with the boys, they all drank Budweiser, clutching the red white & blue cans. We were trying to see if the baby really had that tattoo but we didn't want them to catch us looking. Stormy was getting drunker and drunker and horsing around with the boys and the baby was crawling around like a wind-up toy, down the stairs, headed for the sidewalk. It was terrifying that this girl was a mother. Anyone could have just scooped that kid up and been gone with it. Justine eventually did, before the baby ended up squashed by someone running for the bus. She lifted the child and brought it back up the stairs and Stormy was immediately there, furious, Budweiser can in hand. We had touched the baby. Now she had to kill us.

That's when it got bad, when we forced them to acknowledge us by touching the tattooed baby. They knew we were scared. They were like dogs, a pack of mean dogs. Once they smelt us shrink back we were doomed. They took two of us, Mike and Yvonne. They were like the king and queen of our little gothic world, not because they were benevolent or good leaders but because they both had the biggest black hair and seemed considerably more disturbed than the rest of us, and that com-manded respect. They huddled together and cried a lot. The skinheads took Mike and Yvonne and dumped them in the river. Just lifted them, kicking and screaming, and dropped them in. It was so humiliating it was nearly impossible to imagine. Part of Mike and Yvonne's dignity was they barely ever spoke. It was blasphemy that they had been made to yell and beg and scream.

I personally missed most of the big skinhead scares that summer. Since quitting my job at the Square Deal I'd been hired and fired by a gourmet ice cream shop in Fanueil Hall, so I had no money to get into Boston and of course no money to drink. It was hot like it gets in Boston, the air all thick and wet and sitting heavy on your skin. School was out and I hung out at home eating Kraft macaroni and cheese and playing Trivial Pursuit with my sister. So I wasn't there for the big attack, when they got Rachel on the ground and tried to rip her boots from her feet. They were always threatening to steal our boots but that was the first time they actually tried it. We all wore Doc Martins and the skinheads thought Doc Martins were skinhead things and we had no right. They ripped out chunks of Rachel's spidery hair, and another girl also got punched and had her hair ripped out. It was so scary to hear about; these were my friends. Peter was there, he ran to his car, pulled it up to the front of the library and yelled for everyone to jump in. Everyone ran, all these big hairdos darting towards safety and the skinheads right behind them kicking Peter's car, grabbing onto it as if they could stop it from moving.

I was petrified. I told my parents about it. I wanted a knife and my father was a big fan of self-defense, he had a couple of knives, I thought they'd want to help me out. They went crazy. What kind of war zone was I hanging out in. I wasn't allowed to go into Boston anymore. I was crying in my living room, my parents were drunk, had been out at this shabby bar called Dick's that had an adjacent pizza parlor, and the scene just spun out of my grasp. It was manic, my parents yelling about how I ask for trouble, looking so weird. It was not the first time I'd gone to my parents for help and ended up worse than I'd started. *A knife!* My mother kept yelling. *A knife!*

I had this habit then, of scratching my neck when I was scared or had lost control of my surroundings, and I was sitting in the worn wool armchair just digging at my neck with my fingernails. I wanted them to stop me but they didn't. They were just insane, the both of them but especially my mother, because her mother had just died of cancer and she had enough to deal with without me and knives. Joez was over that night, she was cowering in the doorway like they were going to come after her next. *Come on* said my mother, *we're going for a drive*. She was wrecked. What about Joez I asked and she said *Joez, wait here*.

I went out front, I was barefoot, my mother was crying. She kept yelling at me. I just turned and left. Amazing to realize I could do that. Even as my naked feet carried me to the park down the street I couldn't believe I was getting away with it. I sat on a swing and cried. I didn't understand what had happened A gang of nazis had attacked my friends and I was scared and then my parents lost it. And I had left poor Joez alone with them. I had to go back. I snuck up the back stairway and into my room where Joez sat on the floor, listening to records and writing her name on the linoleum in wet blobs of black nail polish. I sat down beside her and lit a Marlboro Light and cried and said She's Crazy She's Crazy She's Just Crazy and Joez lit a stick of incense, Courage the package read, I had bought it at one of the secret witch shops in Salem. *Yeah*, she said, *I've never seen anyone so crazy*.

I need to get back to Joez and tell you more things. I have to tell you about the house she lived in, in Salem, with her mom with the poverty agenda, her dad that didn't talk, and her two older sisters – the one who helped run Dukakis's run for president and the reason for all the Dukakis propaganda on the fridge and in the window, and the other one who liked folk music and was boring, seemed kind of lesbian to me though I never said this to Joez. Joez's sisters thought she was a mess, between them and her parents she barely left her room all week, she shut herself in there and listened to records, practiced her bass, and cried a whole lot. Sometimes she'd call me, all hiccupy in the middle of one, and sometimes she'd just mention it later, when she was calm again.

Joez's house wasn't like my house, but then Salem wasn't like Chelsea. Chelsea was poor, a bad city getting worse, Getting Out Of Chelsea was something my family talked about a lot, a kind of sport. Keeping tabs on who was winning, what families recently Got Out, you either rooted for them, *Good fa them*, or you hated them, *Ah, money goes to money*. Joez's family wasn't very rich at all, but Salem was a calm and pretty place to live, and they owned their house and it was beautiful. It was a big wooden castle with a brilliant stained glass window, fan-shaped and every color.

Salem, as you know, is a very historical city, and tourist trolleys would cruise by and people would take pictures of Joez's fancy house. Her parents had tried to get it declared a historical monument but the Chamber of Commerce said it wasn't old enough, so they were bitter. Joez would stand in her front yard and stick her middle finger up at all the tourists' cameras. Many years ago the house had been a boarding house, so all the bedrooms had these small white sinks with little mirrors. Joez's was covered with a soft film of the baby powder she dusted her face with to keep it looking dead. She had Siouxsie posters on her walls and lots of good records.

One 4th of July she got her parents to let her throw a BBQ party and invite all her friends from the city. We packed Peter's truck with cases of wine coolers for later when we would go to the beach and take acid and drink. It was weird to be at Joez's house with all the kids from the library steps. Joez's mom was tense and smiling, bringing plates of grilled chicken and bowls of onion dip onto the porch. Peter was running around with his video camera and the *Rocky Horror* people were choreographing dances on the lawn. Everything was perfect and then it went Splat.

Percy was scheduled to show up later with acid, he called during the party to ask how many hits he should bring. Of course Joez's mother was listening on the other line. I was in the living room when I heard Joez scream my name, a loud sob. Upstairs, Joez was in her mother's room, shades down, lights off. It was dark and she was crying, covering her round powdered face with her hands. Her mother looked at me. *I just heard my Jennifer make a drug deal* she said dramatically. Kind of accusingly. *Please tell your friends to leave. MOM!* Joez wailed. *You can stay* she said sternly, *but everyone else goes.* Downstairs Joez's father was clapping his hands together saying *party's over.* Peter caught that moment with his video camera, the big white-haired Dad and all the nervous *Rocky Horror* kids solemnly collecting their things from the lawn. I did not want to stay. It was like I was being punished too and they weren't even my parents. I had 10 bucks invested in the booze in

Peter's trunk and I knew everyone would get drunk without me. Joez's parents stood on the porch observing the silent departure. You could tell they thought we all were trash. In the living room I facilitated the dysfunctional family therapy session. Joez sobbed, her mother said sharp, mean things about her hair, and her father sat unspeaking. I tried to explain. I was kind of Joez's lawyer. It was so tragic. Joez had never even done acid before. It was going to be her very first trip and of course no one believed her. Now her mom thought she was a junkie. *I knew you were hanging out with druggies* she spat. *We're not druggies, do we look like druggies?* Joez cried. *No Jenny you look like bankers!* She didn't get punished. I think her parents thought she was too far gone for punishment, but she had to live there in that house with them thinking she was such a loser. Joez eventually got to try acid and it was terrible, she was paranoid the whole time. She kept saying *what if I have a bad trip* right up until she peaked. Someone commented that people with chemical imbalances shouldn't do drugs, and people started calling Joez 'Chemicals" and she hated it.

We all kept getting a little older and Joez kept getting a little more depressed. She would cry and tell me how sad she was and then yell at me for never sharing my own sadness with her. But I wasn't sad. I was actually a little embarrassed at my cheerfulness. I felt like a poseur. I should have been wearing pink. Joez sat in her dark dark clothes and drank with Renee Blue Hair who was giving her valium or xanax or something. Joez Don't, I said *Oh what do you know Michelle* she said and bitterly ate her pill. Renee turned out to be a dyke so I guess that's why she was so upset. I saw her years later at a pro-choice rally and I could tell she'd been anorexic by the way her teeth sat so large in her face. Joez was always badly wanting a boyfriend. Who wasn't. For a little while she was obsessed with Chris, who looked so much like Morrissey I'm sure he was gay. All the boys looked like Morrissey or else like Robert Smith and certainly all of them were gay. Joez said she was going to marry the first guy who asked her. Joez Don't, I said, and she rolled her eyes. Big gray eyes framed by all that makeup. At night in my room she'd have wads of toilet paper, wiping all the paint from her face. She'd leave smudgy tissues all over the floor, I'd walk around barefoot with one stuck to my heel. They were in my bed amongst the blankets. Sometimes, I'd be half dozing off and feel the mattress lift as Joez stumbled out of the room and into the bathroom to puke. Joez's hangovers were heavier than mine. It was hard to get her up in the morning. So I'd lie there for awhile, reading. Sometimes my mother would open the door and say *up and at 'em. Rise and shine. You're not going to sleep the day away you two, this isn't a flophouse. This room smells like alcohol breath*, she sniffed. Mom, I groaned. She was petrified of me ending up an alcoholic like everyone else in the family.

When did Joez become too much. She was truly tormented now, and made the biggest deal about drinking. We all did it, but the way she talked about it so much. If we didn't want her to come along we'd lie and say we weren't going to drink and she'd get pissed and say *Fine*, all snippy. She thought it was a sell-out thing to do, like when I started wearing colors. She felt so betrayed, but I couldn't sit there in time with her forever. I was wearing jeans and she was yelling at me for it. Angry at my red shirt. She started hanging out with these mean looking industrial kids who had an industrial computer band. She was with them at a party, they all glared at me. Joez, I said, catching her in the hallway. I Don't Want To Be Your Enemy. *You're not* she said simply, and that was it. They used to crank call me at 3 in the morning, threatening to kick my head in, telling me to brush my teeth. I was hurt and scared but really I couldn't be too upset because I crank called people too. Eventually they stopped.

Sunless

Chris Marker

This morning I was on the dock of Pidjiguiti, where everything began in 1959: when the first victims of the struggle were killed. It may be as difficult to recognize Africans in this leaden fog as it is to recognize struggle in rather dull activity of tropical longshoremen. Rumor has it that every third world leader coined the same phrase the morning after independence: *Now the real problems start.* Cabral never got a chance to say it, he was assassinated first. But the problems started, and went on, and are still going on. Rather unexciting problems for revolutionary romanticism: to work, to produce, to distribute, to overcome postwar exhaustion, temptations of power and privilege... History only tastes bitter to those who expected it to be sugarcoated.

My personal problem was more specific: how to film the ladies of Bissau? Apparently the magical function of the eye was working against me there. It was in the market places of Bissau and Cape Verde that I could stare at them again with equality... I see her – she saw me – he knows that I see her – she drops me her glance, but just at an angle where it is still possible to act as though it was not addressed to me – and at the end of the real glance, straightforward, that lasted a twenty-fourth of a second, the length of a film frame.

All women have a built-in grain of indestructibility, and men's task has always been to make them realize it as late as possible. African men are just as good at this task as others, but after a close look at African women, I wouldn't necessarily bet on the men.

He told me the story of the dog Hachiko: A dog waited every day for his master at the station. The master died, and the dog didn't know it, and he continued to wait, all his life. People were moved and bought him food. After his death, a statue was erected in his honor, in front of which suchis and rice cakes are still placed so that the faithful soul of

Hachiko will never go hungry.

Tokyo is full of these tiny legends, and of mediating animals. The Mitsukoshi lion stands guard on the frontiers of what was once the empire of Mr. Okada, a great collector of French paintings, the man who hired the chateau of Versailles to celebrate the hundredth anniversary of his department stores. In the computer section, I've see young Japanese exercising their brain muscles like the young Athenians at the palestra. They have a war to win (the History books of the future will perhaps place the battle of integrated circuits at the same level as Salamis or Agincourt) but are willing to honor the unfortunate adversary by leaving other fields to him: men's fashions this season are placed under the sign of John Kennedy.

Like an old votive turtle stationed in the corner of a field, every day Mr. Akao, the president of the Japanese Patriotic Party, trumpeting from the heights of his rolling balcony against the international communist plot. He wrote me: the automobiles of the extreme right with their flags and megaphones are part of Tokyo's landscape, Mr. Akao is their focal point. I think he'll have his statue like the dog Hachiko, at this crossroads from which he departs only to go on the battlefields. He was at Narita in the sixties: peasants fighting against the building of an airport on their land, and Mr. Akao denouncing the hand of Moscow behind everything that moved… Yurakucho is the political space of Tokyo. Once upon a time I saw a bonze pray for peace in Viet Nam there. Today, young right wing activists protest against the annexation of the Northern Islands by the Russians. Sometimes they're answered that the commercial relations of Japan with the abominable occupier of the north are a thousand times better than with the American ally who's always whining about economic aggression.

On the other sidewalk, the left has the floor. The Korean Catholic Opposition leader, Kim Dae Jung, kidnapped in Tokyo in '73 by the South Korean Gestapo, is threatened with the death sentence. A group has began a hunger strike, some very young militants are trying to gather signatures in his support.

I went back to Narita for the birthday of one of the victims of the struggle. The demo was unreal, I had the impression of acting in *Brigadoon,* of waking up ten years later in the midst of the same players, with the same blue lobsters of Police, the same helmeted adolescents, the same banners, the same slogans: DOWN WITH THE AIRPORT! Only one thing has been added: the airport, precisely. But with its single runway and the barbed wire that chokes it, it looks more besieged than victorious.

My pal Hayao Yamaneko has found a solution: if the images of the present don't change, then change the images of the past. He showed me the clashes of the Sixties treated by his synthesizer. Pictures that are less deceptive, he says, with the conviction of a fanatic, than those you see on television. At least they proclaim themselves to be what they are: images – not the portable and compact form of an already inaccessible reality.

Hayao calls his machine's world: the Zone – a homage to Tarkovsky.

What Narita brought back to me, like a shattered hologram, was an intact fragment of the generation of the Sixties. If to love without illusions is still to love, I can say that I loved it. It was a generation that often exasperated me, for I didn't share its Utopia of uniting in a common struggle those who revolt against poverty and those who revolt against wealth, but it screamed out that gut reaction that better adjusted voices no longer knew how, or no longer dared, to utter … I met peasants there, who had come to know themselves through the struggle. Concretely, it has failed. At the same time, all they had won in their understanding of the world could have been won only through the struggle.

As for the students, some massacred each other in the mountains in the name of revolutionary purity, while others had studied capitalism so thoroughly to fight it that they now provide it with its best executives. Like everywhere else, the Movement had its posturers and its careerists – including and there are some, those who made a career of martyrdom – but it carried with it those who said, like Che Guervara that *they trembled with indignation every time an injustice is committed in the world.* They wanted to give a political meaning to their generosity, and their generosity has outlasted their politics. That's why I will never allow it to be said that youth is wasted on the young.

The youth who get together every weekend at Shinjuku obviously know that they are not on a launching pad to real life, that they *are* life, to be eaten on the spot, like fresh donuts. It's a very simple secret, the old try to hide it, and not all the young know it. The ten year old girl who threw her friend from the 13th floor of a building after having tied her hands, because she had spoken badly of their class team, hadn't discovered it yet. Parents who demand an increase in special telephone lines devoted to the prevention of children's suicides find out a little late that they had kept it all too well. Rock is an international language that's spreading the secret. Another is peculiar to Tokyo...

For the Takenoko, twenty is the age of retirement. They are baby Martians. I go to see them dance every Sunday in the park at Yoygi. They want people to look at them, but they don't seem to notice that people do. They live in a parallel time sphere, a kind of invisible aquarium wall separates them from the crowd they attract, and I can spend a whole afternoon contemplating the little Takenoko girl who is learning, no doubt for the first time, the customs of her planet. Beyond that, they wear dog tags, they obey a whistle, the Mafia rackets them, and with the exception of a single group made up of girls, it's always a boy who commands.

One day he writes to me: description of a dream. More and more my dreams find their setting in the department stores of Tokyo, the subterranean tunnels that extend them and run parallel to the city. A face appears, disappears, a trace is found, is lost, all the folklore of dreams is so much in its place that the next day when I'm awake, I realize that I continue to seek in the basement labyrinth the presence concealed the night before. I begin to wonder if those dreams are really mine, or if they are part of a totality, of a gigantic collective dream of which the entire city may be the projection. It might suffice to pick up any one of the telephones that are lying around to hear a familiar voice, or the beating of a heart – Sei Shonagon's for example... All the galleries lead to stations, the same companies own the stores and the railroads that bear their name, Keio, Odakyu, all those names of ports. The train inhabited by sleeping people puts together all the fragments of a dream, makes a single film of them, the ultimate film. The tickets from the automatic dispenser grant admission to the show.

Video games are the first stage in a plan for machines to help the human race, the only plan that offers a future for intelligence. For the moment, the insufferable philosophy of our time is contained in the

Pac-Man. I didn't know, when I was sacrificing all my coins to him, that he was going to conquer the world. Perhaps because he is the most graphic metaphor of Man's Fate. He puts into true perspective the balance of power between the individual and the environment, and he tells us soberly that though there may be honor in carrying out the greatest number of victorious attacks, it always comes a cropper.

He was pleased that the same chrysanthemums appeared in funerals for men and for animals. He described to me the ceremony held at the zoo in Ueno, in memory of the animals that had died during the year: For two years in a row this day of mourning has had a pall cast over it by the death of a panda – more irreparable, according to the newspapers, than the death of the prime minister that took place at the same time. Last year people really cried. Now they seem to be getting used to it, accepting that each year death takes a panda, as dragons do young girls in fairy tales. I've heard this sentence: *The partition that separates life and death does not appear so thick to us as it does to a Westerner.* What I have read most often in the eyes of people about to die is surprise. What I read right now in the eyes of Japanese children is curiosity. As if they were trying, in order to understand the death of an animal, to stare through the partition.

I have returned from a country where death is not a partition to cross through, but a road to follow. The Great Ancestors of the Bijago archipelago has described for us the itinerary of the dead, and how they move from island to island according to rigorous protocol, until they come to the last beach, where they wait for the ship that will take them to the other world. If by accident one should meet them, it is above all imperative not to recognize them. Hayao Yamaneko invents video games with his machines. To tease me, he puts in my best-beloved animals: the Cat and the Owl.

He claims that electronic texture is the only one that can deal with sentiment, memory and imagination. How can one claim to show a category of Japanese who do not exist? Yes, they're there, I saw them in Osaka, hiring themselves out by the day, sleeping on the ground, ever since the Middle Ages they've been doomed to grubby and backbreaking jobs, and their real name, *etas*, is a taboo word, not to be pronounced. They are non-persons, how can they be shown, except as non-images?

The Bijagos are part of Guinea-Bissau. In an old film clip, Amilcar Cabral waves a gesture of goodbye to the shore – he's right, he'll never see it again. Luiz Cabral made the same gesture fifteen years later on the canoe that was bringing us back. Guinea has by that time become a nation and Luiz is its president. All those who remember the war remember him. He is the half-brother of Amilcar – born as he was of half Guinean and Cape Verdean blood and like him, a founding member of an unusual party – the PAIGC, which by uniting the two colonized countries in a single movement of struggle wishes to be the forerunner of a federation of the two states. I have listened to the stories of former guerrilla fighters, who had fought in conditions so inhuman that they pitied the Portuguese soldiers for having to bear what they themselves suffered – that I heard, and many more things that make one ashamed for used lightly, even inadvertently, the word guerrilla to describe a certain breed of filmmaking ... A word that at the time was linked to many theoretical debates, and also to bloody defeats on the ground. Amilcar Cabral was the only one to lead a victorious guerrilla war – and not only in terms of military conquests. He knew his people, he had studied them for a long time, he wanted every liberated region to be also a precursor of a different kind of society. The socialist countries send weapons to arm the fighters, the social-democracies fill the people's stores: may the extreme left forgive history, but if the guerrillas are like fish in water, it's thanks to Sweden. Amilcar was not afraid of ambiguities, he knew the traps. He wrote: *It's as though we were at the edge of a great river full of waves and storms, with people who are trying to cross it and drown, but they have no other way out. They must get to the other side.*

And now the scene moves to Cassaca, the 17th of February 1980 – but to understand it properly one must move forward in time. In one year, Luiz Cabral the president, will be in prison, and the weeping man he has just decorated, Major Nino, will have taken power. The party will have split, Guineans and Cape Verdeans separated one from the other will be fighting over Amilcar's legacy. We will learn that behind this ceremony of promotions, which in the eyes of visitors, perpetuated the brotherhood of the struggle, there lay a pit of post-victory bitterness, and that Nino's tears did not express an ex-warrior's emotions, but the wounded pride of a hero who felt he had not been raised high enough above the others. And beneath each of these faces, a memory, and in place of what we were told had been forged into a collective memory, a thousand memories of men who parade their personal laceration in the great wound of History...

In Portugal, raised up in its turn by the breaking wave of Bissau, Miguel Torga, who had struggled all his life against the dictatorship, wrote: *Every protagonist represents only himself... In place of a change in the social setting, he seeks simply, in the revolutionary act, the sublimation of his own image...* That's the way the breakers recede, and so predictably that one has to believe in a kind of amnesia of the future that History distributes, through mercy or calculation to those whom it recruits. Amilcar murdered by members of his own party, the liberated areas fallen under the yoke of bloody petty tyrants liquidated in their turn by central power to whose stability everyone paid homage until the military coup. That's how History advances, plugging its memory as one plugs one's ears. Luiz exiled to Cuba, Nino discovering in his turn plots woven against him, can be cited reciprocally to appear before the bar of History - she doesn't care, she understands nothing, she has only one friend: the one Brando spoke of in *Apocalypse*: horror – and horror has a name and a face.

I am writing you all this from another world, a world of appearances. In a way, the two worlds communicate with each other. Memory is to one what History is to the other. An impossibility. Legends are born out of the need to decipher the indecipherable. Memories must make due with their delirium, with their drift. A moment stopped would burn like a frame of film blocked before the furnace of the projector. Madness protects, as fever does. I envy Hayao and his Zone. He plays with the signs of memory. He pins them down and decorates them like insects that would have flown beyond time which he could contemplate from a point outside of Time – the only eternity we have left. I look at his machines, I think of a world where each memory could create its own legend.

In Iceland, I laid the first stone of an imaginary film. That summer, I had met three children on a road, and a volcano had come out of the sea... The American astronauts came to train, before flying off to the Moon, in this corner of Earth that resembles it. I saw it immediately as a setting for a science fiction, the landscape of another planet... or rather no, let it be the landscape of our own planet for someone who comes from elsewhere, from very far away. I imagine him moving slowly, heavily, above the volcanic soil that sticks to the soles. All of a sudden, he stumbles, and the next step, it is a year later, he is walking on a small path near the Dutch border, along a seabird's sanctuary.

That's for a start. Now why this cut in time, this connection of memories? That's just it, *he* can't understand. He hasn't come from another planet, he comes from our future, 4001, the time when the human brain has reached the era of full employment. Everything works to perfection, all that *we* allow to slumber, including memory. Logical consequence: total recall of memory is anesthetized. After so many stories of men who had lost their memory, here is the story of one who has lost forgetting… and who, through some peculiarity of his nature, instead of drawing pride from the fact and scorning mankind of the past and its shadows, turned to it first with curiosity and then with compassion. In the world he comes from, to call forth a vision, to be moved by a portrait, to tremble at the sound of music can only be signs of a long and painful prehistory. He wants to understand. He feels these infirmities of Time like an injustice, and he reacts to that injustice like Che Guevara, like the youth of the Sixties, with indignation. He is a third-worlder of Time, the idea that unhappiness has existed in his planet's past is as unbearable as to them the idea of poverty in their present.

Naturally, he will fail. The unhappiness he discovers is as inaccessible to him as the poverty of a poor country is unimaginable to the children of a rich one. He has chosen to give up his privileges, but he can do nothing about the privilege that has allowed him to choose. His only recourse is precisely that which threw him into this absurd quest: a song cycle by Moussorgski. They are still sung in the 40th century. Their meaning has been lost, but it was then that for the first time he perceived the presence of that thing he didn't understand, which had something to do with unhappiness and memory, and towards which slowly, heavily, he began to walk.

On May 15, 1945, at 7 o'clock in the morning, the 382nd US infantry regiment attacked a hill in Okinawa they renamed *Dick Hill*. I suppose the Americans themselves believed they were conquering Japanese soil, and that they knew nothing about the Ryukyu Civilization. Neither did

I, apart from the fact that the faces of the market ladies at Itoman spoke to me more of Gauguin than of Utamaro. For centuries of dreamy vassalage, Time had not moved in the archipelago. Then came the break. Is it a property of islands to make their women into the guardians of their memory? I learned that, as in the bijagos, it is through the women that magic knowledge is transmitted: each community has its priestess, the Noro, who presides over all ceremonies with the exception of funerals. The Japanese defended their position inch by inch, at the end of the day the two half-platoons formed from the remnants of L Company had only got halfway up the hill. A hill like the one where I followed a group of villagers on their way to the purification ceremony. The Noro communicates with the gods of the sea, of the rain, of the earth, of fire. Everyone bows down before the Sister Deity who is the reflection, in the absolute, of a privileged relationship between brother and sister. Even after her death, the sister maintains her spiritual predominance. At dawn, toppled into the modern world. Twenty-seven years of American occupation, the re-establishment of a controversial Japanese sovereignty, two miles from the bowling alleys and the gas stations the Noro continues her dialogue with the gods. When she is gone, the dialogue will end. Brothers will no longer know that their dead sister is watching over them.

In filming the ceremony, I knew I was present at the end of something. Magical cultures that disappear leave traces to those who succeed them. This one will leave none. The break in History has been too violent. I touched that break at the summit of the hill, as I had touched it at the edge of the ditch where 200 girls had used grenades to commit suicide in 1945, rather than fall into the hands of the Americans. People had their pictures taken in front of the ditch, as souvenirs.

On Hayao's machine, war resembles letters being burned, shredded in a frame of fire. The codename for Pearl Harbor was *Tora, tora, tora* – the name of the cat the couple in Go To Ku Ji was praying for. So all of this will have begun with the name of a cat pronounced three times.

Off Okinawa, kamikazes dived on the American fleet. They were likelier material for it, obviously, than the special units who exposed their prisoners to the bitter frost of Manchuria and then to hot water so as to see how fast flesh separates from the bone. One would have to read their last letters to know that the kamikazes weren't all volunteers, nor were they all swashbuckling samurais. Before drinking his last cup of sake, Ryoji Uebara had written: *I have always thought that Japan must live free in order to live eternally. It may seem idiotic to say that today, under a totalitarian regime. We kamikaze pilots are machines, we have nothing to say, except to beg our compatriots to make Japan the great country of our dreams. In the plane, I am a machine, a bit of magnetized metal that will plaster itself on an aircraft-carrier, but once on the ground, I'm a human being, with feelings and passions... Please excuse these disorganized thoughts. I am leaving you a rather melancholy picture, but in the depths of my heart I am happy. I have spoken frankly. Forgive me.*

Everytime he came back from Africa, he stopped at the island of Sal, which is in fact a salt rock in the middle of the Atlantic. At the end of the island, beyond the village of Santa Maria and its cemetery of the painted tombs, it suffices to walk straight to meet the desert.

He wrote me, I've understood the visions. Suddenly you're in the desert, the way you are in the night. Whatever is not desert no longer exists. You don't want to believe the images that crop up.

Did I write you that there are emus on the Ile de France: this name, Island of France, sounds strangely on the Island of Sal. My memories superimpose two towers: the one at the ruined castle of Montepilloy that served as encampment for Joan of Arc, and the lighthouse tower at the southern tip of Sal, probably one of the last lighthouses to use oil.

A lighthouse in the Sahel looks like a collage until you see the ocean at the edge of the sand and salt. Crews of transcontinental planes are rotated on Sal. Their club brings to this frontier of nothingness a small seaside resort which makes the picture still more unreal. They feed the stray dogs that live on the beach.

I found my dogs pretty nervous tonight. They were playing with the sea as I had never seen them before. Listening to Radio Hong Kong later on, I understood. Today was the first day of the lunar New Year, and for the first time in sixty years, the sign of the dog met the sign of water.

Out there 11,000 miles away, a single shadow remains immobile in the midst of the long moving shadows that the January light throws over the ground of Tokyo: the shadow of the Asakusa-bonze.

For also, in Japan, the Year of the Dog is beginning. Temples are filled with visitors that come to toss down their coins, and to pray, Japanese style: a prayer which slips into life without interrupting it.

Brooding at the end of the world on my island of Sal in the company of my prancing dogs, I remember that month of January in Tokyo, or rather I remember the images I filmed of the month of January in Tokyo. They have substituted themselves for my memory, they *are* my memory. I wonder how people remember things who don't film, don't photograph, don't tape. How has mankind managed to remember?.... I know, it wrote the Bible. The new Bible will be an eternal magnetic tape of a Time that will have to reread itself constantly, just to know it existed. As we await the year 4001 and its total recall, that's what the oracles we take out of their long hexagonal boxes at New Year may offer us: a little more power over that memory that runs from camp to camp, like Joan of Arc, that a shortwave announcement from Hong Kong radio picked up on a Cape Verde island projects to Tokyo, and that the memory of a precise color in the street bounces back on another country, another distance, another music endlessly.

At the end of memory's path, the ideograms on the Island of France are no less enigmatic than the kanji of Tokyo in the miraculous light of the New Year. It's Indian Winter. As if the air were the first element to emerge purified from the countless ceremonies by which the Japanese wash off one year to enter the next one. A full month is just enough for them to fulfill all the duties that courtesy owes to time. The most interesting, unquestionably, being the acquisition, at the Temple of Tenjin, of the Uso Bird who, according to one tradition, eats all your lies of the year to come, and according to another, turns them into truths.

But what gives the street its color in January, what makes it suddenly different, is the appearance of kimonos. In the street, in stores, in offices, even at the Stock Exchange on opening day, the girls take out their fur-collared winter kimonos. At that moment of the year other Japanese may well invent extra-flat TV sets, commit suicide with a chainsaw, or capture two-thirds of the world market for semi-conductors – good for them! All you see are the girls.

The 15th of January is Coming of Age Day, an obligatory celebration in the life of a young Japanese woman. The city governments distribute small bags filled with gifts, date-books, advice: how to be a good citizen, a good mother, a good wife. On that day, every 20 year old girl can phone her family for free, no matter where in Japan. Flag, home and country, this is the anteroom of adulthood. The world of the Takenoko and of rock singers speeds away like a rocket. Speakers explain what society expects of them. How long will it take to forget the Secret?

And when all the celebrations are over, it remains only to pick up all the ornaments, all the accessories of the celebration, and by burning them, make a celebration.

This is Dondo-yaki. A Shinto blessing of the debris that has a right to immortality, like the dolls at Ueno. The last state before their disappearance, of the poignancy of things. Daruma, the one-eyed sprit, reigns supreme at the summit of the bonfire. Abandonment must be a feast, laceration must be a feast and the farewell all that one has lost, broken, used, must be ennobled by a ceremony. It's Japan that could fulfill the wish of that French writer who wanted divorce to be made a sacrament. The only baffling part of this ritual was the circle of children striking the ground with their long poles. I only got one explanation – a singular one – although for me it might take the form of a small intimate service: it was to chase away the moles.

And that's where my three children of Iceland came and grafted themselves in. I picked up the whole shot again, adding the somewhat hazy end, the frame trembling under the force of the wind beating us down on the cliff, everything I had cut in order to "tidy up" and that said better than the rest what I saw in that moment, why I held it at arm's length – at zoom's length – until its last 24th of a second. The city of Heimaey spread out below us, and when, five years later, my friend Haroun Tazieff sent me the film he had just shot in the same place, I lacked only the name to learn that nature performs its own Dondo-yakis. The island's volcano had awakened. I looked at those pictures, and it was as if the entire year '65 had just been covered with ashes.

So it sufficed to wait, and the planet itself staged the working of Time. I saw what had been my window again, I saw emerge from roofs and balconies, the landmarks of the walks I took through town every day down to the cliff where I had met the children. The cat with white socks that Haroun had been considerate enough to film for me naturally found its place, and I thought of all the prayers to Time that had studded this trip, the kindness of the one spoken by the woman at Go To Ku Ji who said simply to her cat Tora: *Cat, wherever you are, peace be with you.*

And then in its turn, the journey entered the Zone. Hayao showed me my images already affected by the moss of Time, freed of the lie that had prolonged the existence of those moments swallowed by the spiral.

Women, Homosexuals and Youth:
Latent Sexual Liberation

Kate Millett

A sexual revolution begins with the emancipation of women who are chief victims of patriarchy, and also with the ending of homosexual oppression. Part of the patriarchal family structure involves the control of the sexual life of children; indeed, the control of children totally. Children have virtually no rights guaranteed by law in our society and besides, they have no *money* which, in a money-economy, is one of the most important sources of their oppression. Certainly, one of children's essential rights is to express themselves sexually, probably primarily with each other but with adults as well. So the sexual freedom of children is an important part of the sexual revolution. How do we bring this about? The problem here is that when you have an exploitative situation between adults and children as you have between men and women, cross-generational relationships take place in a situation of inequality. Children are in a very precarious position when they enter into relationships with adults not only in a concrete material sense but emotionally as well because their personhood is not acknowledged in our society.

Mark Blasius: Do you think that a tender loving erotic relationship can exist between a boy and a man?

Kate Millet: Of course, or between a female child and an older woman. Men and women have loved each other for millennia, as have people of different races. What I'm concerned about is the inequitous context within which these relationships must exist. Of course, these relationships can be non-exploitative and considering the circumstances they are probably heroic and very wonderful; but we have to admit that they can be exploitative as well – like in the prostitution of youth.

Don't you think that the age of consent laws are barriers to exploring possibilities for non-exploitative cross-generational relationships and, more importantly, serve to further deny the right of youths to sexual expression?

Well, they were originally meant to protect the child from exploitation. But what's interesting is that the right to child sexuality is not being approached *initially* as the right of children to express themselves with each other, which was the issue in the 30's with early sexual liberationists. Instead, it's being approached as the right of men to have sex with kids below the age of consent and no mention is made of relationships between women and girls. It seems as though the principal spokespeople are older men and not youths.

That's probably because children and youths have no political voice. But most gay male youth groups seem to support a lowering or abolition of the age of consent as a first step. How prevalent are erotic relationships between women and girls, do you think?

In general, women are given more freedom than men within patriarchy to love across generations. But I don't see the correlative of the man/boy relationship existing in lesbian culture as I know it. There's a lot of cross-generational contact among lesbians and even heterosexual women – for example between older and younger women artists – but they're mainly as friendships or as mentor relationships. And cross-generational sexual relationships are more of a topic within the male homosexual movement than the female homosexual movement and women in the movement often condemn its advocates. As women, we're probably more protective of children. Also, having been exploited we're more sensitive to the possibility of exploitation – we've been minors all of our history. We're more sexually repressed than men, having been given a much more strict puritanical code of behavior than men have. Men engage in sexual activities that women often regard as promiscuous – it's as though men don't have the defenses that women have against mutual exploitation – against sexual use to the degree of abuse. So as women, we've experienced a great deal of sexual repression; at the same time, we're less exploitative. It's possible also that the conditioning of lesbians had been so repressive that it prevents them from seeing female people below the age of consent as sexual partners. There's still, I think, a holding back among lesbians from converting that Platonic/mentor relationship across generations into an erotic one because of the enormous and potentially catastrophic complications involved in doing so. Catastrophic not only in the personal sense but also in terms of the persecution inflicted by the outside world.

The dialogue about these issues within the lesbian and homosexual male movements raises very interesting issues. Have you thought about incest taboo as an issue taboo? I've always wondered about the power of the incest taboo because as child and adult sexuality reaches out to greater and greater freedoms, the proximity of family members make one experiment and challenge this taboo. The incest taboo has always been one of the cornerstones of patriarchal thought.

We have to have an emancipation proclamation for children. What is really at issue is children's rights and not, as it has been formulated up to now, as merely the right of sexual access to children.

But shouldn't one of the rights of children be that of choosing to have an erotic relationship with an older person?

Oh, sure, part of a free society would be that you could choose whomever you fancied, and children should be able to freely choose as well. But it's very hard to be free if you have no rights about anything, if you're subjected to endless violence – both physical and psychological, if you're already governed by a whole state system which demands that you put in forced attendance in school whether you want to be there or not. I would think that given the conditions under which you're a young person in this society, many things would be at least as important to you as sexuality.

It strikes me that there is a contradiction in supporting children's liberation while maintaining paternalistic age of consent laws and stigmatizing adults who have erotic relations with young people.

If you don't change all social condition of children you still have an inescapable inequity. That's like the story of the 1917 revolution. Men and women were declared equal one morning and everybody could divorce each other by postcard. It's just that the women had the babies and getting divorced by postcard when you've been given no means to earn a living and no education and you're in an enormously inferior economic situation meant that you were only being *declared* an equal while not being given the *substance* of equality.

I can see how gay youth groups would be very interested in abolishing the age of consent law because it must be very oppressive for them. But it just seems to me that this has been mainly an issue for older men rather than for gay youth.

The rhetoric of pedophilia – that of older men speaking out for the sexual freedom of boys – reflects the underlying powerlessness of children. One could say that is symptomatic of the powerlessness. Boy lovers are directly and acutely cognizant of social and economic conditions which crush kids. But it is these same conditions which prevent kids both from having real political visibility and from acting on their own behalf.

But what is our freedom fight about? Is it about the liberation of children or just having sex with them? I would like to see a broader movement involving young people who would be making the decisions because it's their issue and their fight. Their's is the authentic voice.

—

Ohio
Section 2907.01
Definitions
"Sexual conduct" means vaginal intercourse between male and female, and anal intercourse, fellatio, and cunnilingus between persons regardless of sex. Penetration, however slight, is sufficient to complete vaginal or anal intercourse.
"Sexual contact" means any touching of an erogenous zone of another, including without limitation the thigh, genitals, buttocks, pubic regions,

*or, if such person is female, a breast, for the purpose of sexual arousing
or gratifying either person.*

New Hampshire
Section 632-A:2
Aggravated Felonious Sexual Assault
*A person is guilty of a class A felony if he engages in sexual penetration
with another person under any of the following circumstances: When
the victim is thirteen years of age and the actor is a member of the same
household as the victim or is related by blood or affinity to the victim
or is in a position of authority over the victim and the actor used this
authority to coerce the victim to submit.*

The Exegesis
Chris Kraus

Entry 52 shows that Fat at this point in his life reached out for any wild hope which would shore up his confidence that some good existed somewhere.
—Philip K. Dick, Valis

3/4/95
Thurman

Dear Dick,

1. Some Incidents in the Life of a Slave Girl

How do you continue when the connection to the other person is broken (when the connection is broken to yourself)? To be in love with someone means believing that to be in someone else's presence is the only means of being, completely yourself.

And now it's Saturday morning and tomorrow I'll be 40 which makes this the last *Saturday Morning in Her 30s* to quote the title of an Eileen Myles and Alice Notley poem that I've thought of with a smile maybe 60 times while making phone calls, running errands during scattered Saturday mornings over the last ten years.

Yesterday afternoon I drove back here from New York. I was disoriented and confused (and I'm confused now, too, whether to address you in the declarative or narrative; that is, who'm I talking to?). I got back to New York on Tuesday night after spending those five days in LA "with" you. And then Sylvere and I spent Wednesday, Thursday, moving all our stuff from Second Avenue to Seventh Street. All through the move I was regretful, and I'm trying not to be regretful still.

In the late '70s when I was working in the New York topless bars there was this disco song that stayed around forever called Shame by Evelyn Champagne King. It was perfect for that time and place, evoking the emotion without owning it –

Shame!
What you do to me is shame
I'm only tryna ease the pain ..,
Deep in your arms
Is where I want to be

Cause shame was what we always felt, me and all my girlfriends, for expecting sex to breed complicity. ("Complicity is like a girl's name," writes Dodie Bellamy.)

"Is that what you wanted?" you asked me Friday morning. It was nearly 10. We'd been arguing in bed without our clothes for hours. And you'd just charitably, generously told me a sad story from your life to make amends for calling me a psychotic. To try and make things right, "Is that what you wanted? A ragged kind of intimacy?"

Well yes and no. "I'm just trying to be honest," I'd confessed to you that morning, and it sounded oh so lame. "Whenever someone makes a breakthrough into honesty," David Rattray'd said in an interview I'd arranged for him with the editor Ken Jordan, "that means not just self-knowledge but knowledge of what others can't see. To be honest in a real absolute way is to be almost prophetic, to upset the applecart." I was trying to promote his book and he was ranting in a way that made me cringe about his hatred for everyone who'd kept him down, who were out to silence "every bright young person who comes along with something original to say." The interview was made just three days before he collapsed on Avenue A with a massive and inoperable brain tumor.

"Because after all," I typed, following his deep and unmistakable patrician voice, "the applecart is just an endless series of indigestible means and social commitments that are useless and probably shouldn't even be honored and futile pointless conversations, gestures, and finally to die abandoned, treated like a piece of garbage by people in white coats who are no more civilized than sanitation workers ... that's what the applecart means to me."

Shame is what you feel after being fucked on quaaludes by some artworld cohort who'll pretend it never happened, shame is what you feel after giving blowjobs in the bathroom at Max's Kansas City because Liza Martin wants free coke. Shame is what you feel after letting someone take you someplace past control – then feeling torn up three days later between desire, paranoia, etiquette wondering if they'll call. Dear Dick, you told me twice last weekend how much you love John Rechy's books and you wish your writing could include more sex. Because I love you and you can't or you're embarrassed, maybe this is something I can do for you?

At any rate in order not to feel this hopelessness, regret, I've set myself the job of solving heterosexuality (i.e. finishing this writing project) before turning 40. And that's tomorrow.

Because suddenly it seemed, after arriving from LA, jetlagged and moving boxes between apartments, that there was so much more to understand and say. Was this the bottom of the snakepit? In the restaurant Monday night we talked about our favorite Fassbinder movie, *The Bitter Tears of Petra Von Kant*. I was wearing a white long-sleeved tailored shirt, looking pointedly demure, the whore's curveball, and I felt like suddenly I'd understood something. "Fassbinder was such an ugly man," I said. "That's the real subject of his films: an ugly man who was wanting, looking to be loved."

The subtext rested on the table in between us like the sushi. Because of course I was ugly too. And the way you took this in, understanding it without any explication, made me realize how everything that's passed between us all came back to sex and ugliness and identity.

"You were so wet," Dick _'d said to me in the bar that Monday night about the sex we'd had on Thursday. My heart opened and I fell beneath the polite détente that we'd established in the restaurant, your black, Italian jacket, my long-sleeved buttoned shirt. Were you seducing me again or just alluding to things I'd written in my manifesto *Every Letter is a Love Letter* which you'd finally read that afternoon? I didn't quite know how to take this. But then Dick glanced brusquely at his watch and turned to look at someone else across the room. And then I knew you never wanted to have sex with me again.

I came back devastated by the weekend, begging Sylvère to give me some advice. Even though his theoretical side is fascinated by how this correspondence, love affair, has sexualized and changed me all his other sides are angry and confused. So can I blame him when he responded like a cut-rate therapist? "You'll never learn!" he said. "You keep looking for rejection! It's the same problem that you've always had with men!" But I believe this problem's bigger and more cultural.

We looked great together Monday night walking into the Ace of Diamonds Bar. Both of us tall and anorexic and our jackets matched. "Here comes the Mod Squad," the barman said. All the regulars looked up from their beers. How hilarious. You're a mod and I'm a modernist. "Buy you a drink?" "Sure." And then suddenly I'm back in 1978 at the Nightbirds Bar, drinking-smoking-flirting, shooting sloppy pool with my then-boyfriend Ray Johannson. Ha ha ha. "You can't sit on the pool table! You've gotta keep both legs on the floor!" Within minutes of arriving we trashed the whole agreement of mature neutrality we'd worked out in the sushi bar. You were flirting with me, anything seemed possible. Back to English rules.

Later, legs pressed close under one of those tiny barroom table we were talking one more time about our favorite ghost, David Rattray. And I wanted to explain how I made allowances for David's bad behavior, all those years on alcohol and heroin, how he got bigger while his wife who'd been on the scene with him shrank until she nearly disappeared. "He was part of the generation that ruined women's lives," I told you. "It's not just that generation," you replied. "Men still do ruin women's lives." And at that time I didn't answer, had no opinion, took it in.

But at 3 a.m. last Wednesday night I bolted up in bed, reaching for my laptop. I realized you were right.

"J'ACCUSE" (I started typing) "Richard Schechner."

Richard Schechner is a Professor of Performance Studies at New York University, author of Environmental Theater and several other books on anthropology and theater and editor of The Drama Review. He was once my acting teacher. And at 3 a.m. last Wednesday night it occurred to me that Richard Schechner had ruined my life.

And so I'd write this broadside rant and wheatpaste it all around Richard's neighborhood and NYU. I'd dedicate it to the artist Hannah Wilke. Because while Hannah's tremendous will to turn the things that

bothered her into subjects for her art seemed so embarrassing in her life
time, at 3 a.m. it dawned on me that Hannah Wilke is a model for
everything I hope to do.

"J'ACCUSE RICHARD SCHECHNER who through SLEEP DEP-
RIVATION amateur GESTALT THERAPY and SEXUAL MANIPU-
LATION attempted to exert MIND CONTROL over a group of 10
students in Washington DC."

Well, it was a plan. And at that moment I believed in it as strongly
as the plan Sylvere and I made one night on 7th Street when I was so
depressed and he joined me in my suicide attempt. We each drank some
wine and took two percosets and decided to read Chapter 73 of Julio
Cortazar's book *Hopscotch* out loud into your answer phone. "Yes but
who will cure us of the dull fire, the colorless fire that at nightfall runs
along the rue de la Huchette..." At the time it seemed so daring, apropos
and brilliant but Dick, like most conceptual art, delirium can get so
referential.

At Richard Schechner's Aboriginal Dream Time Workshop in
Washington DC, he and I were the only people in the group who got
up before the crack of noon. We drank coffee, shared the *Post* and *New
York Times* and talked about politics and world events. Like us, Richard
had some kinds of politics and in that group I was the only other
person interested in the news. I was a Serious Young Woman, hunched
and introspective, running to the library to check out books about the
Aborigines – too dumb to realize in that situation that the Aborigines
were totally beside the point.

Richard seemed to like our morning conversations about Brecht
and Althusser and Andre Gorz, but later on he turned the group against
me for being too cerebral and acting like a boy. And weren't all these
passionate interests and convictions just evasions of a greater truth, my
cunt? I was an innocent, a de-gendered freak, cause unlike Liza Martin,
who was such a babe she refused to take her platforms off for Kundalini
Yoga, I hadn't learned the trick of throwing sex into the mix.

And so on Perilous Journey Night I went downtown and took my
clothes off in a topless bar. Shake shake shake. That same night Marsha
Peabody, an overweight suburban schizophrenic who Richard'd let into
the group because schizophrenia, like Aboriginal Dream Time, breaks

down the continuum between space and time, decided to go off her medication. Richard spent Perilous Journey Night on the football field behind the changing sheds getting a blowjob from Maria Calloway. Maria wasn't in our group. She'd come all the way from NYC to study with Richard Schechner but she'd been shunted into Leah's workshop on Body/Sound because she wasn't a "good enough" performer. The next day Marsha disappeared and no one asked or heard from her again. Richard encouraged me and Liza Martin to work together in New York. I gave up my cheap apartment and moved into Liza's Tribeca loft, topless dancing several nights a week to pay her rent. I was investigating the rift between thought and sex or so I thought, letting lawyers smell my pussy while I talked. This went on for several years and Dick, on Wednesday night I woke up realizing you were right. Men still *do* ruin women's lives. As I turn 40 can I avenge the ghost of my young self?

To see yourself as who you were ten years ago can be very strange indeed.

On Thursday afternoon I walked over to the Film/Video Arts on Broadway to make a copy of the videotape of *Readings from the Diaries of Hugo Ball*, a performance piece I'd staged in 1983.

Though he's remembered as the person who "invented" Dada at Zurich's Cabaret Voltaire in 1917, Ball's art activities lasted only about two years. All the other years were fractured, restless. He was a theater student, factory worker, circus attendant, journalist for a leftist weekly and amateur theologian chronicling the "hierarchy of angels" before his death of stomach cancer at age 41. Ball and his companion Emmy Hennings, a cabaret performer, puppet maker, novelist and poet, zigzagged across Switzerland and Germany for 20 years recanting and revising their beliefs. They had no steady source of income. They moved around Europe looking for the perfect low-rent base where they could live cheap and work in peace. They broke with Tristan Tzara because they couldn't understand his careerism – why spend your life promoting one idea? – and were it not for the publication of Ball's diaries, *Flight Out of Time*, all traces of their lives probably would've disappeared.

Morphine
What we are waiting for is one last fling
At the dizzy height of each passing day
We dread the sleepless dark and cannot pray.
Sunshine we hate, it doesn't mean a thing.

We never pay attention to the mail,
The pillow we sometimes favor with a silent
All-knowing smile, between fits of violent
Activity to shake the fever chill.

Let others join the struggle to survive
We rush helplessly forward through this life,
Dead to the world, dreaming on our feet.
The blackness just keeps coming down in sheets.

Emmy Hemmings wrote this poem in 1916 and Dick, it was just so thrilling to discover there were people in the past like Ball and Hemmings, making art without any validation or career plans when my friends and I were living in the East Village, New York City in 1983.

Reading about them saved my life, and so to stage the diaries I invited the nine most interesting people that I knew to comb through Ball and Henning's writings for the parts that best described themselves. There were the poets Bruce Andrews, Danny Krakauer, Steve Levine and David Rattray. There were the performers Leonora Champagne and Linda Hartinian, the actress Karen Young, the art critic Gert Schiff and me.

And since three of these nine people are dead now, and since I'd recently read Mick Tausig's account of Ball in his book *The Nervous System* (who regrets the historical absence of Dadaist women, but doesn't look too hard to find them – Dear Dick, Dear Mick, I'm just an amateur but I found three: Emmy Hennings, Hannah Hoch and Sophie Tauber) I wanted to take another look at the play.

As instigator of the piece I played the role of hostess/tour guide, giving my friends a chance to speak and filling in the expository holes. To do this I stole the character Gabi Teisch, a German high school history teacher created by Alexandra Kluge for her brother's film *The Patriot*. Because she is unhappy in the present, Gabi Teisch decides to excavate the whole of German history to find out what went wrong. I was unhappy too. And until we own our history, she thought, I thought, there can be no change.

To get into the role I found a sensible tweed skirt flecked with tiny rhinestones and a long-sleeved lacy blouse: a costume that reminded me of an arcane archetype, the Hippie Intellectual Highschool Teacher, of her, of me.

So on Thursday afternoon I stood around the Film/Video Arts dub room watching myself at 28 as Gabi Teisch: a scarecrow with bad hair, bad skin, bad teeth, slouched underneath the weight of all this information, every word an effort but one worth making because there was just so much to say.

To perform yourself inside a role is very strange. The clothes, the words, prod you into nameless areas and then you stretch them out in front of other people, live.

Chris/Gabi was a mess, persona-less, trying to lose herself in talking. Her eyes were open but afraid, locked in neutral, not knowing whether to look in or out. While she was in rehearsal for the play, Chris/Chris had started having sadomasochistic sex with the downtown Manhattan luminary Sylvère Lotringer. This happened about twice a week at lunchtime and it was very confusing. Chris would arrive at Sylvère's Front Street loft after doing errands on Canal Street, She'd be ushered into Sylvère's bedroom, walls lined with books and African water bags and whips and he'd push her down unto the bed with all her clothes on. He held her, squeezed her tits until she came. He never let her touch him, often he wouldn't even fuck her and after awhile she stopped wondering who this person even was, revolving on his bed deeper through time tunnels into memories of childhood. Love and fear and glamour. Browsing through his books she realized she was up against some pretty stiff competition, reading some of the inscriptions: "To Sylvère, The Best Fuck in the World (At Least to My Knowledge) Love, Kathy Acker." Afterwards they'd eat clam soup and talk about the Frankfurt School. Then he showed her to the door ...

So what was Chris performing? At that moment she was a picture of the Serious Young Woman thrown off the rails, exposed, alone, androgynous and hovering onstage between the poet-men, presenters of ideas, and actress-women, presenters of themselves. She wasn't beautiful like the women; unlike the men, she had no authority. Watching Chris/Gabi I hated her and wanted to protect her. Why couldn't the world I'd moved around in since my teens, the underground, just let this person be?

"You are not beautiful but you are very intelligent," the Mexican gigolo says to the 38 year old New York Jewish heroine of the film *A Winter Tan*. And of course it's at that moment that you know he's going to kill her.

All acts of sex were forms of degradation. Some random recollections: East 11th Street, on the bed with Murray Gorman: "Swallow this mother 'til you choke." East 11th Street, in the bed with Gary Becker: "The trouble with you is, you're such a shallow person." East 11th Street, up against the wall with Peter Baumann: "The only thing that turns me on about you is pretending you're a whore." Second Avenue, the kitchen, Michael Wainwright: "Quite frankly, I deserve a better-looking, better educated girlfriend." What do you do with the Serious Young Woman (short hair, flat shoes, body slightly hunched, head drifting back and forth between the books she's read)? You slap her, fuck her up the ass and treat her like a boy. The Serious Young Woman looked everywhere for sex but when she got it it became an exercise in disintegration. What was the motivation of these men? Was it hatred she evoked? Was it some kind of challenge, trying to make the Serious Young Woman femme?

2. The Birthday Party

Inside out
 Boy you turn me
 Upside down and
 Inside Out ...
  Late '70s disco song

Joseph Kosuth's 50th birthday party last January was reported the next day on *Page 6* of the *New York Post*. And everything was just as perfect as they said: about 100 guests, a number large enough to fill the room but small enough for each of us to feel among the intimates, the chosen. Joseph and Cornelia and their child had just arrived from Belgium; Marshall Blonsky, one of Joseph's closest friends and Joseph's staff had been planning it for weeks.

Sylvère and I drove down from Thurman. I dropped him off outside the loft, parked the car and arrived at Joseph's door at the same moment as another woman, also entering alone. Each of us gave our names to Joseph's doorman. Each of us had names that weren't there. "Check Lotringer," I said. "Sylvère." And sure enough, I was Sylvère Lotringer's "Plus One" and she was someone else's. Riding up the elevator, checking makeup, collars, hair, she whispered, "The last thing you want to feel before walking into one of these things is that you're not invited," and we smiled and wished each other luck and parted at the coat-check. But luck was something that I didn't feel much need of because I had no expectations: this was Joseph's party, Joseph's friends, people, (mostly men, except for female art dealers and us plus-ones) from the early 80s art world, so I expected to be patronized and ignored.

Drinks were at one end of the loft; dinner at the other. David Bryne was wandering across the room as tall as a Moorish king in a magnificent fur hat. I stood next to Kenneth Broomfield at the bar and a said a tentative hello; he hissed and turned away. A tightened grip around the scotch-glass, standing there in my Japanese wool dress, high heels, and makeup …

But look! There's Marshall Blonsky! Marshall greets me at the bar and says that seeing me reminds him of the party we attended some 11 years ago when I was Marshall's date. And of course he would remember because the party was given by Xavier Foucade to celebrate the publication of Marshall's fist book *On Signs* at Xavier's Sutton Place townhouse. It was late winter, early spring, Aquarius or Pisces and I remember guests tripping past the caterers and staff to walk around the green expanse of daffodils and bunny lawn that separated us from the river. David Salle was there, Umberto Eco was there, together with a stable load of Foucade's models and a reviewer from the New York Times.

At that time I was living in a tenement on Second Avenue and studying charm as a possible escape. Could I be Marshall Blonsky's perfect date? I'd given up trying to be as sexual as Liza Martin but I was small boned, thin, with a New Zealand accent trailing off to something that sounded vaguely mid-Atlantic. Perhaps something could be done with this? By then I'd read enough that no one guessed I'd never been to school. Marshall and I'd been introduced by our mutual friend Louise Bourgeois. I loved her and he was fascinated by her iron will and growing fame. "It is the ability to sublimate that makes an artist," she told me once. And: "The only hope for you is marrying a critic or academic. Otherwise, you'll starve." And in the interest of saving me from poverty, Louise had given me, for this occasion, the perfect dress: a straight wool-boucle pumpkin-colored shift, historically important, the dress she'd worn accompanying Robert Rauschenberg to his first opening on East 10th ... Most of Marshall's friends were men – critics, psychoanlysts, semioticians – and he liked that he could walk me round the room and I'd perform for them, listening, cracking jokes in their own special languages, guiding the conversation back to Marshall's book. So French New Wave ... Being weightless and gamine, spitting prettily at rules and institutions, a talking dog without the dreariness of a position to defend.

Dear Dick, It hurts me that you think I'm "insincere." Nick Zedd and I were both interviewed once about our films for English television. Everyone in New Zealand who saw the show told me how they like Nick better because he was more sincere. Nick was just one thing, a straight clear line: *Whoregasm*, East Village gore 'n porn, and I was several. And-and-and. And isn't sincerity just the denial of complexity? You as Johnny Cash driving your Thunderbird into the Heart of Light. What puts me off experimental film world feminism, besides all its boring study groups on Jacques Lacan, was its sincere investigation into the dilemma of the Pretty Girl. As an Ugly Girl it didn't matter much to me. And didn't Donna Haraway finally solve this by saying all female lived experience is a bunch of riffs completely fake, so we should recognize ourselves as Cyborgs? But still the fact remains: You moved out to the desert on your own to clear the junk out of your life. You're skeptical of irony. You are trying to find some way of living you believe in. I envy this.

Jane Bowles described this problem of sincerity in a letter to her husband Paul, the "better" writer:

August 1947:

> *Dearest Bupple,*
>
> *... The more I get into it ... the more isolated I feel vis-a-vis the writers whom I consider to be of any serious mind ... I am enclosing this article entitled New Heroes by Simone de Beauvoir ... Read the sides that are marked pages 121 and 123. It is what I have been thinking at the bottom of my mind all this time and God knows it is difficult to write the way I do and yet think their way. This problem you will never have to face because you have always been a truly isolated person so that whatever you write will be true which is not so in my case.... You immediately receive recognition because what you write is in true relation to yourself which is always recognizable to the world outside.... With me who knows? When you are capable only of a serious approach to writing as I am it is almost more than one can bear to be continually doubting one's sincerity....*

Reading Jane Bowles' letters makes me angrier and sadder than anything to do with you. Because she was just so brilliant and she was willing to take a crack at it – telling the truth about her difficult and contradictory life. And because she got it right. Even though, like the artist Hannah Wilke, in her own lifetime she hardly found anybody to agree with her. You're the Cowboy, I'm the Kike. Steadfast and true, slippery and devious. We aren't anything but our circumstances. Why is it men become essentialists, especially in middle age?

And at Joseph's party time stands still and we can do it again. Marshall walks me over to two men in suits, a Lacanian and a world banker from the UN. We talk about Microsoft and Bill Gates and Timothy Leary's brunches in LA until a tall and immaculately gorgeous WASP woman joins us and the conversation parts away from jokes about interest rates and transference to make room for Her.

(As I write this I feel very hopeless and afraid)

Later Marshall made an academic birthday speech for Joseph that he'd been scribbling on all night. And Glenn O'Brien, looking like Steve Allen at the piano, performed a funny scat-singing recitative about Joseph's legendary womanizing, wealth, and art. Everybody clapping, laughing, camp but serious and boozy like in the film *The Girl Can't Help It*, men in suits playing TV beatniks but where's Jayne Mansfield as the fall girl? Then David Byrne and John Cale played piano and guitar and people danced.

Sylvère got drunk and teased Diego, something about politics, and Diego got mad and tossed his drink in Sylvère's face. And Warren Niesluchowski was there, and John and Anya. Later Marshall marshalled a gang of little men, the banker, the Lacanian, and Sylvère, to the cardroom to drink scotch and talk about the Holocaust. The four looked like the famous velvet painting of card-playing dogs.

And it got late and someone turned on some vintage disco, and all the people young enough never to've heard these songs the first time got up and danced. *Funky Town*, *The Freak is Chic* and *Inside Out* ... the songs that played in topless clubs and bars in the late 70s while these men were getting famous. While me and all my friends, the girls, were paying for our rent and shows and exploring "issues of our sexuality" by shaking to them all night long in topless bars.

Gabi Teisch's life was very hard.

She hardly slept or ate, she forgot to comb her hair. The more she studied, the harder it became to speak or know anything with certainty. People were afraid of her; she forgot how to teach her classes. She became that word that people use to render difficult and driven women weightless: Gabi Teisch was "quirky."

On New Year's Eve in Germany, 1977 it was snowing very hard. Gabi Teisch invited several of her women friends around to celebrate the holiday. The camera keeps it's distance, circling around the table of drinking smoking laughing talking women. It's happiness. A bright island in the snowy night. A real cabal.

This morning it's my birthday and I drove out to Garnet Lake.

Upstate March is the moodiest, most desolate time of year. February's glistening cold becomes unsettled. Water in the streams and brooks begins to move under melting ice: stand outside and you can hear it rushing. The Torrents of Spring. But the sky's completely gray and everybody knows the snow'll be around at least until the end of April. The weather's dull, resentful. I drove out through Thurman, Kenyon-town, past the "burnt-down store" (a landmark and epistomological joke – in order for it to mean anything you would've had to be here 20 years ago when the store was standing), the Methodist church and schoolhouse where as recently as 30 years ago local kids between the ages of 5 and 17 arrived by foot and horse from within an 8 mile radius. "What do you consider to be the greatest achievement of your life?" a teenager from the Thurman Youth Group asked George Mosher, a 72 year old trapper, farmer, handyman and logger. "Staying here," George said. "Within two miles of where I was born." Dear Dick, The southern Adirondacks make it possible to understand the Middle Ages.

There were two guys out ice fishing on Garnet Lake, skinny speckled fish, pickering or mackerel. My long black coat open, dragging through the snow as I walked around the lake's perimeter. When I was 12 it occurred to me for the first time it might be possible to have an interesting life. Yesterday when I phoned Renee up over at the trailer to find out if her brother Chet might be able to come over and unfreeze the kitchen pipes she said Yeah, but I don't want to put a time on it because I'm high.

In all the books about the 19th century New England Transcendentalist Margaret Fuller they tell this story about her and the English critic George Carlyle. When she was 45 she ran away to join the Italian liberal revolution of 1853 and fell in love with Garibaldi. "I accept the universe," Margaret Fuller wrote in a letter postmarked out of Italy. "Well she'd better," Carlyle replied. She was drifting further and further on a raft out into the Caspian Sea. Today I'm going to New York,

Love,
Chris

Becoming-Woman
Félix Guattari

In the global social field, homosexualities function somewhat as movements, chapels with their own ceremony, their initiation rights, their
myths of love as Renée Nelli puts it. Despite the intervention of groupings of a more or less corporatist nature like Arcadia, homosexuality
continues to be tied to the values and interactional systems of the
dominant sexuality. Its dependence in regard to the heterosexual norm
is manifested in a politics of the secret, a hiddenness, nourished by
repression as well as by a feeling of shame still lively in "respectable"
milieus (particularly among businessmen, writers, show-biz people etc.)
in which psychoanalysis is presently the reigning master. It enforces a
second degree norm, no longer moral, but scientific. Homosexuality is
no longer a moral matter, but a matter of perversion. Psychoanalysis
makes an illness of it, a developmental retardation, a fixation at the pre-
genital stage, etc.

On another, smaller and more avant-garde level is found militant
homosexuality, of the FHAR type. Homosexuality confronts heterosexual power on its own terrain. Now heterosexuality must account for
itself; the problem is displaced, phallocratic power tends to be put into
question; in principle, a conjunction between the actions of feminists
and homosexuals then becomes possible.

However, we should perhaps distinguish a third level, a more molecular one in which categories, groupings and "special instances" would
not be differentiated in the same way, in which clear cut oppositions
between types would be repudiated, in which, on the contrary, one would
look for similarities among homosexuals, transvestites, drug addicts,
sado-masochists, prostitutes, among women, men, children, teenagers,
among psychotics, artists, revolutionaries, let's say among all forms of
sexual minorities once it is understood that in this realm there can only

be minorities. For example, it could be said at the same time 1) that all forms of sexuality, all forms of sexual activity are fundamentally on this side of the personological homo-hetero oppositions; 2) that, nonetheless, they are closer to homosexuality and to what could be called a feminine becoming.

On the level of the social body, libido is caught in two systems of opposition: class and sex. It is expected to be male, phallocratic, it is expected to dichotomize all values – the oppositions strong/weak, rich/poor, useful/useless, clean/dirty, etc.

Conversely, on the level of the sexed body, libido is engaged in becoming-woman. More precisely, the becoming-woman serves as a point of reference, and eventually as a screen for other types of becoming (example: becoming-child in Schumann, becoming-animal in Kafka, becoming-vegetable in Novalis, becoming-mineral in Beckett).

Becoming-woman can play this intermediary role, this role as mediator vis-a-vis other sexed becomings, because it is not too far removed from the binarism of phallic power. In order to understand the homosexual, we tell ourselves that it is sort of "like a woman." And a number of homosexuals themselves join in this somewhat normalizing game. The pair feminine/passive, masculine/active therefore remains a point of reference made obligatory by power in order to permit it to situate, localize, territorialize, control intensities of desire. Outside of this exclusive bi-pole, no salvation: or else it's the plunge into the nonsensical, to the prison, to the asylum, to psychoanalysis, etc. Deviants, various forms of marginalization, are themselves coded to work as safety values. Women, in short, are the only official trusteés of a becoming-sexed body. A man who detaches himself from the phallic types inherent in all powerful nations will enter such a becoming-woman according to diverse possible modalities. It is only on this condition, moreover, that he will be able to become animal, cosmos, letter, color, music.

Homosexuality, by the very nature of things, cannot be disassociated from becoming-woman – even non-oedipal, non-personological homosexuality. The same holds true for infantile sexuality, psychotic sexuality, poetic sexuality (for instance: the coincidence, in Allen Ginsberg's work, of a fundamental poetic mutation together with a sexual mutation). In a more general way, every "dissident" organization of libido must therefore be directly linked to a becoming-feminine body, as an escape route from the repressive socius, as a possible access to a "minimum" of sexed becoming, and as the last buoy vis-a-vis the established order. I emphasize this last point because the becoming-feminine body shouldn't be thought of as belonging to the woman category found in the couple, the family, etc. Such a category only exists in a specific field that defines it. There is no such thing as woman per se, no maternal pole, no eternal feminine....The man/woman opposition serves as a foundation to the social order, before class and caste conflicts intervene. Conversely, whatever shatters norms, whatever breaks from the established order, is related to homosexuality or a becoming-animal or a becoming-woman, etc. Every semiotization in rupture implies a sexualization in rupture. Thus, to my mind, we shouldn't ask which writers are homosexual, but rather, what it is about a great writer – even if he is in fact heterosexual – that is homosexual.

I think it's important to destroy "big" notions like woman, homosexual.... Things are never that simple. When they're reduced to black-white, male-female categories, there's an ulterior motive, a binary-reductionist operation meant to subjugate them. For example, you cannot qualify a love univocally. Love in Proust is never specifically homosexual. It always has a schizoid, paranoid component, a becoming-plant, a becoming-woman, a becoming-music.

Orgasm is another over-blown notion whose ravages are incalculable. Dominant sexual morality requires of the woman a quasi-hysterical indentification of her orgasm with the man's, an expression of symmetry, a submission to his phallic power. The woman owes her orgasm to the man. In "refusing" him, she assumes the guilt. So many stupid dramas are based on this theme. And the sententious attitude of psychoanalysis and sexologists on this point doesn't really help. In fact, it frequently happens that women who, for some reason or other, are frozen with male partners achieve orgasm easily by masturbating or having sex with another woman. But the scandal would be much worse if everything were out in the open. Let's consider a final example, the prostitute movement. Everyone, or just about, at first yelled "Hurrah, prostitutes are right to rebel. But wait, you should separate the good from the bad. Prostitutes, OK, but pimps, people don't want to hear about them." And so, prostitutes were told that they should defend themselves, that they're being exploited, etc. All that is absurd. Before explaining anything whatsoever, one should first try to understand what goes on between a whore and her pimp. There's the whore-pimp money triangle. But there also is a whole micropolitics of desire, extremely complex, which is played out between each pole in this triangle and various characters like the John and the cop. Prostitutes surely have very interesting things to teach us about these questions. And, instead of persecuting them, it would be better to subsidize them as they do in research laboratories. I'm convinced, personally, that in studying all this micropolitics of prostitution, one might shed some new light on whole areas of conjugal and familial micropolitics – the money relations between husband and wife, parents and children, and ultimately, the psychoanalyst and his patient. (We should all recall what the anarchists of the turn of the century wrote on this subject.)

Translated by Rachel McComas and Stamos Metzidakis

LIFE IN THESE UNITED STATES

Home Training to Crash Pad
Tisa Bryant

home training

    I never had a chance to rue the day I grew tall enough to reach the kitchen sink. At seven, my mother gave me a crate to stand on. Maybe she saw my path. I was already predisposed to redecorating the room I shared with my brother. He'd come in from playing and find his bed moved, the dresser realigned, a new strip of masking tape dividing the configuration. I'd give him a quick orientation. He couldn't have cared less. My mother always cleaned his side of the room anyway. In evenings after dinner she instructed me on plate washing, how to remove food stuck between fork tines, to arrange the dishes in the rack and pour scalding hot water over them for a final, soap free rinse. When my mother started working nights, she'd find the dishes done by her little elf in the morning. My weekend chores were to vacuum and dust, to polish the bar and all its contents after making my bed with expert hospital corners, cleaning my room. Wiping down bottles of gin, olive jars, bitters, brandy snifters, highballs were the highlight of it all. It seemed so glamorous, the fancy shaped glasses, the multi-colored liquids. My brother would dawdle until my mother told him to beat it. I strove to be the perfect Junior Miss, asked to help, asked for more. "Did I do a good job?"
(Do you love and accept me now, in this clean and shining moment?)

playing house

    After my mother, or girl cousin-babysitter inspected my work and found it satisfactory, I was free to go to my desk and play with Lite-Brite.

I'd push transparent colored pegs through stenciled black paper and into a grill of holes, creating a pleasing neon-like picture (clown, house, flower) lit from behind by a 75-watt bulb, a proto-monitor for kids. I was a born recruit.

In addition to real chores, my little girly life in Domestic Boot Camp was laden with the appropriate tools for more "play": Baby Alive, who ate and went poo; an E-Z Bake Oven and forty-piece tea set; a giant Black Barbie head with non-toxic make-up, combs and hair curlers. I had a Shoppin' Sheryl doll, a thunder-thick baby haus frau, who "walked" guided by my hand down the grocery aisle. When I pushed the button on her back, her magnetized right palm "grabbed" little realistically branded groceries off the shelves. When I released the button, she dropped the items into the shopping cart she gripped with her left. My dad growled for hours as he helped me put together the shelves that made the aisles, fold and label the boxes and cans, stick magnets on them all and place them on the wobbly shelves, only to see the force of the doll's hand destroy everything in one fell swoop. Shoppin' Sheryl soon became an outlet for repressed sex-role rage, as she not only wreaked havoc in her toy supermarket, she could also knock my brother's G.I. Joe flat with a single whack to the head. However, I do recall actually begging for these "toys," which, beyond the financial terror they created, and the fist-fights with my brother as he raided my E-Z Bake catered tea parties, must have pleased my mother to no end.

(Bend. Stretch. Reach. Like us like us like us. Cut like this, serve like that. Pour from the left. Stretch. The walls are at your sides, feminine curvings, this crack is yours to fill. Repeat the exercises of your days, like this, like this, like this. Bow to this synchronized womanhood. This is the proper stroke, here, between the lines. See power. See darkness. You are here.)

I read indiscriminately at an early age, from my mom's bodice-rippers like *Cashelmara* to my dad's copy of *Naked Lunch* swiped from their bed's headboard bookcase (latch-key kids *are* smarter), but somehow "toys" were different. I didn't want robots, like my brother, probably because I was already becoming one, adapting by rote to the tasks assigned to my sex. Mother's Little Helper. And how else would she get help besides training her progeny? Are there mothers now who teach their daughters the finer points of day trading, product marketing, chemical engineering? If so, who's mopping the floor? Hazel? Maria-Luisa? Dad? My grandmother cleaned kitchens, took in sewing, to keep the family living. My mother said, "Never." My grandmother must have thought, "Well, that's the point," but I'm not privy to such conversations. West Indian families like mine lived by the unspoken rule of ambitious pragmatism. My Gram was trained to be a paralegal, but she never got the chance to work in that field. Discriminating tastes overruled her desires, and touch-typing was replaced by scrubbing floors. She, in turn, trained my mother to keep house, who then learned to keypunch after high school. Data entry and other clerical functions was the field Black women were shunted into during the 60s and 70s, after someone else's kitchen and cash crops, after white women moved on to higher paying jobs. My Gram's fingers absently tapped steno key beats on the armrest while she read the Bible and made "casual" comments about dusty furniture. I kept my room clean and the coffee table gleaming, ever watchful for the slight aimed at me through my mother. Later I learned to keypunch in a 7th grade computer class. My mother and I bonded momentarily over my homework, the stacks of long rectangular colored cards scientifically punched to correspond with letters and numbers. "A single medical record could take a hundred cards, depending on how much information has to be stored," she said. I felt proud for a moment. Busing, then a final move "up" to home owning in the sticks had made this moment, this acquisition of knowledge, possible. I was following in a family tradition, something reserved for us, a way of fulfilling my grandmother's promise.

(O dutiful womanhood, how I tried, still try, to be a good girl in my mother's image, to work hard within the cracks of the broken mold.

A promenade of women holding mirrors, Suppliers of Knowledge, showing me how to give, never speaking of the cost of doing so, never fully revealing the chain of hands that take and take, the fingers fearing reprisal, starvation. Not faceless, not unnamed. Mother. Auntie. Cousin. Friend. Showing me the ropes, the cords of care never ever really cut. Are those my wrists, my flexing thumbs, catching the flow-chart marked in red, the paper towels, the dry-erase pens? Familiar as a mother's skin, or a monotonous task, this constant flipping of palms. Dropping into. Catching. Tasks. How we became grown, our skill sets set in stone.)

home training 2

I had no choice but to help my mother. No one else would in the way she needed. By my mid-teens, I took care of my baby sister (9 years younger), did the dishes, the laundry, cleaned the house, started dinner after school (unless I was working) while my brother was out shooting hoops or whatever. My mum's response to my contributions to the functioning of the household ranged from a muted 'thank you,' to "That's what you're *supposed* to do." I resented it, especially during the summer when I was supposed to be on vacation from school, from everything, and I let my mother know.

"She's not my kid, she's yours."

"I gotta work."

"You knew that when you had her."

"Knew that when I had you."

"Too late now, ain't it. So what am I supposed to do? You act like this is the Depression or something, and you got eight brats."

"What am I supposed to do, you ungrateful little bitch?"

"Is this what you want for me, to be a housewife?"

"I want you to be responsible and independent. "If you knew how to drive–"

"I wouldn't have a car because I can't afford one because I work here for you, for them, not for me. And like you'd let me drive yours. Ya right. I'd drive you to work, then pick you up. I'd be Dad and you."

"You miserable wretch. What the hell do you want from me, huh? Christ almighty..."

"Looks like the same thing you want from me."

We stood there, nostrils flaring, chests out, heads raised, ready to really throw down, tears in our eyes, my Mum's ham fists quivering at her rock-hard thighs. She could have killed me and gotten it over with, but she needed me too much at that moment, or, more likely, didn't want to go to jail, and she did love me, after all. I was her inheritance, and she was mine. We were all we had, and hated the fact that if she didn't keep the house together, it would fall apart, and if I didn't help her, she would. The men in our family, father and brother, were no help, not in this area. Other girls I knew were off gallivanting at camps or hanging out at the beach, or working. How they managed their house-hold responsibilities was a mystery to us. We were stuck. It amazes me how we two formidable mouths and bodies didn't demand participation from the other two people who generated dirt and housework, my brother and father. My mother and I had silently and tacitly agreed it was out of the question, not worth the hassle, or the inevitable training, supervision, ruined clothes, dishes, etc. So, after I demanded it, my mother paid me for my services, although less than she would've paid an outside person. I feel kind of bad about that now, but at the time my actions were and still are in line with my responsibility to myself to confront The Boss, no matter how difficult, at the slightest indignity, even if The Boss was my mother. That was how I was raised. Yet keeping this in practice became increasingly difficult. I only knew about these kinds of cut-and-dry, straight-up situations with my no-nonsense mother. I knew nothing about the kinds of manipulative, head-trip dynamics that were to come and build a pyramid on my head.

power (prelude)

For my first paying job outside home, I had to apply for "working papers" because I was 14 and underage. I slung pizza and bussed tables at Papa Gino's, a medium-sized chain of restaurants in mostly Metro Boston and points southwest. Punctuality, efficiency, team work, money were the orders of the day. There was only one other Black girl, Heidi, working there besides me. Six months or so into the job, a new manager came on board, replacing the one who trained us. On his second day he said Heidi and I lacked experience and had to prove our skills. He cut our hours from 15–20 per week to 5 or less. This went on for 2 months; we worked hard under his scrutiny without the reward of more shifts. We were pissed. It wasn't worth the walk to work after school, and not worth the point: cash for clothes, school supplies, and that life-or-death line item, hair products. We told our mothers. They were pissed, too. "It never fails," my mother growled. "Samo shit." We went to the Massachusetts Council Against Discrimination and filed a complaint, threatening to sue. In the end Heidi and I won back our lost wages, then we quit, which from two hours a week, was simply a symbolic gesture. The offending manager was transferred, no doubt to a more color-blind atmosphere.

li'l lady

After the small victory over the pizza people, I went to work at a huge supermarket chain, Purity Supreme, after school (during which I drank, got stoned, and zoned out, except in English and sometimes history classes) and on weekends. I bagged groceries. I made a lot of money in tips in addition to the $3.35/hour wage, because at that time we wheeled one or two carts out to customers' cars and loaded their purchases for them. It was very physical work, and made me feel capable, strong, a little butch. I was the only girl. The carts were about four feet high, maybe four feet wide, and maybe six feet deep, with two wheels in back, two triangle-shaped feet in front. You either pushed or pulled it, like a hand-truck. Within a few weeks, I could handle two without a problem, like the guys, pushing one in front, pulling one from the back, because if they helped me, they cut into my tips. The male customers never failed to crack me up, and I played right into it, feigning difficulty with the weight of their bags full of beer, Dinty Moore stew, Hormel Chili, potatoes and toilet paper. "You sure you got that, li'l lady?" "Umm," I'd say, trying to sound unsure, voice high. "I *think* so." Then, with the customer leading me to his van or whatever, I'd whip the carts out, quick and smooth. "Careful, that's pretty heavy. Hey, you must be strong. This is hard work, even for the guys. Here." Usually I landed a nice 5 spot from these sexists when they shopped for themselves, but when their bags were full of Kleenex, fresh produce, spices and other items from a neatly inked grocery list, my tip was considerably less, especially on a Saturday afternoon. Women tended to tip less, and some of them acted like it was a privilege for me to haul out their month's worth of groceries. Bags full of premium meats, four kinds of breakfast cereal, nothing generic, no coupons. They stood by and supervised, squawking advice and admonitions, especially those with mile long register tapes waving out from the top of a jam-packed bag, the white snake of affluence, covered in numbers. I felt closest to those women who shopped like my mother, like they were playing a game on The Price Is Right: *How* much? Oh. (eyes survey the conveyer belt for potential casualties.) Take that, off, ah, and that, and that, and this too, they can do without. How much now? That's better. The women at the registers always asked me, especially when it was raining or snowing out, why I didn't want to become a ringer, and I told them I didn't want to stand in one place for hours on end. Sometimes, when it was slow, I did shelving or facing, which I hated. Somehow I had cultivated the notion that the only real labor was physical labor, that I was only really working when my body felt it during the day, not just at the end of one. Which is why I hustled at Purity Supreme. I was also competing with Nate, the only brotha at the store and fellow bagger, and the other guys. Fast turnaround from bagging to car and back meant more money on busy days. One thing that drove me nuts was the way men always seemed to park so far from the store. Last thing I needed was to get dragged into a Ford Econoline with no plates after loading some perv's groceries, and who knows how close I came to that? My fear gave me a rule: hand male customers their groceries and let them load up, keep the cart between you and him. Even with women, I was cautious. Sometimes they left their men, or *some* man, sitting in the car, waiting. But I survived, and my survival made me feel rich and responsible. My Madewells (working class pants from a textile mill in Fall River, MA) bulged and chinged with bills and coins by the end of the night. My dad always laughed at the showdown at the O.K. Corral sound of my noisy, swaggering approach when he picked me up, and I'd give him money for gas before I dumped out my pockets on my bed and stacked my cash, bills, quarters, dimes, nickels, pennies tossed in the jar. From this cash, I bought my own notebooks, personal care and hair products, designer jeans, makeup, lunch at school and, of course, music, in addition to kicking in money for food and stuff at home. This is how I've come to understand working middle class. Being a good worker came first, before school, and although my parents never said as much, my grades were ultimately my problem, not theirs, as long as my bad grades didn't cost them any money. Now, my good grades would have, could have, or should have, depending on the class you might relate to this from, cost my parents something. We weren't bourgie in the strictest sense, but we never wanted for anything. Tons of toys, nice clothes, decent food, safe housing full of books, but my parents didn't come from the sort of Black family stock that had what we understood as bourgie pride/pretensions. No one in our posse was the first Black this or that, had been a teacher or other lauded professional, and we weren't Southern, so the up-from-slavery American ethos was out. (Only the 90s would herald a full on appreciation for all things Caribbean.) Going to college wasn't drilled into our heads as an imperative. There was no "family name" to uphold, no tradition to follow except one: Working and being self-sufficient (keep a roof over your head and food on your table, don't depend on nobody for nothing). We knew our roles, and as we got older, it mattered less to my parents *how* we played them, just that we did.

entry level

To begin working for money at a level equal to one's...gender? Class? Experience? What would have been fair to ask me when I was newly escaped from the sticks of Plymouth, MA into the teen-wild streets of Boston's Fens, Class of '84 high school yearbook under my arm, three years of paid labor under my belt? How was it that I was just then entering the workforce at the bottom, anyway? So. What are my strengths? "Well, I was a dietary aid in a nursing home until a few months ago. I like to write. I keep my books in alphabetical order and occasionally dust them. My weaknesses? Well, um, I graduated near the bottom of my class. I guess I get bored easily. What? You're going to time me while I put this stack of library card files in ascending order? Okay..." *have to remember to ask Mum about this*. By the end of the appointment I was just glad I could quit selling cookies by the quarter-pound at Au Bon Pain/Cookie Jar downtown and walk to John Hancock Mutual Life Insurance Company. I heard a magical word: Salary, zipping in my ear. I had a "title": File Clerk. The company owned four buildings on the block: three of old stone surrounding The Tower, 60 floors of icy blue glass and those famed faulty, falling windows. The buildings were huddled like conferring heads of state, endlessly reflecting themselves in each other. A long tunnel connected the Berkeley Building, "my" building, to The Tower, so that employees wouldn't have to go outside during winter, or at all.

(Mirror halls, promenades of Knowledge, the cost of monotony, suppliers of skin and task, the women of my line acknowledge the curve alight with traffic, with feminine providers of support, conducted by procurers, humming with progress, the colored strain of working)

My mother and godmother had worked at John Hancock in high school. My aunt and uncle still did, and my older cousin and running buddy had just started. I was secretly proud of the negligible nepotism that I thought had gotten me the position, so happy to join my blood in the fields of Adulthood, convinced they'd had some power to get me the job, only to learn later they hadn't been asked a thing. A young Black woman, Edwina, not much older than me, showed me the ropes in "my" new department, in that staccato, telegraphic speak that hides the keys of how to survive at work within the banal minutiae of how to do the job.

(New women enter the field of business here.)

"First file room older files four-foot shelves starts at 1000 and ends here [points to doorway] at 6224."

(Skills setting, skills set.)

"Footstool's over there, the next room newer ladders built into shelves, much higher maybe eight feet, in general pull in the morning." (promenade, tasks tasks tasks, passing palms, produce invisibly, progress)

"Shelve in the afternoon when it's slow, but keep busy Dee the supervisor's watching. She tells Mary, the manager, everything."

(here are the ropes, the ropes, learn the ropes that pull you in, hold you back)

"They won't tell you nothing now, but when you get your review, every little thing will come back to you."

looks and moves

Edwina wore a skirt suit every day. "I don't care what I do. I have to look *good*," she said. The women within earshot, skirts pressed and nylons fresh, nodded and looked me over. Edwina was a third degree black belt. Her "master" was Billy Blanks, pre-TaeBo. When no one was around, she'd do splits, or stretch one leg over my head, holding her skirt down in the middle. She talked very quickly, especially when she was excited or being nosy. Melinda always slid in at 10 past 9 with an excuse about her son, her husband, her mother, her priest. We'd lean over the "to be filed" bin to hear what excuse she would give the supervisor this time. Edwina thought Melinda was hooking on the side. "Wouldjajustlookitthemshoes?!"

From time to time, a haughty, stocky blonde in unflattering white stockings and flat shoes would come over from somewhere and ask one of us about a file in a snotty way. "Who's that?" I asked Edwina. "That's Muriel. One of Mary's old pets. She got promoted to the Tower. She shits ice cream now."

(Bend. Stretch. Reach. Repeat the exercises of your days, like this, like this, like this, like us. Hand over fist. Relay breath, gesture, letter openers probe the slit, extract our accrued lives. Bend. Stretch. Like this. Like this. Like this. That's right. Looking good.)

I kept things orderly, robotically pulling and replacing annuity files yellowed and dusty as old tobacco as inquiries arrived in the mail, often written in a shaky, Palmer Method hand, searched a mechanized, Toyota-sized Rolodex card file if an annuity number was in doubt. Afternoon shelving passed slowly. Most talk was prohibited, not to mention our radio station of choice, Black-owned WILD. Instead, Muzak. Leo Sayer. Helen Reddy. The Beatles. The Fifth Dimension. All reformulated, ever more digestible. I felt that pressure in an unspeakable, vague way, to reformulate my dress, my talk, under duress, but I was yet to cave. Ain't was my spice; my eyes rolled of their own accord. I couldn't, or didn't bother to, read any stricken looks as having a warning for me. Dee, a white woman head clerk, smoked incessantly, complained about a boyfriend I just couldn't believe she had; a girlfriend was more like it. Another woman, Cassie, white and also higher up than a clerk, scared us with a story of a cyst under her arm, how the doctor did the biopsy with a long needle. Edwina, Melinda and I were the Black file clerk back-ups. I sang Muzak songs to myself, underpinning the reedier notes of Edwina's, the sighs and murmurs of the other women unseen but heard in the stacks.

(Bend. Stretch. Reach. Like us like us like us. Repeat the exercises of your days, like this, like this, like this. You looking? Good. Mirrors flash up in Olympic judgement. I bow to your synchronized woman-hood.)

crash pad

After work, I trotted quickly on my heels 15 minutes to Westland Ave. I didn't want anyone to see me, but there was no way around it. I lived in a rooming house with a bunch of kids around my age. The room was 9x12 with a single bed. Four of us slept across its width. Some of my friends on the Ave saw me in my new get-up and were crass, wondrous and suspicious all at once.

"What the hell you got on?"

"You should let *me* cut your hair."

"Where you work at?"

"So you big time now?"

"Tsk. Fuck that. They try to change you and shit. Look at you, man."

"How much you make?"

"*That's* what your legs look like?"

Occasionally, a whisper, "You think you can get me in?"

"They got a mailroom or somethin'?"

When I wasn't writing in my notebooks in a delusional and impenetrably cryptic imitation of Anaïs Nin (though I was bummed out from her writings about 'Negresses,' her condescension to her Black maid). I ran the streets, squirmed my underage ass into The RamRod, Jumpin' Jack Flash, The 1270 Club, and did a lot of drugs. I had to balance things out. Most of my friends had odd jobs, none of them were writers or wanted to be, as far as I knew. We didn't get that deep. We just made money somehow and partied. Dying fast was romantic. Getting old, especially in an office, was just not. The other girls, the roommates, and me moved upstairs in the rooming house 20x20-foot spread. Random kids, our breakdancing, tagging, boom-box-having friends, were less constantly sleeping on the floor. With the new job, I kept food coming in for the hotplate. They got dependent and resentful. We fought. Someone stole some of the move-out money I was stashing in a box of Stayfree. It was time to go.

The Popling
William Burroughs

Audrey and Jerry set out to isolate and capture a popling. An old steam railroad takes them to a desolate town in northern Canada. A trading post. A few cabins. A group of adolescents stand in front of the trading post. They snigger and giggle and nudge each other as the two boys pass them on the way into the trading post. One of the local youths twists his head to one side and rubs his crotch. Audrey feels a blush burning the back of his neck.

The clerk is a youth with one eye slate gray, the other black. He puts out his hand.

"I'm Steve… you two are looking for the Piper brothers, right? Well, just follow that wagon road outside, you can't miss it, there's only one road. Walk about two miles and take the path to your right. It's a mile from the fork to the Piper place…"

Outside, the boys are sitting in a line, leaning against the wall, knees up, wobbling their knees back and forth and rubbing their crotches. One calls after them.

"We'll be seeing you, milk boys."

The wagon road, which was also passable for trucks in dry weather, was yellow gravel winding between birch and pines. Wild flowers grew by the side of the road, and a mourning dove cooed softly from woods. As they walked they swatted at deer flies that lit on their necks and hands and faces. Stinging like sparks of fire.

"They can even bite you on the palms of the hand," Audrey said. "And the big horse flies can bite through jeans."

"You know this country pretty well…"

"The cabin we're going to still belongs to my father, but I haven't been here since I was thirteen. We always needed a guide to find it… this must be my turn off."

They turned into a narrow footpath and the shadow of deep woods. Weeds and bushes brushed them as they passed. And now clouds of voracious mosquitoes took over from the biting flies. They stopped and rubbed citronella on their faces and hands. The mosquitoes hovered around them, buzzing in frustration.

They stepped finally into a clearing by a lake, and there on a high rocky bank over the lake was the Piper cabin. The mosquitoes fell away behind them. The younger Piper, who was about 20, was cutting wood. He drove his axe into the block and came over to greet them.

"You're Audrey and Jerry. I'm Carl Piper."

The older brother, who was around thirty, was sitting in the open door of the cabin tying a fly. He looked up and nodded gravely. Both the Pipers had yellow hair, bright blue eyes, and curiously pointed ears. The older Piper went back to his fly. He finished it. Held it up to the light and looked at it critically, turning it in his hands. He put it into a fly box.

"Well," he said at last. "So you want to go to your father's cottage and find a popling. You know that a popling has already found you?"

He looked at Jerry and added "Both of you."

"Well yes, we know that and that's why, well hang it all, we have to come to terms with this thing."

He nodded. "Yes, if that's what you want."

"When can we start?"

"Right away. All preparations have been made."

The trip took three days, with back-breaking portages every few miles. At the end of the day Jerry and Audrey would fall asleep immediately after supper, which was black bass or walleyed pike with biscuits and dried fruit. The Pipers sat up drinking coffee and playing on their wooden flutes. Audrey drifted off to sleep with the strange wild music in his ears. The pipes of Pan.

Late afternoon on the third day they came to a wide lake after a three mile portage. As the canoes glided out into the clear blue water, Audrey could see great boulders on the bottom, some fifty feet in height. He shivered slightly – there was something chilling about the silent blue depths and the shadows of those boulders, rolled down by glaciers millions of years ago. He knew that the lake was more than a thousand feet deep in the middle.

They paddled for two hours, and at sunset he could see ahead a little pier and a sandy inlet. He knew that the house was set in a grove of pine and birch a few hundred feet above the pier. They tied up at the pier and jumped out. The pier ended in ten feet of water. Audrey remembered fishing from the end of it for rock bass and yellow perch. The bank sloped steeply from the end of the pier into clear blue depths. Audrey led the way up the path to the house.

It was just as he remembered it. A screened porch in front, two pine chairs on the porch. His key opened the lock and they stepped into the living room. Pine paneling, small windows, pine furniture, low table. A book case with some of Audrey's old books still there. *The Book of Knowledge,* some copies of *Adventure* and *Amazing Stories,* and a stack of Little Blue Books. The kitchen had a wood-burning stove and pine table with chairs.

Up the steep stairs on the second floor there were two bedrooms over the living room and a smaller bedroom over the kitchen. There was a bathroom with running water and flush toilet and bathtub. Water flowed from a two-hundred-gallon tank in the attic, which was filled by a pump from the lake. There was a boiler that could be heated by a small stove to provide hot water. On the back porch, which was also screened, there was an ice box and a wood bin.

Behind the house was a wood shed and an ice house and a long low building with a beamed ceiling that had been his father's workshop. The tools were still there – some lumber, a drum of kerosene, and a coil of rope. Audrey looked up at the beams and remembered an incident that had occurred on his last stay here, when he was thirteen. His father and brother had rowed to the other side of the lake to fish. Audrey had watched them go with a tingle of anticipation in his crotch and the pit of his stomach. He was going to jack off. But there was no hurry now. He could take his time about it.

He went out to his father's workshop, looking up at the smooth round beams. His father planned to nail planks to the beams to form an attic and storeroom to the workshop, but this was never accomplished. Looking up at the beams, Audrey suddenly felt a feeling of weakness in his chest. He was starting to get a hard-on as he remembered something he had read in an old medical book he found in a trunk in the attic of the family house in St. Louis. It was about death by hanging.

"Ejaculation in young male subjects during hanging is so frequent as to be the rule. This generally occurs twice, once immediately after the drop when the neck is broken and once just before the blood stops circulating and the heart stops. However, in some cases ejaculation may occur three times and sometimes as often as five times. Full consciousness may persist for as long as three minutes with the neck broken, and as long as twelve minutes in cases where the neck is unbroken or lightly fractured. Ejaculation is thought to result from pressure on the vagus nerve."

Audrey was standing up at the attic window when he read this. He became quite dizzy, and silver spots boiled in front of his eyes and he went off in his pants. Well, now was his chance to try it. Heart pounding, breath whistling through his teeth, he fashioned a hangman's knot and threw the rope over a beam. He stripped off his clothes, his cock hard and lubricating as he adjusted the knot behind his left ear, reached up as far as he could on the loose end of the rope, and pulled himself up on tip toe. Then he arched his feet, swinging a few inches off the floor. Blood pounded and sang in his ears and the room blacked out and he went off.

He came to himself lying on the floor, his neck very sore and a taste of blood in his mouth. Hastily he dressed and undid the knot and coiled the rope. He went back to the house and looked in the mirror. There was a red mark around his neck. How would he explain it to his father? He got an idea. He took a pail and went out to pick some blackberries. When his father came home just before sunset and asked, "What happened to your neck Audrey?"

"Well uh I was picking blackberries and I fell and a branch got tangled around my neck."

His father looked at him speculatively for a moment, and Audrey felt himself blushing. But nothing more was said. All this came back to him as he stood in the work room with Jerry and the Piper brothers and glanced up at the beam.

Audrey picked up a shovel and a can. "Let's catch some fish for dinner?"

He knew exactly the spot to dig for worms. This was a compost heap of garbage and humus for the wildflower garden at the side of the house. Violets and forget-me-nots and even some of the iris his father had brought in still bloomed there. Every shovel of dirt turned up thick red worms. Audrey could see the fish flapping on the pier, feel the jerk and vibrating weight on the line. Jerry and Audrey got their fishing poles and walked down to the pier.

The Pipers were busy unpacking gear from the canoes. The sun was setting across the lake, and three geese flew north in v-formation. Somewhere in the distance the laugh of a loon. The water was smooth as glass. Audrey baited his hook and let the line slide into the blue water. Jerry was fishing from the other side of the pier. Almost at once Audrey felt the tug on his line and pulled out a one-pound rock bass. In twenty minutes they had six rock bass and seven yellow perch. They cleaned the fish in the lake and carried the entrails in a pan and dropped them on the compost heap. A fire was already burning in the kitchen stove.

In the days that followed they fished and swam and hiked and canoed around the lake.

"The presence of human bodies will draw the popling," Leif told Audrey. "Sooner or later he will show himself."

For a week nothing happened. And then one afternoon as Jerry and Audrey were coming back from a walk around the edge of the lake with two black bass and a walleyed pike Audrey suddenly stopped and put his hand in front of Jerry. He knew that just ahead was a little sandy inlet between two boulders. You could easily miss it because there were bushes growing around the boulders that almost concealed the inlet. He knew it was there because three days before, he and Jerry had stopped here for a swim.

The water was shallow for about twenty feet, and then the bank fell away sharply into deep water. Somehow Audrey could never bring himself to swim out into the deep water, and anyway the water was much too cold to stay in for more than a few minutes. So they swam close to shore and then came out and stood on the sand, running the water off their bodies and shivering. As the sun warmed them they stood with their arms around each other's shoulders, looking across the lake, and three geese flew over, heading north. Audrey became aware that someone or something was looking at him. He felt a sudden rush of blood to his crotch. Jerry glanced down, grinning.

"You're getting a hard-on, Audrey."

"Yeah, I suddenly got hot for some reason."

"Me too. Look." He pointed down to his stiffening phallus.

They stood their with their arms still around each other's shoulders, as if they were having a picture taken, and Audrey realized that it felt exactly like someone was taking a picture. Next take showed the two boys jacking off, bodies contracted, looking down as they ejaculated and Audrey thought of a picture he had seen in Paris of a little boy pissing into the water... "Ne Buvez Jamais D'eau" as their semen slashed into the water like salmon roe.

Now he knew that whatever had been watching them was there in the inlet. They moved forward cautiously and parted the bushes over the inlet and peered down. At first they saw nothing, then Audrey made out a figure lying in the sand. The figure seemed almost transparent, and was exactly the color of the sand, webbed feet trailing in the water. At this moment a breeze rustled across the lake between the creature's legs, stirring sand-colored pubic hairs, and the creature got an erection and ejaculated with a low whistling sound. The breeze died and the creature lay there as if dead.

Trying to make as little noise as possible the boys dropped down onto the sand between the popling and the water. The creature leaped up, and when he saw his way to the water was cut off he gave a whistling sigh of fear, turned green, and shit on the sand. Audrey could smell it as he moved forward. Quickly stripping off his belt and pinioning the creature's arms. It smelled like humus, stale flowers, and stagnant water with Accent sprinkled over it. They carried the popling several hundred yards back to the house. The green color slowly subsided. The creature was looking at Audrey, who was carrying his legs, and he gave a little cooing giggle that sent a shiver down Audrey's spine. Carl opened the door and they carried the popling into the living room. Carl bolted the door.

"They've got him."

Leif came out of the kitchen where he had been preparing the evening meal. A smell of frying fish came out with him as he opened the door. Now the popling began to struggle like an impatient dog as he whistled out... "Fish fish fish."

Audrey untied the creature's arms and set him gently on his feet. He sniffed through the open door of the kitchen, where Leif had already laid out plates of fried fish with biscuits and rice. The popling grabbed a plate off the table and carried it into a corner of the kitchen, where he squatted down eating the fish with delicate voracity, cramming rice and biscuits into his mouth with his hands. In a few seconds he had picked the bones clean. Audrey handed him another plate and he ate that too. Then he curled up in his corner and went to sleep.

After they had finished eating, Audrey stepped over to the popling and touched his shoulder. The popling looked up at him, turned a salmon pink color and rolled over on his back with his legs in the air and made a strange popping sound in his throat. His penis surged erect like some pink translucent fish. Audrey and Jerry carried him upstairs to the bedroom and laid him down on the bed with a bath towel under his ass. The popling writhed ecstatically. He turned bright red and shit. Audrey and Jerry stripped off their shorts, dropped the bath towel on the floor and began caressing him, running light fingers over his nipples and nuts and ass. The popling turned purple, orange, salmon, pink – the colors washed through his body so that Audrey ached to look at him. Kicking his legs spasmodically in the air, the colors flashing through him faster and faster, he came in a shrill whistle of ecstasy that brought the two boys off with him.

Audrey's note on the popling: physical characteristics: he is quite tall, almost six feet, but so slender that he could not weigh more than 110 pounds. His neck is serpentine and flexible, his head comes to a point and is quite hairless. However, he has pubic and rectal hairs. When he swims, his penis and testicles are retracted into his body, leaving a smooth slit. Normally he is a silver gray translucent color, with huge clear gray shimmering eyes. His body gives off a gray ghostly underwater sperm smell. He defecates from sudden fear or pleasure, but has now learned to use the toilet at other times. He is an instant chameleon, changing color in a split second to match his surroundings. Pleasure is always manifested by red and fear by green. The pubic and rectal hairs change color with the skin. He can see with his whole body and often turns around and bends over to look at me with his ass. This method of perception produces a physical impact, like soft erogenous spanks. I can tell if he is looking at me with my back turned.

Jerry and I are naked most of the time, and we are slowly learning how to see with our bodies. The ass, nipples and genitals are the most sensitive seeing areas, and the lookout is different according to which areas are used. Above all, the popling wants to be seen with other bodies and to see other bodies. When he looks at me with his nipples, my nipples become erect. Today I was in the workshop and the popling came in. He looked at the beams and made a little chirping giggle sound that vibrated in my throat, and then he looked at me with his neck where a red line like a rope mark appeared, and jerked his head to the left and I ejaculated. His whistles and chirps vibrate in my body like some sonar language.

He can make himself transparent and show his viscera, like a tropical fish. He seems to be able to ejaculate any number of times, achieving erotic frenzies that are almost painful to watch. These frenzies are more and more frequent. However, he will not allow Jerry or me to fuck him. If we try to fuck him, he turns green and shits. Carl has explained to me that it is fatal for a popling to be fucked. "He will pop all the way and die."

"What happens if he fucks me?"

"That you will find out soon enough."

Abduction and Rape – Highway 31, Elkton, Md – 1969
Cookie Mueller

"They were just three sluts looking for sex on the highway," the two abductors and rapists said later when asked to describe us.

This wasn't the way we saw it.

A lot of other people didn't see it this way either, but these were women. Most men who know the facts say we were asking for it.

Obviously you can't trust every man's opinion when it comes to topics like rape. A lot of honest men admit that they fantasize about it and that's healthy but the ones that do it to strangers, unasked, ought to have hot pokers rammed up their wee wees.

The worst part is there's no flattery involved in rape; I mean, it doesn't much matter what the females look like; it doesn't even seem to matter either if they have four legs instead of two. Dairy farmers have raped their cows even.

"It's great to fuck a cow," they say, "you can fit everything in... the balls... everything."

So I guess it just depends on your genital plumbing as to how you see the following story.

True, we were hitchhiking. True, we were in horny redneck territory, but we hadn't given it a thought.

It was a sunny day in early June, and Mink, Susan and I were on our way to Cape Cod from Baltimore to visit John Waters who had just finished directing us in his film *Multiple Maniacs*.

When we told him we were going to thumb it, he said incredulously, "You three? You're crazy! Don't do it."

"He's just overly paranoid," I told Susan and Mink. "Hitchhiking's a breeze."

It made sense anyway because we only had about fifty dollars between us and above all we needed a beach.

Mink, the redhead, was dressed casually as always in a black leather jacket with chains, black fingernail polish and tight black Levis. Susan, the brunette, was dressed as was her normal wont, in a daytime low cut evening gown, and I, the blond, was dressed conservatively in a see-through micro-mini dress and black velvet jacket.

This was not unusual for us, in fact benign, but in Baltimore at this time, the height of fashion was something like lime green vinyl pants suits, or other petroleum-based togs in chartreuse plaid or paisley that melted when the temperature was above 98.6. These clothes became one with Naugahyde car seats on a hot day. So people stared at us. They laughed right in our faces when they saw us.

"I hate to tell ya this," somebody would always take us aside, "but this ain't Hallor-ween."

To this day I can't figure out why we looked so odd to them. What did they see when they looked at their own outfits in their full-length mirrors?

In Susan's thrift store Victorian mirror that was about as useful as looking into a huge silver wrapped stick of Wrigley's, we put on our Maybelline black eyeliner lines and mascara, and were looking much better than any of the other displaced hillbilly beau monde on South Broadway that day.

"FINE MAKEUP, SENSIBLY PRICED" the Maybelline ad on TV said. I thought to myself how true it was. Couldn't beat it for a long trip; water-proof, smudge-proof, it sure held up.

For the twelve hour trip, we didn't forget our two quarters of Jack Daniels and a handful of Dexadrine Spantuals (they were new on the pharmaceutical market), and twenty Black Beauties. Aside from these necessities we had a couple of duffle bags of Salvation Army and St. Vincent de Paul formals and uniwear. We were all set.

On the street, we had no problem getting a ride due north.

The trouble started after about an hour into the journey. We had been traveling in an old green Plymouth with a salesman and his Gideon Bible. He had run off the road into an embankment. Trying to follow our conversation, he'd gotten too drunk on the Jack Daniels, so we left him after he passed out behind the wheel.

"I don't think he was ready for us," Susan said, as we tumbled out of his car laughing.

"Let's make sure the next ride is going to Delaware or Connecticut," Mink suggested, "or at least a little further north."

We had no idea that we were standing smack in the middle of a famous love zone, Elkton, Maryland, the quickie honeymoon and divorce capital of the eastern seaboard.

Men whose eye pupils were dilated with goatish desire stopped before we could even free our thumbs. We decided to be selective. Apparently we weren't selective enough.

After a long dull lull in traffic, we hopped right into the back of a burgundy Mach 4 Mustang with two sickos, gigantic honkies, hopped up and horny on a local joy ride. They told us they were going to New York City, the Big Apple, they said.

It is a fact that retarded people do not know they are retarded; they just know that some people do not talk about stuff that interests them.

The conversation we were having in the back was beyond their ken; after a quart of liquor and five Black Beauties apiece, we were a bit hard to follow, even for people who read all the classics.

I suppose they got jealous. They decided to get our attention by going around in circles, north, then south, then north again, passing the same toll booth four times.

Mink, the most astute of us, realized that her instinctive internal migratory compass was awry.

"We're trying to go north," she reminded them.

They just laughed.

"We see that you're playing some kind of circling game with your car." She was trying to make herself heard over the din of some backwoods hard rock bubblegum music that was blaring on the radio.

"Yeah, guys, I saw this same cheesy truck stop whiz by twice already," Susan pointed to a roadside diner that was whizzing by for the fourth time.

"I think they're just trying to get our attention," I said, taking the psychological angle.

"No," said Mink, "these guys are assholes. They're wasting our road time."

She should not have said that, but Mink has never been afraid of telling people about their personality flaws.

"Assholes, huh?" the driver scoffed, and he veered the car right off the highway and into a field of baby green beans and then got back on the blacktop and headed north again. The tires squealed the way they hardly ever do in real life, only in squalid car chase movies.

"Round dees parts we don't call nobody assholes," he said. "That's kinda impolite. We call 'em heiny holes." And they laughed and laughed.

"Well at least we're going north again," I said and in the very moment I said it I realized that it was a ridiculous thing to say.

There comes a time when even the most optimistic people, like myself, realize that life among certain humans cannot be easy, that sometimes it is unmanageable and low down, that all people are quixotic, and haunted, and burdened and there's just no way to lift their load for them. With this in mind I wanted to say something to Mink and Susan about not antagonizing these sad slobs, but right then the driver turned to me.

"You ain't going north, honey, you ain't going nowhere but where we're taking you."

These were those certain humans.

"Let's ditch these creeps," Susan said.

"We're getting out at the next truck stop," said Mink and she gathered her duffle bag like a career woman in a taxi with her attaché case.

"Shut the fuck up," the driver said as a Monarch butterfly was creamed on his windshield. The wings mushed into his wipers as the blades squeaked over the splattered glass.

"Fucking butterfly guts," he said.

"We have knives," the guy riding shotgun said and he grinned at us with teeth that had brown moss growing near the gums.

"Big fuckin' deal," said Susan, "so do I," and she whipped out a buck knife that was the size of my mini skirt.

The driver casually leaned over and produced a shot gun and Susan threw the knife out the window.

Suddenly the effects of the Jack Daniels were wearing thin and the black reality of a speed crash was barreling in.

Mink began scribbling a note on a Tampax paper; "HELP!!! WE ARE BEING ABDUCTED BY ASSHOLES!!! CALL THE POLICE

IMMEDIATELY!!!"

It was a note for the woman at the toll booth.

When we stopped there Mink started screaming and threw it at the woman. The note fluttered back into the car as we sped away.

"Have you ever fucked calves' liver?" Mossy Teeth said.

"How the hell ya supposed to fuck calves' liver?" the driver asked.

"Well, ya buy some fresh liver and ya put it in a jar and ya fuck it. It's better than a pussy."

Now that's disgusting, I thought, almost as disgusting as a popular practice in 17th century France when men took live ducks and placed the heads of the ducks in a bureau drawer, put their dicks in the ducks and then slammed the drawer shut at the moment of their (not the duck's) orgasm. Men will fuck anything.

I supposed they also cooked the duck and ate it too.

They pulled into this long driveway. The dust was rising and matting the mucous membranes of our noses. Everybody sneezed.

I began to realize that for them we were party girls, that this wasn't something unusual, that girls around these parts were game for a good time, a gang bang, and that threats of murder might just be considered all part of the fun.

We bounced full speed down this backroad for quite awhile, passing vast stretches of young corn plants rustling and reflecting the sun on their new green leaves. I remember getting sliced by young corn plant leaves once, the same kind of painful wounds as paper cuts.

Mink and Susan and I couldn't even look at each other, our eyes hurt.

A white clapboard house came up near diseased elm trees in the distance. Some chickens ran away from the fenders. A rusted-out pickup truck was growing weeds and a blue Chevy was sitting on four cinder blocks right next to a display of greasy old auto parts and an old gray dog that was trying to bark. We pulled up right to the house and from the front door, screen door slamming, came a big acne-scarred man in his BVD underwear, a plaid flannel shirt with a sawed off shotgun.

"I told you once before, Merle, get off my property," the man hollered, "I'll blow your fuckin' heads right off your shoulders."

"My cousin's a little crazy," the driver said to us and he laughed.

"You wouldn't do no such thing," he bellowed to his cousin with the yellowish drawers on.

"Oh yes I would," the cousin said and aimed his gun at the windshield.

"You think he'd shoot us, El?" the driver asked his buddy.

"Sheet," the other one said, "he'd shoot his granny."

The screen door slammed again and then next to the cousin was a woman with dirty blond hair and dirty bare feet. She was wearing blue jean cut-offs and a tee shirt that said MARLBORO COUNTRY on it. She looked forty-five but she was probably twenty.

A toddler of about two came to the door, pushed it, and fell out into the dirt. The baby started crying but nobody in the yard noticed. The baby got to his feet and stopped crying when he picked up a piece of car tire and put it in his mouth. He was teething, I guessed.

The woman grabbed the shotgun nuzzle. "Put that fucking gun down, Henry," she said.

"Leave goa dis gun, woman," Henry said and shook her off, aimed again. She jumped for it again, and in this moment the three of us, Mink, Susan and I started diving out of the car windows. Mink and Susan got out but Mossy Teeth, El, grabbed my thigh and held me fast. Merle spun the car around and we took off, making corn dirt dust in all the faces of everyone who was standing there in front of the house.

Susan and Mink tried to run after the car, yelling to me to jump, but I wouldn't now. It was too late. We were burning rubber up the gravel path while Merle and Ed were pulling me back into the car. They got me in the front seat with them. I was straddling the bucket seats.

I wondered what was going to happen to Mink and Susan, but I bet they wondered more what was going to happen to me.

What happened was this: I began to feel the mood change. As they were talking to each other I noticed that they sounded scared; El even wanted to get out and go home.

After a lot of fighting, Merle finally did let El go. He let him out at a backwoods package store.

Now Merle and his little brain began to wonder what to do with me. His buddy was gone. Who would fuel the fire?

I assumed that he would rape me. He wouldn't let me get away without that at least. Of course I didn't want to get raped, so I began to think of a plan.

I have always been an astute observer of sexy women and unsexy women, and in all my years I've never seen a crazy woman get chased by a man. Look at bag ladies on the street. They rarely get raped, I surmised. And look at burnt-out LSD girls. No men bothered with them much. So I decided that I would simply act crazy. I would turn the tables. I would scare him.

I started making the sounds of tape recorded words running backwards at high speed. This shocked him a bit, but he kept driving further into the woods, as the sun was setting and the trees were closing in.

"What the fuck are you supposed to be doing?" he asked me nervously. "You a maniac or something?"

"I just escaped from a mental hospital," I told him and continued with the backward tape sounds, now sounding like alien UFO chatter.

I think he was believing me, anyway he pulled off into the bushes and unzipped his pants and pulled out his pitifully limp wiener. He tried to get it hard.

For a second I saw him debating about whether or not he should force me to give him a blow job.

"Ya devil woman, ya'd bite my dick off wouldn't ya?"

He tried to force his semi-hard pee-wee rod into me as he ripped my tights at the crotch. I just continued with the sounds of the backward tape as he fumbled with his loafing meat.

This infuriated him. "I'm going to ask Jesus to help me on this one. Come on, sweet Jesus, help me get a hard on. Come on."

He was very serious.

This struck me as deeply hilarious. Praying to the Lord for a hard on was asking for the ultimate Bible text rewrite.

Not waiting to see whose side the Lord was on, I pushed his wiener quickly aside and threw open the door and dove out into the darkness. I ran faster than I'd ever run and I wasn't a bad runner.

As my eyes grew accustomed to the half-moon light, I saw that I was running into very deep woods. Aggressive brambles grabbed at my thighs, poison ivy licked at my ankles and yearling trees slapped me in the face.

After a long time I decided to stop running, so I got under a bush next to a pile of rocks. I felt a bunch of furry things scuttle away. Rats, or possums or raccoons, I guessed.

I laid there for awhile trying to see things in the darkness. And then I heard his voice.

He was far in the distance yelling, "Girl! Girl! Where the hell are ya?"

Did he think I was really going to answer?

As he got a little closer I saw that he had a flashlight and I got scared again. If his light found me there would be no hope. My white skin was very bright in the bluish flood of the half moon.

I had a black velvet jacket on with a black lining, so I ripped out the lining in two pieces and wrapped one around my head and the other on my almost bare legs. Those brambles had shredded my stockings.

No light would bounce off me now.

I was awake for a long time and then I just fell asleep, sure that he had given up the search.

At sunrise, or thereabouts, I woke up. I didn't even have a hangover.

I felt very proud that I had melted so well into the underbrush, just like Bambi.

Without too much trouble I found this little dirt road and I started walking to the right.

"All roads lead to Rome," I told myself.

I guess I was walking for almost an hour when I heard a vehicle rumbling up behind me. For a second I thought maybe I better dive back into the woods, maybe it was Merle again but I turned and saw it was a little country school bus, a sixteen seater, a miniature version of the long yellow city buses. I stood in the middle of the road and waved it to a stop.

A woman was driving the bus and there was a load full of kids. I stood in the front of the bus and whispered my predicament; I didn't want to alarm the kids. She drove me to a ranger station and the ranger's wife gave me a cup of Lipton's.

I told my story and they were really peaceful sympathetic people. The ranger called the police station and I found out that Mink and Susan were there.

The ranger's wife liked me, I could tell, and they both drove me to the police station.

When they let me off the wife kissed me and said, "I hope everything goes well for ya, honey. That's a nasty thing ta happen. Watch yasself round these parts, there's some hanky-panky round every corner here abouts. I know. My husband deals with it everyday."

They drove off. I liked her.

Inside the police station the police weren't so nice, but they were patient with my story. They knew the guy. It was a small town.

"He was just released from Jessups Cut," they said. "He's a bad ass for sure, always in trouble."

"His daddy's a religious man, though, had one hell of a religious upbringing," one of them said.

Don't I know it, I thought. He believed the Lord would raise the dead even.

It was good to be reunited with Mink and Susan. They told me that they were beside themselves with worry until about ten o'clock. That was about the time I was finally relaxing in the bush, I told them.

The police brought Merle in for questioning. They wanted to hold a kangaroo court right there in the next building. The law is quick in Elkton, Maryland.

In the courtroom I didn't press charges. That would mean lawyers and coming back there and a whole long drawn-out scene. I would lose anyway. I just wanted to leave that town as quickly as possible; anyway Merle was going back to jail for a false insurance claim, or something like that.

The cops then drove us to the bus station and told us that they better not ever see us on a highway again.

While we were waiting for the bus we decided to go to Washington, D.C. to the airport where we could maybe hitchhike a ride on a plane.

"Let's go in style," I said. "No more cheap highways."

At the airport bar we met a marine biologist who was working in Woods Hole, Massachusetts.

"I'm flying back to work, I'm working with endangered bass," he said. "But my buddy's flying right into the P-town airport. He'll take you there. No problem. He should be landing here in about twenty minutes."

In mid-air we told them the story. We laughed a lot.
His friend flew us right into Provincetown.
"Wow, what luck!" Susan said.
I didn't think it was luck. Innocent people are sometimes rewarded.
Anyway, after everything we'd been through, we deserved it.

LSD...Just the High Points

Ann Rower

The following transcript is a conversation between the writer Ann Rower and members of The Wooster Group, a Manhattan-based theater company, held in 1984. At that time, The Wooster Group were preparing a play about Timothy Leary, witch-hunts and drug culture, which they eventually staged as *LSD...Just The High Points*. The Group was curious about Rower's experience as a sometime-babysitter and early participant in Leary's psilocybin experiments in Cambridge during 1961. Everyone in The Wooster Group participated in the conversation in some way. The afternoon flowed from serious inquiry to druggy nostalgia back to philosophy and social history. Rower's comments became the text spoken by one character in the play, "The Babysitter," played by Nancy Reilly. They also became the basis for a story published by Rower in *If You're A Girl*.

LIZ (LECOMTE)

Um, what we want then, is just for you to remember what you can about any... any images. Anything you can remember... it doesn't need to be about him.

ANN

Yeah, I just sort of started jogging my memory and stuff is still coming up. I jotted some of it down. Should I read what I wrote and we can take it from there? Some of it is a little self-indulgent.

LIZ

Honey, we're used to it. (laughter) There's a lot of that around here.

ANN

I decided to call it LSD…Just the High Points …or Leery about Leary
(PEYTON SMITH laughs) which I was.

KATE VALK

We've all been wantin' to say it.

ANN

Which I was, though it might not be useful to your sense of Leary as
victim of witch hunt. You could call it King Leary. … So – I'll just read
what I wrote, okay? The thing is, the fact that Leary struck me as an
asshole, such a jerk, had nothing to do with the fact that people in command were so scared by his wanting to expand society's consciousness,
bringing peace and harmony through LSD. There was a certain dis-
honesty, something unconnected, some ability he had to dissociate
internally. He was a prophet of LSD who didn't do it because it
depressed him. And this is what he was trying to sell? So when I met
him he was running from Berkeley to Harvard, partly to get away from
the place where his wife and mother of his two kids had killed herself,
partly 'cause he got a grant. He thought everyone thought he had driven
her to suicide. His message preceded him, of course, to the East. Mostly
I heard about him from the poets. But none of us were interested in his
message. We were interested in his pills. (PEYTON chortles.) In fact,
this hurt Tim very much, I think.

There was a story that got back to him of everyone hanging out in
Ginsberg's apartment. Allen, Peter, Jack Kerouac's ghost. Allen was
cooking chicken soup and everyone was just waiting for the weird professor from Harvard with the little pink pills. Leary heard about this
cartoon image and was hurt. But then everything was hurting him in
those days. I met him in the early spring of '61. But this time I was
already a drinker, a heavy amphetamine addict and a heavy pothead. I
mean, I was ready. I remember one morning in the big kitchen on the
wide proper New England street. It must have been late spring, maybe
May, 1961. I was squeezing orange juice for me, Robert, my husband,
and William Burroughs, who was visiting Tim. Susan, Tim's daughter
came down for breakfast and asked us, "Did you take pills?" I shook

my head no. "Then how come you have those funny eyes?" That's what she called being high, "having funny eyes." Come to think of it, that was the last morning I ever spent in Tim's house, or with Tim. He had just spent the whole day and night before moving house, from this one to the one in Newton Center. And the reason Robert and I were there was not to babysit the kids but for William Burroughs. At the time Burroughs was still living in Tangiers. Until now, no one could get him to put in an appearance on our shores. But Tim had organized a conference on hallucinogens. He invited everyone and all the experts on drugs were to be there. Tim did get him to accept. The lure was Aldous Huxley, who was teaching at MIT that year. So Burroughs was flying in from Tangiers, his first time in America in years and coming directly to Tim. And Tim was moving that night so he couldn't be home. Typical. Tim called us and asked us to be there and babysit Burroughs. Typically, he'd made no provisions for Burroughs. Here Burroughs was, an ex-junkie, hashhead, traveling, wisely, without anything and coming to Tim's house where there was nothing for him to smoke. We ransacked the house. There was nothing. No psilocybin. Nothing. Tim had no understanding of the drug culture he was founding at all. It bothered me.

PEYTON

How much time were you involved with Leary, babysitting?

ANN

Well I met him in January of '61 and I left Cambridge in August that year. I was involved probably every weekend. There were just these crazy weekends at his house –

MICHAEL (STRUMM)

What were you doing in Cambridge?

ANN

I was at Harvard on a Woodrow Wilson Fellowship, uh, and anyway, the first time I met Tim I was living in Boston and Ben, a friend of ours in the math department had known Tim from Berkeley when Tim came out to Boston that year. Tim's specialty was creativity or because he went to Harvard, he was trying to come on like he had a specialty. Trying to be very serious. Anyway Ben took us over there this afternoon. It was a beautiful afternoon, sort of late. There was this beautiful sort of late, strong winter sun. And we came in and I remember Tim standing there with his arms around the kids and they all looked very depressed. They were all really very down, I guess the suicide of the wife was, whatever, fairly recent. I don't know, you could just sort of feel there was this kind of air of, you know, everything was kind of held in. And there was this little small Japanese woman uh, who did everything. And we all went inside.

    This was one of those breaks when there were no pills. They would come in from Sandoz, see, coming in from Switzerland, these little shipments of pink psilocybin pills ... uh, and this was a dry period. Tim had this candy dish. It was amazing. A three-tiered candy dish that had these little round dishes on each level going up and they sort of swung around and they were always full of these little pink pills. But the candy dish was empty that weekend and there was this atmosphere of waiting. We went into the study and I remember sitting down in front of the window. There I was, a sort of young newlywed with newly washed hair and the sun was coming in through the window onto my hair and Tim looks at me and says "Get the camera, get the camera." The Japanese woman runs and gets the movie camera. 'Take it, take it, the sun's going down, hurry up." She looks through the camera and starts to shoot the sun coming through my hair and suddenly she drops the camera and it shatters on the ground. That was my first memory, the first day. Tim was sort of running around like a tyrant, he was horrible to her. He was very bossy anyway.

                              LIZ
Was she young?

                              ANN
Yeah, she seemed like she was twenty-seven or so. She was young and sort of attractive, not flashy but very small and solid, compared to him ...

LIZ

Was he considered handsome?

ANN

I guess there's a certain tweedy Irish type, umm, except he wasn't really handsome. He was sort of gangly and all over, he had salt and pepper hair, lean and lanky if you like that type, but he didn't have a nice face or anything. He just wasn't attractive as a person. He had these very unattractive eyes. Maybe it was something coming out of him. He always struck me as false. He was also, I think, very defended. And really hurting at this point. You could tell. He didn't take psilocybin himself at that time because he was in a real depression and he was afraid that it would bum him out. And that bothered me, the fact that that was happening and still he was continuing to proselytize.

LIZ

Was this around the time he was working with convicts?

ANN

Yeah. I remember an afternoon we were over there. Tim wasn't home and we were sort of babysitting, I guess. Alice, I forget her name, the Japanese woman's name, was with him. He was going to get home late. And he walked in an hour after we'd gotten there and we didn't know why he came home so early. He had given the convicts this big dose of psilocybin and brought them all into the rec. room or something but he got depressed and left, sending the convicts back to their cells tripping their brains out. That was the thing.

The second time I met him was also hysterical. In all these scenes Leary is in the background, because that's what he was: an observer. He was a scientist, a psychologist. He was giving everybody these questionnaires. It took weeks of fawning before he would give us any drugs to take home. We would have to do it there, sit around and record our experiences afterwards. It was all right. It was interesting because there was no literature on it at the time so nobody knew what to feel.

I have this memory that's very clear, the first time that we took it, of all of us standing around the living room. I was standing with my elbow on the mantelpiece, very casually holding myself up and feeling I have absolutely no boundaries and I just loved this woman who was standing next to me who I had never met before. I was her. All these things ... I guess we had been reading Alan Watts so it didn't come completely out of the blue. But there were no magazine articles on what it was supposed to feel like and at first it seemed to me a coincidence that it turned out everyone was feeling the same thing at that point, but that was the point. And also nobody knew how many to take. I mean one night I took two, one night I took twenty. We had no idea what we were doing. Fortunately with these drugs, there's a point at which you take a lot, nothing else happens, unless it hasn't happened yet. I think that was always my experience on LSD.

Also, that night, a Richard Alpert was there. It was also the first time he had ever done it ... and he had a toothache ...

Before Alpert was Baba Ram Dass he had no cool, he was just a grad student, a psychology grad student at Harvard. And he had this horrible experience, eight hours of toothache. We were all somehow forced by Tim to stand around him – he was lying on the dining room table – and support him ... He'd be brave and moan and all ... it was terrible. There was something very ritualistic about it, too. Alpert was lying out, sort of like a corpse, and we were all standing around him and there were these candles, and he was moaning. An asshole. I mean he also struck me as a real jerk.

WILLEM (DAFOE)

At this point were you a friend or a babysitter or somebody who just walked in?

ANN

I was never a friend. There were just lots of people who were sort of around. A group of ten people that were in and out, on my level, friends of friends, but that became like fixtures, who were there regularly. Baby-sitters.

WILLEM

How was it presented?

ANN

Very ritualistically. Atmosphere was very important to Tim at that point. And that everyone would be supported. We would all sit down. He would build everybody up around him and everybody would take it, and then he didn't take it ...

LIZ

He wouldn't take it?

ANN

No.

PEYTON

Would he not take it on the guise of monitoring what you were doing?

ANN

Yeah, I guess so. But there were other people who'd volunteered to monitor.

LIZ

They used to talk about the person who would come ...

PEYTON

The guide.

MICHAEL

The babysitter.

LIZ

Do you remember someone called Lisa Beaverman? She she was involved with LSD in a serious quote way, and it seems there was a competition between them, she was very annoyed by the way he pros-elytized ...

ANN

I don't have any specific memory of that. But like I said, I was really only interested in the drugs. But there was this amazing man who Tim was working with who should have been Tim. Frank Barron was this mystic, a mystic Irish poet. Also with the psychology department at Berkeley, and into probability theory. He tested his probability theories on the tables at Las Vegas all the time he was in California. He was a poet, a genius, gorgeous, loose. He had this amazing kind of theoretical underpinning about taking drugs that also involved the idea of getting high which was completely foreign to Tim. There was this feeling that Frank should have been Tim. But that also Frank had the sense not to be Tim, because Tim had this amazing ego, this irritating King Leary thing.

Then there was this crazy, crazy weekend that I remember. It may have been building up to the big convention where Burroughs finally came. But Arthur Koestler was there and Allen Ginsberg and Peter Orlovsky and Watts and his girlfriend were there. Koestler had never done this drug and had some kind of attitude about it. Everyone was very nervous about whether he would come, whether he would do it. He was very critical of it all.

He didn't believe that you should become psychedelic, ecstatic by ingesting a chemical. So he was very anti. Right, that was it. He was coming from a more mystical end. He was very skeptical but he came and he did take some. And the first thing that happened was he ran upstairs and walked into his bedroom and somehow by mistake Allen Ginsberg and Peter who, I think, had been there for a week already, were in Arthur Koestler's bedroom and they were, um, fucking and sucking each other on Koestler's bed and he got real upset ...

LIZ

He was there?

ANN

He walked into the room. He took this psilocybin and he became very spiritual and he wanted to go up to his room (laughs) and meditate.

MICHAEL

And he opened the door and bang –

ANN

Yeah, screaming and running around and really freaking out. I don't know why I keep thinking of a comb. Allen came out combing his hair, or maybe Arthur was looking for a comb. Anyway it was very bizarre and also the same weekend Alan Watts was there and Watts of course was one of the supporters. But again there was all this kind of apprehension amongst the establishment Buddhists and Leary. Watts came because he was planning to get high, not with his wife but with his girlfriend. This was supposed to be very hush-hush. He had just written, *Nature, Man and Woman*. That's the book everybody was reading at the time. And he comes in with this young thing, and everybody takes pills. And at one point there's this screaming coming from the downstairs bathroom and everybody's banging. And I come in and there's this line of people, Watts, Arthur Koestler, Allen and Peter, Tim, everybody, Frank Barron, Richard Alpert – all of them, huddled outside the bathroom door saying "let us in, let us in" because this woman was screaming and screaming inside. Finally somebody says to her, "What's the matter, what's the matter?" and she says, "They're coming. They're after me. They're coming." "Who's coming?" "They're coming. They're trying to steal my shit. They're trying to steal my shit." And finally they burst the door open and she points to the wallpaper which has these little birds on it that she had hallucinated into horrible vultures that were coming down, to try and steal her shit ... (laughter)

LIZ

What was the house like?

ANN

It was very comfortable ... There was the first house I was in the night we had to babysit for Burroughs, and then there was the house in Newton Center that became infamous. There were a lot of different couples living there and it was like a commune ... you know, with kids and people of all ages. Tim eventually got thrown out of it when he was thrown out of Harvard. But the first house was a real traditional, spacious center-hall colonial, very comfortably furnished. It was obviously one of those academic sublets. But it was a very beautiful house with opulent, dark shining woods and carpets and curtains and a big yard with apple trees, And then the room where Jackie, Tim's son, put all his toys. People were always coming up to people, asking if they were high. I can't remember much about the kids, partly because they were usually in their rooms and partly because I was high.

KATE

Didn't you have to take them on outings?

ANN

No. I only started out as a babysitter but I became more of a participant in the great experiment. So I didn't have a lot of contact with the kids, they weren't really around a lot. You had the sense that they had been hit over the head or something.

KATE

This is a rude question, but how old are you?

ANN

Forty-five.

NANCY (REILLY)

God, you look like you're thirty-five ...

PEYTON

See what drugs and alcohol will do for you?

ANN

If I weren't forty-five, I would not have been in Cambridge in 1961. That's all I can tell you ... That's the only consolation.

PEYTON

What kind of music did everybody listen to?

ANN

I don't remember anybody listening to any music ... This is before music.

MICHAEL

A little – Brahms?

ANN

I don't remember any Brahms at all ... I don't remember any music.

RON (VAWTER)

What was it like after you distributed the drugs? What went on in the room? Would there be a lot of talk?

ANN

There would be a lot of talk and a lot of silence, I guess, and the talk would be about what people were ...

RON

Thinking about?

ANN

Thinking and feeling ...

LIZ

Here it is – (reading) "they talked about Hindu symbolism, the Euclidean mysteries, Tantric cults –

ANN

I don't remember that ...

LIZ

– "and the ancient secrets of Tibet."

ANN

I don't remember any of that.

PEYTON

But it was clinically monitored?

ANN

Mostly it wasn't and the point is it became increasingly less and less clinical ...

In the beginning he did it that way but in his house he was a little more casual and it became much looser, and eventually he gave us stuff and we took it home. We had to say we were going to experiment creatively ... So, you know, we'd just come over and pick up a bottle of ... fifty of 'em or whatever ... I mean it was very crazy, very irresponsible ... though it didn't look that way at the time.

NANCY

Did you take a lot of it? How many times a week?

ANN

Oh, usually once. Just on those weekends and when I had it at home. That's not a lot, is it?

RON

Would you stay in the same room with everyone else or would you wander around?

ANN

Well, we would wander around. There was this huge house and it had this whole upstairs with all these bedrooms and then it had a den, and then this room with a fireplace, and then a dining room and this big kitchen and then there was outside ... there was a lot of wandering around.

PEYTON

Was there, uh, sexual stuff?

ANN

Not while I was there, and it didn't feel like there would be. It was a very puritanical kind of atmosphere. Tim seemed very kind of tight-assed. And Alice ... There was something about them as a couple.

LIZ

Alright, I wanna know something and I want the straight dope on this. Were you ever in the sack with this guy?

ANN

With Leary? No, no, not my type, really.

PEYTON

Were you tripping there with your husband?

ANN

Huh?

PEYTON

I asked if you were there with your husband?

WILLEM

Ah, here it is (reading from Leary's autobiography) "And then Ann and I ambled up and went into the bedroom ..."

ANN

Ahh ... He was a liar ... He's so dishonest ... that's what I was saying.

NANCY

That's what the book implies, that he was a liar ...

ANN

He was ... He was obviously a psychopath in many ways. I mean, he was a classic paranoid –

MICHAEL

Doctor Tim?

ANN

Ya, but then again, like most paranoids, he turned out to be right. He talked such a big game, I mean about women. Like he was having all this sex. But I knew he wasn't taking the pills so I had a feeling he wasn't really having the sex. But he had this rap and on a certain level, it didn't matter, and maybe it doesn't matter. He just seemed very tormented and defended as I said, like a little king, only he wasn't little. I mean, he was kind of a big man. Leary had this amazing status, you know … there was that thing about him at that point, that he was special. It was all special, and you were special to be allowed to take it. He was doing research into creativity. That was his experiment. The experiment was to give artists psilocybin and have them record their responses. And so he had this idea of giving it to thousands and thousands of people, and they came through his house.

RON

Would you characterize those weekends as good times?

ANN

Yes, I would characterize them as good times.

RON

Why?

ANN

Well, you know, they were very cosmic.

RON

Would you drink?

ANN

No, I don't think anyone would eat or drink … Maybe a section of an orange or two …

RON

Then it was not a party.

ANN

No, it was not a party. But it was a party in a way. It just wasn't a wild party. Um, it was sort of a very internal party. I mean there was all this stuff going on inside everybody's head and all. I think everybody was having a party separately. It was more than a party ... It was like a revolution or something. On a certain level everyone believed that if you could give this to everyone it would change the world. It's so hard to get back to that feeling exactly ...

MICHAEL

And where did it come from?

PEYTON

California ...

LIZ

Ya, I remember that ... Sunshine ... and everybody's name was Sunshine and every shop was named Sunshine ...

ANN

Then there was Windowpane which was very beautiful acid. After a certain point, I used to take it when I was crashing from speed.

KATE

You used to take acid when you were crashing from speed?

February 1984
33 Wooster Street, NYC

Death Mask

David Wojnarowicz

It's February, 1989, several years before the introduction of AZT and other pharmaceutical treatment cocktails for HIV. George Bush is the president, and AIDS equals death. David Wojnarowciz has only recently tested positive for HIV, but already he is sick and well intermittently. More often, he is sick. His close friend, the photographer Peter Hujar, died of AIDS in 1989 and David is now occupying Peter's cavernous loft above Second Avenue in 11th Street. The owner of the building is vigorously trying to evict David, and he spends many days in court. The rage he feels against the US government and medical establishment is something he needs to have heard. But he is ambivalent to talk about himself. French photographer Marion Scemama, who is his friend and has been working with him for a number of years, asked me to make this interview with David because her and I have already collaborated on some video-projects. Besides I already have met David a few times, so we can make a team. Once again, David is ambivalent. He is distrustful of "theorists." Outside, the traffic roars and we can barely hear each other. My French accent doesn't help. What follows is the transcript of lateral conversation often conducted at cross-purposes, in which David asserts the origins and logic of his work against the intellectual tradition which he thinks I represent. It turns out to be his last interview. David died in 1992.

In 1989 David is notorious and renowned in the East Village art world (he has been publicly attacked by the Christian fundamentalists), but he has yet to have a major museum show. A major retrospective of his work was presented at the New Museum in New York in 1999.

David Wojnarowicz: I guess I feel a little intimidated, mostly because my experience with intellectuals has always been that they use language like a hammer.

Sylvère Lotringer: [Thinking of Nietzsche.] *Sometimes you need hammers, too.*

True, but not when you're the one who's getting hammered on the head. I've always been attracted to people with information and to the idea of language. Most of my life has been without words. I feel like everything I respond to is on either an intuitive or primitive level. It still shocks me that people would think things similar to me. I'd get so obsessed when I was younger that if I looked at this table and you looked at this table, we would both think we're seeing the same thing. Are we really? Then I would think well, the only way to know is to take a photograph of it and I'd say, Does this look like what the table looks like? And if you said yes, then it would confirm that I'm seeing the same thing. But then I'd think what's the difference between the photograph and the real thing? I can't get inside your eyes and look through them. It still shocks me that people would think similar things to me because I've always been so isolated. I don't think I ever believed that paintings could change people. I always thought they were signs that people who felt similarly or differently could identify with and get some comfort from.

What about your relationship with the photographer Peter Hujar? You were very close to him. Did that change anything about the way you look at things?

I had a very powerful relationship with Peter Hujar. He was somebody who I felt saw the world the same way I did, and he was twenty years older. He taught me a lot of things, and he connected instantly to what I felt about the world myself. But beyond him, I've always felt like a stranger among people. I'll spend years in the company of certain people and I'll always feel like I just don't understand them. There are certain things that are familiar, but then once I get beyond that, it's like I don't have the faintest idea of where they're coming from, or how they're looking at things. It just wouldn't make any sense to me.

I did this painting recently called *My Father was a Sailor, My Father was the Century*. For me it's the same thing. It was not only about my father being a sailor, but also about transportation. It was about moving out where a century ago most people wouldn't know what was beyond the bend in the road outside their door. Now you turn on the TV and you're in China, you're a thousand feet below the ocean looking up at things that exist. The painting touched on that as well as on my father's psychosis. It was a world that was extremely dangerous, extremely death and destruction oriented. All of these activities about destruction or self-destruction in the household I grew up in, shaped my first experience. First, if you believe that embryos pick up thoughts – I wouldn't accept that argument because of its anti-abortion implications, but just thinking of the possibilities in the world, or the possibilities in forms of life, communicating without words – then that was the world I was born into. My mother, when I was fourteen, told me that she had just prayed that I would die when I was in her belly, that I would abort, or that I would be stillborn. Because of everything she felt about my father and her two other children I just wasn't wanted when I arrived. My father constantly beat and threatened her with guns. I was born with the umbilical cord wrapped around my throat. I was almost strangled. I only recently found that it happens to a lot of children whose parents want them to die. They're born with the umbilical cords around their throats.

I grew up in a society that basically wanted to kill me, and every sign I picked up as a kid growing up, whether in the structure of my household, of schools, or of the world at large, everything was aimed at extermination. Especially when at the age of eight I had my first homosexual experiences with a thirty year old guy. I knew what my family would do. I knew what people beyond my family would do, whether it was the police or the hospitals, any of these things. I knew that they would try to destroy this if they found out. I've met people who experienced just the opposite. The moment they realized they were homosexual, or that they were inclined towards that experience, they were immediately open about it, immediately talked about it. Yes, they were beaten up and yes, they had rejection from their families, but they never questioned for a moment that this was who they were. For me, I remember inventing all these reasons why this was happening. Then, from the age of eight on, I kept thinking, Well when I hit puberty I'll start having relationships with women. I didn't have hair on my body, so I thought this was why I was making it with men. That excuse failed by the time I hit puberty. I realized I was still like that.

I know I turned a lot of death towards myself. I had attractions to death. I took myself into situations where it was possible to die. Some of them were reactions to what I understood homosexuality is. I remember going to the library trying to find out what a homosexual is and reading books that said that I had to put bottles up my ass and wear a dress. I was horrified. That wasn't what I wanted, but then I thought I had no choice. I thought by the time I'm seventeen I'll be wearing dresses and putting bottles in my ass. It was upsetting. I didn't want to be a "sissy." It was also an ugly torture against somebody that society hates, somebody who's effeminate. The whole thing was informed with rage. On some level, I wanted to be accepted, but on another level it was impossible. I tried very hard to be normal and to get loving, touching gestures. It was a terrific waste of time.

What about Peter?

Peter, in his Buddhist leanings, always encouraged me to meditate and I tried it for a period of time. But it made everything I did worthless. I no longer wanted to paint these images, and I no longer wanted to deal with violence. I was on this health diet. I'd given up smoking, sugar, salt, meat, all these things. I did it for four months and it scared the shit out of me. I was at a total loss as to what to do, what to paint, what to make. None of it made any sense. I can't think of an interesting way to present beauty unless it's inside of death or violence. That's where I make violent things beautiful. There have been times that I've painted flowers or landscapes, and it's actually been nice to give myself that freedom, but in the end it's not something I'm really interested in showing other people. They can go out and look at the same. Somehow it's just not potent to me; it doesn't express something. So I gave up meditation and went back to eating sugar and pancakes. I became violent again. It made me feel much better. Actually, I remember having had an image of bathing my brain, holding it under running water out in the woods. It just became a beautiful image, being able to wash your brain like you wash your pants and squeeze it out and start fresh.

TV does that too, in another way...

I've always had a strong reaction to the sound of TV. If I watch it for five minutes during the morning or afternoon hours, it colors the rest of the day. It hits something in the head that makes me numb. For the rest of the day I feel uncomfortable. It's more about frequencies. It makes me want to throw up. So I've gone through periods of watching TV just trying to drown things out. It's just so ugly and the sound waves are so distorting. Then all the information puts me in a rage and there's nothing I can do about it. That's why I scream at the TV, "Fuck you!" Sometimes I draw things on the front of the screen, like a big dick, so that every announcer has this dick going into his mouth, or into his face. It's like fucking with the images so that they mean something else. I'm always sitting there in a dialogue with this box. I imagine murdering these people on TV. I confront them at every turn. [He grabs a gun on the table nearby and starts pulling the trigger mechanically. Click. Click. Click.]

[Pointing.] Where did you get this gun?

[Looking at his hand, startled.] I got it in Germany. They're now illegal in the United States because they look too real. It's a cap gun or something.
     I think about mass murderers and how they seem to really love death and killing. They keep doing it over and over and over. They even do it with a lot of thought and care. They're in love with it, that sensation of death, or what they imagine death to be. Most people you talk to would be, or at least say that they're horrified at the idea of death, or the idea of killing...

And you?

I think I've worked at rage all my life. I used to feel very self-conscious about it because when I first began showing my work, all the people who worked in the gallery would say, "Can't you, you know, paint something nicer?" Or, "Why can't you be like Keith Haring?" Or, "Can't you create something that's fun?" I was extremely uncomfortable. I felt terrible. All I can do is produce misery.

What about Peter?

Peter had just an enormous rage, incredible rage and ugliness, the last year of his life. It became an ugly spectacle because there was nothing that you could do to touch it. Finally he hit a point where it was as if he had let go of something, and maybe it was a string leading into life. Then he let it go and it was just passivity.

All my life I tried to fit. One of the things that happened with my diagnosis is that I don't care if I fit. There are still parts of me that want to be touched or accepted or embraced, but in the end it's absurd. It's not going to keep me from dying. Part of what I felt in the year of Peter's illness before he died was this incredible rage about everybody I knew. I hated them. I hated them so much because not one of them would ever say anything. And if they ever said anything, they would touch on it once or twice and then never bring it up again. They would look at you with certain eyes. I would feel people looking at me because they knew that I was going through something in relation to Peter's slowly dying. It's the same thing that I feel about memorials for people who die. On some level, it's great to make a private grief public because it makes people more aware and makes them witness to what's happening. But, at the same time, memorials eventually just become this preparation for death, and everybody refines their words about this person who's about to die so that when the day comes and there's a memorial, they get up and say, "This is who this person was. This is what this person meant to me." It's beautiful, but then they all go home and prepare for the next death.

There are moments when I have a slide machine in my head, and suddenly one slide that I carried for years and years gets knocked out and another one comes in. It could be for a minute or five minutes, when suddenly I'm looking at death, seeing the end of my life. My body grows still. I have absolutely no fear. It makes perfect sense and there's nothing loaded or attached to it. And, what am I afraid of? What am I afraid of? I know I'm afraid of losing control mostly because of the rage that I've carried, afraid of that monster coming out. It was loss of control that I was suppressing for years, ever since I was a tiny kid, fear for this thing to suddenly jump out. I think I was always afraid that, if provoked, then I would lose control and I would kill somebody. It's the same thing about my death, or the view of my death, the loss of control or the loss of the ability to mark it, or change it, or shift it, or construct things in order to make it not exist, or exist less. But for that five minutes, it's a wonderful sensation because everything is meaningless.

My friend Keith Davis died two times of a heart attack, and the doctors came in twice and jumped up and down. Finally, they brought him back and then attached him to a machine. The family was trying to get them to remove the machine, but it was a Catholic hospital. They said, "Look, we can't make the decision to take away this life." They stuck him on the fucking machine, and they made a decision to bring him back from death because of their own fear of death. I had to argue. I screamed at these doctors, "What the fuck is wrong with you? Why did you put him on the machine if now you can't make the decision to take him off the machine and why did you suddenly feel that you had the right to do that?" Keith expressed that he never wanted anything like that. Anyway, after five days of fighting with the doctors, most of the family who visited New York to witness his death went out sightseeing around New York. They were in the Empire State Building around the time that his sister and I finally convinced the doctors to pull the plug, and in something like thirty seconds, he was dead. Later on finding out that they were on the observation deck of the Empire State Building, I thought it was wonderful. I loved the idea that they were up in the sky, so high above the ground, and that at the moment of death all that energy just got dispersed and covered everything or mingled with everything and then dissipated. This energy is free of gravity and moving up into the atmosphere, and here are these people looking through binoculars into the sky or into the city and through the depths of this height. I thought it was the perfect death, or the perfect moment for him to achieve death while his family was sight-seeing.

One of the things that I remember Kiki Smith saying to me was that when you die you become fly food. I like that. That's the clearest idea that I've ever heard from somebody, that it's nothing less. The idea that you nourish things in your death is kind of comforting. It's sweet. That's what I've been seizing on lately; that idea of death. That actually makes me fairly comfortable. I'm attracted to the idea of existence after death in the form of objects. I have a pair of Peter's glasses, and they are the saddest things I've ever seen in my life. They're sadder to me than his death because they become totally useless, and yet they possess all of this personality. They're silent.

I had a therapist confront me not too long ago. He said that I found it easier to develop relationships with my objects than with people, that I invest so much emotional energy that I'm afraid to invest in people. It's fairly true. Objects don't speak back. I love animals. I've loved animals all my life because of my early experiences with my family. I would spend all of my time in the forest and watch animals, catch animals, read about animals. I've always loved them more than people, or always trusted them more than people. I bought a bunch of crickets to feed a scorpion that I'd bought to use in a film, and the crickets started eating each other. Within twenty-four hours, two crickets killed the other twelve. I couldn't understand what was going on. What the hell is this? Maybe it's a virus that's attacking the crickets, and they're dropping dead. I didn't realize they were cannibals. Then one day I looked in there, and I saw this cricket bite the leg off of another cricket. There were two left, and I fed them to the scorpion. I didn't feel so bad. The scorpion eats them like popcorn.

I'm having a lot of odd thoughts of what death is at this point. Partly because when I watched Peter and Keith Davis die, I was in the room with both of them when they went, and it confronted all my feelings of what death is. Suddenly everything, every idea I've had about death seemed so stupid. It was so totally about living or life that the words seemed ridiculous. Peter wanted to believe that there's experience and there's travel after death. I even did some little rituals in his house after he died according to some Buddhist papers that somebody gave to me. I made a drawing of him and burned it at some point so that after seven days his spirit can receive all knowledge. I totally believed in those things as I did them. It made me feel calmer about his absence, but now, facing my own death, I don't want to believe that there's an afterlife. This is what they do to enslave people. They tell them, "Oh you get your reward after you die," and not when they can question it, not when they can confront it. I love playing with all the contradictions on the surface. To be limited only by what you experience seems really boring, but then I realize that is one of the things about which I like to write. What I experience, what I think, or what I see in terms of someone else's experience, whatever attracts me, I pull together for my own writing.

When Peter was diagnosed with AIDS I made this enormous construction of what this man was going through, what he was thinking and how he saw life. He gave me an indication early on the first day he got the news that he was diagnosed with AIDS. I came over ten minutes later from my house to sit with him for a few minutes. He went to meet me at the door. There was some mail that arrived, and it fell on the floor. He picked it up and turned saying, "Even something like getting a piece of mail in my home has an entirely different meaning." I felt very distant from him. I felt very sad. I felt angry. I felt fear. And yet the moment I got diagnosed, it was a shock that nothing changed, that people were still running back and forth on the street, that the mail still comes. You wake up in the morning and you have to eat. Other people have the luxury of time where they can abstract it into their nineties, or when they reach fifty. Suddenly I'm doing it at thirty-three.

Right after my diagnosis, the things I appreciated for a period of time about people who were dying from AIDS was their courage in facing death. I thought Peter was courageous. Even in the midst of his rage he was courageous. Everywhere I experienced a friend's death, or knew of a friend's death or illness and experienced part of it, I thought it was with great courage that they were living. Once I was diagnosed, the idea of courage enraged me. I thought this is bullshit really. They're talking about politeness, that the more politely a person dies, the more courageous he is, and contains his experience of his death within himself, the easier he makes it for everybody so that he slips through and dies.

Peter threatened to throw himself in front of a car because he was mad. He talked about killing himself endlessly, brutally. "I want to go to that building across the street, climb to the top and jump off the roof." He would say, "I'm gonna do it, I'm gonna do it." And he said it every day until one day we gave him the number of a doctor who would give him medicine to kill himself. Once I gave him the number, he tucked it away and never spoke about killing himself again.

The persons to whom I feel attracted have the ability to control language that's beyond what I've learned or what I understand. That's where I become overwhelmed or frightened. I've had this fear of getting trapped in language – in doing interviews, talking about AIDS, talking about death, talking about these things. I used to fear my contradictions as I grew up. I didn't understand. I wasn't in contact with enough people to realize that everybody has contradictions.

The first time I explored the promiscuous sex scene in the warehouses, I always stayed away from it and had judgments about it on some level because I wanted a relationship, or I wanted to be connected to somebody and not just run around and have sex for the sake of having sex. I had a friend from high school who was ostensibly straight, but then suddenly admitted to me, after all the years knowing him, that he had fantasies of having sex with men. We were sitting by a river, and he was telling me this when he saw these men going in and out of the warehouse, I mean dozens of men. And he said: "What's that? What's going on?" I said " Oh, you know, they're stupid. They go in there, and they just fuck all over the place." I used to get really frightened by contradictions in people and get really upset at contradictions. Mostly because I was upset at them in myself. Recently I've been enjoying more and more confronting my fear of contradictions, because I love contradiction. It makes perfect sense to me. It's becoming less and less scary, and I'm feeling more strongly about accepting contradictions and holding them or embracing them. The more I think about death, the less I want to find my feet in the cement of one form of thought.

I see myself now living my life in a capsulized in a compression of time. All these things are happening very quickly, it's almost as if the length of my life is suddenly compressed to months and things that I thought were years away, if at all possible, are going boom, boom, boom. I feel like I'm riding on a current of very nervous energy. It's part fear and it's part exhilaration. It's about what I'm approaching, about the possibility of it and also confronting all these fears in myself. Not just about death – it's pretty abstract to think about death. I feel like I'm trying to break down everything at once, cut through the bullshit, cut through all these constructions I made all of my life in order to feel somewhat comfortable, or somewhat safe. It's like breaking all of those down because they're going to become meaningless as death comes close. Suddenly it's just like plowing through everything, and I'm scared to death at moments of confronting these privacies and it is exciting at the same time...

Talking about sexuality is something I've hardly ever done. If I did it, I would always displace it to another person or to something I witnessed. Even in the first book of monologues I wrote, some of those monologues were me, but I was afraid to reveal that, so I would make them be some kid in Times Square at 4 a.m. They really are my stories. Now I write my stories, and it's exhilarating to confront that fear in myself about revealing those things.

Marion and I had a rough fight recently and in part it had to do with documenting myself. On one hand I'm attracted to it. When Peter died, I saw all the photographs he left and how little of himself he left clearly. It was all contained in the photos, but it's also hidden in the photos because it's other people, other images. I have some tape recording where I was trying to do interviews with him. He was having such a hard time with the gallery system that I thought, Well, maybe I could write an interview, but it ended up being too self-conscious and we never did it. There are these pieces of tape that exist in different people's houses. Ten years ago, in one of these tapes, he was talking about what he imagines death is. Things like that are valuable.

I went through a period of eight days in the last month, or in the beginning of this month, where I couldn't function at all. I felt everything shutting down inside me, inside my head, inside my body. It was about making gestures. Making gestures at this point suddenly became meaningless in the face of dying. It was like, "Well, so what." So what if I make a painting? So what if I write? It wasn't going to stop the illness. Those are scary moments because if that's what I was going to feel for the rest of my life, there was no reason for me to live. I've always found reasons to live by making things ever since I was a kid. It's the only thing that remained constant, or the only thing that ever made sense, or gave me proof that I was here because I felt so completely alien; that's one of the reasons I began writing in my late teens. I was writing constantly because I couldn't speak to people.

Recently, I felt everything shutting down and it was scary to shut down. This train of thought relates to my fear of death more than fears about loss of speech, loss of movement, loss of sight, loss of the senses. Maybe I have some claustrophobia and death seems claustrophobic. I got into a fight with Marion about the loss of what's inside of me in terms of videotape or recording, and being trapped in that language that's becoming my existence after I'm dead.

One of the things that happened after my diagnosis is this feeling that this may be the last work I do. Trying to focus everything and channel it into this square or into this photograph or into this thing, that it's all got to go in, and it ends up not being everything. I have the attraction to document things because through Peter I saw how little was documented of him. After he died, as soon as I could get everybody out of the room I shot a super-eight film of his body, maybe a minute and a half, and then took a number of pictures of him, which served like a modern death mask for me.

My early images were all very simple; I just wanted to record things that I didn't see people recording and painting at that time. Part of that desire is my ignorance of art history, but I wanted to record my own history, a different history. That's what painting originally was for me. It slowly unraveled that I always thought painting was a proof of my own existence, that these objects are just proof of my existence to me because of the isolation, or feeling invisible. All the paintings are diaries.

In doing this show what am I facing? I'm facing death. What do I have to lose? The self consciousness was different, and I thought okay, I have this date for this show (David Wojnarowicz retrospective, Normal, 111., 1990) and I'll put in everything that I think of, quiet things, things that are beauty to me and not loaded with violence or confrontation as well as what was confrontational for me to put out there. I usually suppress that aspect in my work. One of the things that I realized in the midst of this is that I am nervous about making certain gestures and putting them in front of people. I am nervous talking about the fact that I have AIDS on film or in public. I've always loved my anonymity, but I also need to be reassured by positions of strength.

One of the most emotional experiences I had when I was a kid hustling was one day being picked up by this guy who was extremely sad and creepy. I mean creepy in a way that unnerved me because he was totally unattractive to me. He was going to give me some money to go to a hotel, and he blew me. I was in this hotel room with him, lying on one of these cheap hotels beds with this guy sucking my dick. His mouth was sticky, and he would kiss my leg, and there would be this gummy stuff on my leg. I was really repulsed by all of this stuff but not enough to not have a hard-on. This guy was blowing me, and at some point I felt incredible emotion for this guy. I just felt so sad for him that at some point I like reached under his arms and pulled him up to me and kissed him on the mouth which was the thing that I least wanted to do. He started weeping when I did that and just said, "Nobody's ever done that." He ended up giving me extra money.

There was something exciting about these people. As a kid it was just so stimulating and so taboo that I always had an instant erection. Pushing those limits or taboos still excites me. It's one of the things I felt about looking at death. Just a week ago I became aware that what's pushing me at this point is defining where my differences are with other people. It's embracing them without the fear and without the guilt, without the sense of taboo that has always informed my work. I'm not there yet, but it's the same sensation of wanting to define myself more clearly that I've always had. I don't know if that means that I'm just trying to break things down so that they become extremely simple before dying, if I do die from this virus. Then, if there is no cure for it and nothing to extend life, that may be part of what it is to just simplify things so that it's easier to detach. What I carry as a living thing may soon die. But, for the first time in my life I feel strongly about the strength in diversity, in finding strength in those differences.

SOURCES

An American Poem by Eileen Myles, taken from her book Not Me, published by Semiotext(e) Native Agents series 1991

Prisoner in the United States by Assata Shakur, taken from the book Still Black Still Strong, ed. by Jim Fletcher, Sylvère Lotringer and Tanaquil Jones, published by Semiotext(e) Foreign Agents series 1992

Our Theater of Cruelty by Jean Baudrillard, taken from The German Issue of Semiotext(e) magazine, ed. by Sylvère Lotringer, 1982

Aliens & Anorexia by Chris Kraus, taken from her book Aliens & Anorexia, Semiotext(e) Native Agents series 2000

Armed Imperialist Struggle by Ulrike Meinhof, taken from the Schizo-culture issue of Semiotext(e) magazine, ed. by Sylvère Lotringer, 1978

Pandora's Box by Nina Zivancevic, taken from her book Inside and Out of Byzantium, published by Semiotext(e) Foreign Agents series 1993

The Empire of Disorder by Alain Joxe, taken from his book The Empire of Disorder, published by Semiotext(e) Foreign Agents series 2002

Algeria by Kathy Acker, excerpt taken from her book Hannibal Lecter, My Father, published by Semiotext(e) Native Agents series 1991

The Culprit by Georges Bataille, taken from the Polysexuality issue of Semiotext(e) magazine, ed. by Francois Peraldi, 1981

SOURCES, CONT.

Energumen Capitalism by Jean-François Lyotard, taken from the
Anti-Oedipus issue of Semiotext(e) magazine, ed. by Sylvère
Lotringer, 1976

Uncle FishHook and the Sacred Baby Poo Poo of Art by Jack Smith.
taken from the Schizo-culture issue of Semiotext(e) magazine, ed.
by Sylvère Lotringer, 1978

In the White Winter Sun by Fanny Howe, taken from her book
Indivisible, published by Semiotext(e) Native Agents series, 2001

Full Stop for an Infernal Planet by Louis Wolfson, taken from
the Schizoculture issue of Semiotext(e) magazine, ed. by Sylvère
Lotringer, 1978

The Wild Celebration by Frederic Rossif, taken from the
Polysexuality issue of Semiotext(e) magazine, ed. by Francois
Peraldi, 1981

We Can't All Die In Bed by Guy Hocquenghem, taken from the
Schizo-Culture issue of Semiotext(e) magazine, ed. by Sylvère
Lotringer, 1978

Friendship as a Way of Life by Michel Foucault, taken from the
book Foucault Live, ed. by Sylvère Lotringer, Semiotext(e)
Double Agents series, 1989, 1996

Goth 'n Roll High School by Michelle Tea, excerpt taken from her
book The Passionate Mistakes and Intricate Corruptions of One
Girl in America, published by Semiotext(e) Native Agents series
1998

<u>Sunless</u> by Chris Marker, taken from the <u>Oasis</u> issue of <u>Semiotext(e)</u> magazine, ed. by Brigitte Vial, Tim Simone, Martim Avillez, et. al., 1984

<u>Women Homosexuals and Youth: Latent Sexual Liberation</u> by Kate Millet, taken from the <u>Man/Boy Love</u> issue of Semiotext(e) magazine, ed. by Sylvère Lotringer, 1980

<u>The Exegesis</u> by Chris Kraus, taken from her book <u>I Love Dick</u>, published by Semiotext(e) Native Agents series 1997

<u>Becoming-Woman</u> by Félix Guattari, taken from his book <u>Soft Subversions</u>, ed. by Sylvère Lotringer, published by Semiotext(e) Foreign Agents series 1996

<u>Home Training to Crash Pad</u> by Tisa Bryant, taken from her novel-in-progress, <u>Playing House</u>

<u>The Popling</u> by William S. Burroughs, taken from the <u>Polysexuality</u> issue of <u>Semiotext(e)</u> magazine, ed. by Francois Peraldi, 1981

<u>Abduction and Rape - Highway 31 Elkton Maryland 1969</u> by Cookie Mueller, taken from her book <u>Walking Through Clear Water in a Pool Painted Black</u>, published by Semiotext(e) Native Agents series 1990

<u>LSD ... Just the High Points</u>, excerpt taken from her book <u>If You're A Girl</u>, published by Semiotext(e) Native Agents series 1990

<u>Death Mask</u> by David Wojnarowicz, taken from his book <u>Collaborator</u>, ed. by Sylvère Lotringer, published by Semiotext(e) Foreign Agents series 2003

PUBLICATIONS BY SEMIOTEXT(E)

PUBLICATIONS BY SEMIOTEXT(E), CONT.